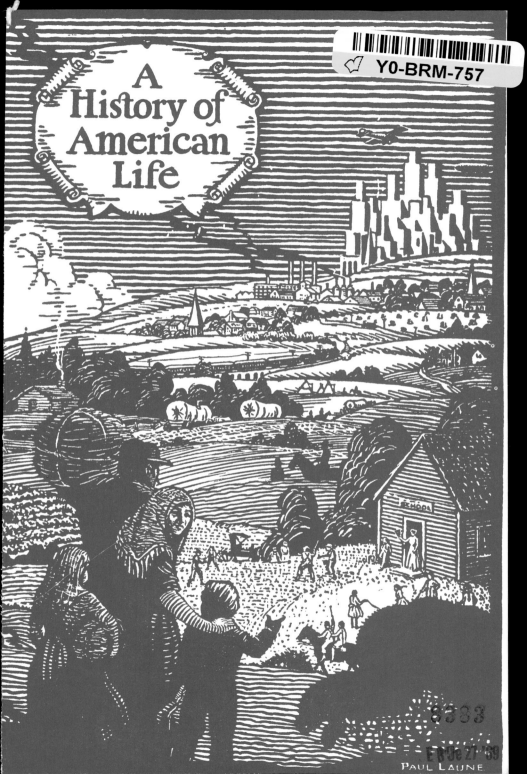

A History of American Life

PAUL LAUNE

A HISTORY OF AMERICAN LIFE

IN

TWELVE VOLUMES

ARTHUR M. SCHLESINGER
DIXON RYAN FOX

Editors

ASHLEY H. THORNDIKE   CARL BECKER

Consulting Editors

THE MACMILLAN COMPANY
NEW YORK · BOSTON · CHICAGO · DALLAS
ATLANTA · SAN FRANCISCO

MACMILLAN & CO., LIMITED
LONDON · BOMBAY · CALCUTTA
MELBOURNE

THE MACMILLAN CO. OF CANADA, LTD.
TORONTO

Aristocracy retreats before THE RISE OF THE COMMON MAN—*A riotous election, 1844.*

A HISTORY OF AMERICAN LIFE
Volume VI

THE RISE OF
THE COMMON MAN
1830-1850

BY

CARL RUSSELL FISH
PROFESSOR OF HISTORY, UNIVERSITY OF WISCONSIN

THE MACMILLAN COMPANY

CONTENTS

Ours is a country, where men start from an humble origin . . . and where they can attain to the most elevated positions, or acquire a large amount of wealth, according to the pursuits they elect for themselves. No exclusive privileges of birth, no entailment of estates, no civil or political disqualifications, stand in their path; but one has as good a chance as another, according to his talents, prudence, and personal exertions. This is a country of self-made men, than which nothing better could be said of any state of society.

[CALVIN COLTON], *Junius Tracts,*
no. vii. (New York, 1844), 15.

ILLUSTRATIONS

(By the Editors)

(b) North Bend, near Cincinnati: From an engraving by W. Woodruff, for the *Ladies' Repository*, I, 193 (July, 1841), One type of Western house, showing Virginia influence (*cf.* picture of Mt. Airy in *A History of American Life*, III). It was seventy feet long. The Whitewater Canal passes in front and tunnels through the hill at the left. The name of the steamboat on the Ohio in the foreground is the *Tippecanoe*. About an inch from the middle of the left-hand edge is a white speck which in the original appears as the monument to Harrison, whose death had occurred not long before the engraving was published. "We do not over estimate his virtues or his fame," observed the *Ladies' Repository*, "when we venture the prediction that North Bend will be the Mount Vernon of the West."

(a) Marcus Whitman's mission at Waiilatpu, 1843: From a painting reproduced in a number of works on Oregon and on Whitman, done apparently from tradition. The building at the mouth of the brook is the mill; in front of it, the first house; next, the blacksmith shop; at the right, the new house. The Walla Walla River shown at the left is by a change of course, now a half mile away from this site. The Editors are indebted to Prof. M. C. Jacobs, of Whitman College, for aid in this identification.

(b) Salt Lake City in 1847: From an illustration in Howard Stansbury, Capt. Corps Topographical Engineers. U. S. Army, *An Expedition to the Valley of the Great Salt Lake of Utah* . . . (Phila. 1852).

(a) Normal School at Lexington, Mass.: From an illustration in the Lexington Historical Society, *Proceeds.*, I, 9 (Lexington, 1890). This first state-supported normal school opened in 1839 with three students; it was the result of a movement carried forward by such men as Horace Mann, Jared Sparks and Robert Rantoul. The building still stands, though much changed.

(b) Ladies Hall, Oberlin College: This was begun in 1834 to house the women students in this first of American co-educational colleges; see Delavan L. Leonard, *The Story of Oberlin* (Boston, 1898), 46. Board and lodging were to be had here at "seventy-five cents a week, if a diet purely vegetable would suffice, or for a dollar with meat twice a day."

(c) Tappan Hall, Oberlin College: This hall was given for theological students by Arthur Tappan, of New York City, on condition that the college would admit blacks as well as whites; see Leonard, 30. It was torn down in 1885 "because of grave imperfections of constitution." See *General Catalogue of Oberlin College* (Oberlin, 1909), 74.

EDITORS' FOREWORD

IN this volume Professor Fish shows American society in the process of remaking itself. The cultural heritage of the American people during these years was essentially an aristocratic one; even the efforts of the preceding generation for cultural independence had affected little the life of the masses.[1]   In the eyes of the new generation it was quite as important to abolish special privileges respecting cultural property as those in respect to   physical   possessions.   It therefore blithely undertook the task of spreading the good things, even the choice things, of life over the whole face of society, and dared to believe, though all history seemed to speak to the contrary, that the common man had his own contribution to make to human welfare.   Indeed, Emerson himself, mourning the "dearth of American genius," had hopes that "the evil may be cured by this rank rabble party, the Jacksonism of the country, heedless of English and of all literature—a stone cut out of the ground without hands;—they may root out the hollow dilettantism of our cultivation in the coarsest way, and the newborn may begin again to frame their own world with greater advantage."[2]   For the first time in history a people faced the problem—today ever with us—of whether the finer fruits of civilization can be democratized without being vulgarized.   Professor Fish's whole volume is an answer to this question, an answer given with fine discrimination, keen insight and an engaging sense of humor.

[1] See D. R. Fox, *The Completion of Independence, 1790-1830* (*A History of American Life*, V).
[2] *The Heart of Emerson's Journals* (Bliss Perry, ed., Boston, 1926), 85.

In contrast with earlier days in America, it was a motley company that crowded the stage in the thirties and forties: Henry Wadsworth Longfellow and P. T. Barnum, Andrew Jackson and Horace Mann, Cyrus H. McCormick and "Father" Miller, Peter Cooper and Henry D. Thoreau, Louis Agassiz and John B. Gough, Horace Greeley and Horatio Greenough, Orestes A. Brownson and Stephen C. Foster, Elihu Burritt and John Tyler, William Lloyd Garrison and Bishop Hughes, and so on without end. They represented a wide variety of activity and achievement; most of them, a lyric belief in the perfectibility of man; and many of them, new visions and new adventures of the human spirit. Though these figures seem to form a distinctively American gallery, the author makes it clear that they and their work cannot be understood without reference to the great economic, humanitarian and intellectual currents that were sweeping through Europe during these same years and registering their victories without regard to international boundaries. Many instances are given of the interchange of ideas and material that occurred between the *entrepreneurs*, reformers, artists and intellectuals of America and western Europe, all leading to the conclusion that, despite the Monroe Doctrine and Clay's "American System," American culture was inextricably bound up with that of the outside world.

Earlier attempts to picture American life in the thirties and forties were made by Edward Channing and J. B. McMaster in their general histories of the United States. Since their main preoccupation, however, was with the affairs of the government, the present volume may be regarded as in a class by itself. Professor Fish does indeed give due attention to political concerns, for government and politics were among the inherited institutions of this generation which the common folk sought to subdue to their own purposes—just as they did the schools and the banking system—but he deals with such matters from the viewpoint of social interpretation. He also shows, as perhaps no one else has, that the constructive genius that went into the work of organizing political machinery and party conventions was equally exemplified in the structure of the reform movements, the development of business corporations and the evolution of an educational system. The Americans developed a talent for extralegal organization that was, in later years, to ramify into all departments of their life. Many readers will leave this volume with mixed feelings as to the significance of this period in the growth of American civilization. But it is clear that the older view, which saw in these years only a lowering of standards, must be offset by the picture, here presented, of a society which in many vital and enduring respects was leveling up as well as down.

A. M. S.
D. R. F.

THE RISE OF
THE COMMON MAN

CHAPTER I

NEW WINDS

IN 1815 new winds had begun to blow over the American people. For more than a decade they buffeted the fortresses of old habits and ideas, and then in 1829, with the elevation of Andrew Jackson to the first office in the land, they gained full sweep. In the twenty years from 1830 to 1850 these new concepts were to dominate American life; they grew established, respectable, venerated. The brash young men of 1830 became the pillars of society. By 1850, however, other forces were rushing to control, younger leaders were worshiping changed gods. It is this span of years, marking the dominance of the generation that came to power in 1830, that is the theme of this volume.

One feature of this era was its outstanding Americanism. Americans have from the beginning differed from the world from which they have been drawn, but they have been at no time detached from that world. Relatively, however, this was the period of least vital contact. The spirit of the Monroe Doctrine was so universally accepted among them that diplomatic relationships were reduced to a minimum. Foreign trade was important, but less than usually contentious. Immigration until the late forties was less a factor than in any period except that immediately preceding. Fewer boys than before or since went abroad for their education.

1

The cultural independence of the United States had to a large extent been attained.

Nor was this a mere state of facts: Americans were vitally conscious of their difference. The Americans of the thirties and forties gloried in their separation from the "monarchical" governments and tax-supported churches which were "enervating" the civilization of Europe. It would not be true, or fair to Americans of other ages, to say that this was the most patriotic of our generations. It was, however, the period of most assertive patriotism, and of a patriotism typical of a certain stage of social development. It was like that which one still finds among the dwellers in new Western towns. Americans had their plans, they knew their power, to them the future was already realized. Their cities did not equal those of Europe, but they would—as they have. They, therefore, resented the criticisms of others, and they bolstered up their own hopes by suppressing their own criticism.

Nor was this aloofness, at least among the thinking, entirely selfish. It is astonishing to find how widespread was the idea, passed on by those who had conceived of American civilization before it existed, that a purified people, with institutions based on the laws of Nature— identified in the words of Webster with the law of God —would, if true to their covenant, found a refuge for the world's oppressed and a model for other nations to copy. In 1848, this generation, now in its old age, believed it saw the world actually copying this model.

Americans were not alone in regarding the United States as unique. No other people have had their opportunity of realizing Burns' ambition to "see oursels as others see us." From about the time of the Revolution until after the Civil War, scarcely a year passed without the publication of a book by some European traveler.

A comparison of these accounts of the thirties and forties with those of the preceding period shows one difference so emphatically pointed out that its real existence can hardly be denied. This is a difference in the speed of life. It is clear that it was at this time that Americans became hustlers. The "quick lunch" was introduced, and everywhere people ate in a hurry. They ate abundantly, from tables groaning with the products of a soil teeming beyond all demands. Breakfast, dinner and supper, practically identical, each with hot breads and meats, and washed down by ice water, confronted nearly all Americans daily, but detained them briefly. The drinking of intoxicants was generally not so hurried, but it was not at the table. It was not always clear what particular task called them away from the board, but there was unquestionably a general urge to be up and doing.

This restless hurry was an outward sign of an inward quality which became apparent as soon as one engaged an American in conversation. This was optimism. Like hustle, this enormous optimism was but newly becoming an American characteristic. It had certainly required faith to bring the first Americans across the Atlantic, but that faith had little of the intoxicating quality of this new spirit. The Indian and French wars of colonial times had severely tested faith and turned many to the habit of fearing the worst. The Revolutionary generation regained confidence, a reasoned philosophic serenity such as Franklin expressed, a belief that America was safe and would be great. Very different was this new exhilaration, this conviction of salvation attained. In matters of politics and economics Americans were nearly all millenarians, believing that they themselves would see the realization of human happiness; in religion the belief that this generation would with their own eyes, living, even see God, went far beyond the confines of the small sect who made that belief an article of creed.

The causes of such optimism are found in the new conditions which the new generation encountered. Its basis was the realization of the unlimited resources of the land. These resources had existed from the beginning, but their relation to the American people had changed. Until 1815 the future of the vast valley of the Mississippi could scarcely be considered as definitely determined. Andrew Jackson's great victory at New Orleans on January 8, 1815, bore the same relation to the whole two-century-long contest for this valley that it did to the War of 1812. For the winning of either it was unnecessary, but it put to the result the seal of finality. The door to the boundless spaces of the continent was now open to them.

It was in more than ownership, however, that the relation of Americans to their land had changed. For nearly two centuries they had literally toiled uphill. A stiff day's walk could generally take a man from the edge of settlement of his boyhood to the edge as it had been advanced during his maturer years; sometimes it receded. During the preceding period the summits had been reached and since then the flood had been pouring down easy slopes into the fertile valley of the Mississippi. The Indian power had been crushed, and the obstacles to the occupation and enjoyment of territory three times as large as that already occupied, were less than they had been to a twenty-mile advance up the valley of the Mohawk or the Chattahoochee. The greatest difficulties in the way of the occupation of their land had been met and surmounted.

What was still more important, this long struggle had taught the Americans the art of breaking a wilderness. Poor indeed was the education of this generation judged by many standards, hopeless would anyone be who relied upon it today, and it was inadequate for many contemporary tasks. For the great task of the period, however, it was the ripe product of generations of effort. As Thoreau said, the Pilgrims were not backwoodsmen, and they had confronted settlement in a new land fearsomely and not too well. Now, the average American plunged joyously into the woods with a confidence, soundly based on inherited and acquired skill, in his ability to sustain himself and to extend perceptibly the civilization that he loved.

It was true that each new portion of the continent presented new problems, and called for new methods and new tools. It was, however, precisely in respect to such requirements that the American's training was most efficient. He was not afraid of the new. By this time the disinclination to change, a characteristic of settled civilizations, had reached the lowest point as a deterrent; the lure of the untried has rarely been so general. The American became an inventor not through scientific research or from peculiar mental gifts, but because of a developed spiritual impulse to try new things, and to rebound and try again if they proved unsuccessful. Travelers all noted the moving of houses. Now the moving of houses is not a difficult mental achievement, but it is the work of a man who is willing to take wide liberties with circumstances, a man undeterred by fear or ridicule.

To the American of the thirties and forties, however, unlimited natural resources and acquired fitness for handling them seemed but incidental blessings. Fundamental was the political system which his fathers had created and which he inherited. For him the political wisdom of the preceding generations had been crystallized and condensed into the Constitution. To him that document had become not a mere instrument of government —it was the reality behind all government. In the next generation tens of thousands would die for it.   It drew to itself not only the strength of people meticulously legal-minded, ready to fight on points, as Webster said, but the devotion of a people who inherited and transmitted a high degree of religious intensity.   As the Ark to the Israelites, so was the Constitution to the Americans; and as David, so, in their own way, the American leaders danced before it.

Down to 1830, the interest was in the Constitution chiefly as an instrument of government and not so much in its bearing upon disputed points of policy.   Later there came a shift and the Constitution came into the center of political conflict.   When that time arrived, however, its sanctity was so well assured that no political party attacked the Constitution itself or surrendered its views because contrary to the Constitution.   Rather, in the manner familiar to the student of fixed creeds, all believed that so righteous a document must favor them and by interpretation found in it what they wished. The aspect of the Constitution as an instrument of government which created genuine enthusiasm was not the machinery it afforded for effective coöperation.   To some, indeed, that was a feature to be admired; but they were the minority.   Not Fraternity, but Liberty, was what appealed most to Americans.   To them the keynote of the Constitution was opportunity for the individual.   In this the Constitution reënforced the economic conditions of the time.   The occupation of the continent which was going forward was an occupation by individuals; the Constitution permitted and protected this process.

Few boys of that generation escaped being told that they might become president.   Few were not told that in the matter of money the future was in their hands. In both of these assertions there was sufficient truth to make them grip the youthful mind and influence many

The Capitol from the White House, 1838. In the second quarter of the nineteenth century the Presidency began to seem attainable by every American boy.

lives. It is really doubtful if such a range of possibilities had ever before been offered to so numerous a field of contestants. Nor was the guerdon snatched early away, as it is today, by the debilitating diagnosis of mental tests, or by the necessity of selecting one's life work in time for a long special training. The more important tasks of the day could be performed by good brains and strong characters, with comparatively little selective training. To be an American was enough to have all doors open. It was something new in the world. No wonder foreigners came to watch its working, and that optimism ruled American life and thought.

Liberty had been a leading ideal of the preceding generation, but then it was a thing to be won or defended; now it was a thing realized, and this realization was impregnated into the very bone and sinew of the Americans. Liberty, moreover, was now linked with another ideal which paired with it in the devotion of the people, and which served to broaden still further the basis of their optimism. Liberty and opportunity, after all, mean responsibility, a sobering thought; one other gift of the American political system involved no personal effort, was complete at birth—equality.

Americans of the thirties and forties were laughed at by foreigners, and still are by their own descendants, for their frequent assertion that every American was a king in his own country. Few remember today, what every schoolboy then knew, that this was not a figure of speech, but a specific provision of the national and of every state constitution. Statesmen indeed wrangled as to whether sovereignty was divided between the state and national governments or wholly absorbed by the former. It was, however, governmental sovereignty of which they spoke. None denied that sovereignty was divided between government and the citizens, and that, in a field well defined in state "Bills of Rights" and in the first ten amendments to the national Constitution, the citizen was as sovereign as, in a wider field, was the czar. From one point of view this meant liberty, from another, essential equality; it was the latter which held the devoted interest of that generation of Americans, for they were the first who felt called upon steadfastly to illustrate it in practical community life.

Of course, the notion of equality went back of the Constitution to the Declaration of Independence, but the two blended in the popular mind.   When Jefferson wrote "All men are created equal," did he state a fact existing, or an ideal to be made real, or an aspiration to be approximated?   Whatever view people took, the phrase had an effective influence on conduct.   It is for the historian to discover what it meant in practice.

In so far as dress may be taken as an illustration, Americans between 1830 and 1850 ran neither to an extreme of individualism nor to uniformity.   Class distinction became less obvious than in earlier days, but did not quite disappear.   Gentlemen had by 1830 given up knee breeches and donned pantaloons, but they still wore coats of blue and buff; they had given up lace, but their shirts continued to be frilled.   Many tried to look like gentlemen by a short cut, such as a detachable collar or shirt front.   Foreign travelers laughed, but after all, even to look clean was something.   As with clothes so with manners.   The formal manners of class became less and less common, at least among those who sought popularity; on the other hand, in part, the thought of equality caused many to imitate the courtesy of those to the manner born.

It was really true that the passion for equality took more the form of an insistence that all could became gentlemen than that gentlemen should cease to be.   Jealousy was not lacking, but there was absent the later bitterness of class feeling.   Of course, as W. T. Sherman wrote,

there were "the people and others," but, in the free
states at least, few felt debarred from any class. There
was so close an approximation to economic equality to
match the political that effort and ability could raise
anyone to the top. The absence of higher professional
training made communion with the intellectual almost
as easy as entrance into the ranks of the opulent. There
were, indeed, circles made exclusive by culture, but, for
the most part, they were not attractive to those not bred
to their habits. The material ideal of all classes was
not far different—a country home of some dignity, set
in a hundred or so acres. Only a few wished to be
without occupation, and only a few wished to coerce
their fellow citizens; it was much more attractive to fool
than to boss them.

The lower aspect of this belief in equality was
expressed by Andrew Jackson in his message to Congress
in 1829: "The duties of all public offices are, or at
least admit of being made, so plain and simple that men
of intelligence may readily qualify themselves for their
performance." [1] Americans were only too prone to
believe that they were at any moment ready for anything; it was the reverse side of their splendid self-
confidence. Failure did not touch them, for with their
ready adaptability they turned from failure in farming
to banking, from the broken bank to law, from law to
mining. The life history of many an American of the
period reveals him adept at many trades, while but few
excelled in any. There was distinct danger that the
ideal of equality would run to seed in futile belief that
all men are created the "same."

It is a relief to find one of the brightest boys growing
up during the period, William T. Sherman, shunning
versatility as a plague, and counseling his young brother

---

[1] J. D. Richardson, ed., *A Compilation of the Messages and Papers of
the Presidents, 1789-1908* (Wash., 1908), II, 449.

John to mix no two occupations, not even engineering and trade, or law and politics.   This was not only a reaction from the evil effects of the Jacksonian doctrine which he saw about him, but in part due to the fact that equality found among certain of Jackson's contemporaries an interpretation different and less likely to abuse.[1]

Penetrating the quiet recesses of Concord, Massachusetts, optimism and equality flamed in Emerson into the doctrine that all men were divine, and could become as God, thus placing equality upon a superhuman plane. While, however, he flung his challenge into the teeth of that Calvinism which had so dominated American thought, he retained Calvinism's practical teaching. This elevation of mankind was open to all, but it could be attained only by effort.   Self-improvement—that it was the duty of man to control his conduct and that he possessed the power to mold his character—had ever been a central feature of Calvinistic discipline and particularly in New England.   Now under the impulse of national elation this conviction became not merely a solemn duty, with fear of failure always present and with escape from damnation as its most insistent motive; it was a thrilling, almost gay, opportunity, a sure key to treasures of earth and heaven.   Seldom have people thronged so merrily to school.

The ultimate tendency of Jackson's view would have been to dull effort by a satisfied sameness.   Equality to Emerson was a reward of striving.   Andrew Johnson, a child of their generation, combined the two: "I believe man can be elevated; man can become more and more endowed with divinity; and as he does he becomes more God-like in his character and capable of governing himself.   Let us go on elevating our people, perfecting

[1] W. T. and John Sherman, *Letters* (Rachel Sherman Thorndike, ed., N. Y., 1894), 6-7, 10-12.

our institutions, until democracy shall reach such a point of perfection that we can acclaim with truth that the voice of the people is the voice of God." [1]

It was more immediately important that both Jackson and Emerson realized that equality was not yet existent. Jackson, therefore, and the confrères and disciples of Emerson set themselves to make it so by throwing down the obstacles they saw in the way, fearlessly breaking old habits and customs with the same confidence that American mechanics were discarding old methods and devising new machines. Restrictions as to the suffrage, long terms of office, the barriers of ignorance, the impediments of blindness, such were the hindrances to the equality of man, and to annihilate them was the dominant idealistic aim of this generation.

In the twenties and thirties these aims were developed, first here, then there, now by one individual, then by another. By the forties there was very general acceptance of the validity of such purposes, and to carry them into effect it was only necessary to overcome inertia, unless they touched some substantial interest, such as the liquor traffic, or some division of interest or of culture, as in the case of slavery. To force such obstacles, organization was resorted to in both politics and philanthropy. The most striking thing about all these campaigns, however, is that their strategy was invariably based on the conception that all might be accomplished at once. To deny that the American system of government would be immediately beneficial if adopted in China, was to commit democratic treason; heredity availed not—opportunity plus effort would produce anything at once. The most exacting, of the people who counted, asked only the infant at birth.

Finally, it must be remembered that the dominant note in all these campaigns was Emerson's. The limit

[1] Andrew Johnson, *Speeches* (Frank Moore, ed., Boston, 1865), 56.

was only at the top.   Nothing was to be dragged down.
The struggle for equality aimed not at all at transferring
one man's wealth to another; no important man thought
of an equal division.   Nor was there any purpose of lim-
iting any man's liberty.   The ideals—that some men's
liberty should be restricted because they are not strong
enough to use it for their own advantage; that some
men's liberty, or at least the liberty of artificial men,
corporations, should be restricted because dangerous to
other individuals or to the body politic; that the body
politic is more deserving of consideration than any of
the individuals who comprise it—were never in America
so weakly held or apologetically presented.   Resources
were limitless.   Free men could be trusted to want what
was right and to get it.

CHAPTER II

THE MATERIAL AND SOCIAL INHERITANCE

THE United States in 1830 was divided into the settled East, which extended from the seacoast to the mountains with New Orleans as a detached fragment, and the settling West. There was little in the material civilization of the East to discourage those who proposed to reproduce it in the wilderness. The most important cities along the Atlantic were New York, with a population of two hundred thousand, Philadelphia, with three fourths as many, Baltimore, with eighty thousand, Boston, with sixty thousand, and Charleston, fifth in size, with thirty thousand. As smaller but similar companions were such towns as Portland, Portsmouth, Newburyport, Salem, New Bedford, Newport and Providence, New Haven, Norfolk and Savannah.[1] New Orleans, the chief city of the Gulf, numbered more than forty-five thousand.

In all these the busy section was the water front, with its wharves, its warehouses and merchants' offices. In some cases, as in Newburyport, a merchant's wharf was at the foot of his estate and his land ran up to higher ground where stood his mansion. New York and

---

[1] In 1830 the population of the cities listed below was as follows: Portland, 12,601; Portsmouth, 8,082; Newburyport, 6,388; Salem, 13,895; New Bedford, 7,592; Newport, 8,010; Providence, 16,832; New Haven, 10,180; Norfolk, 9,814; Savannah, 7,776; Mobile, 3,194. The largest inland cities were Albany, 24,238; Cincinnati, 24,831; Pittsburgh, 12,568; and Louisville, 10,341. J. D. De Bow, comp., *Statistical View of the United States . . . Being a Compendium of the Seventh Census* (Wash., 1854), 192-193.

13

Charleston, with unusual civic sense, beautified their entrances, New York by Battery Park, and Charleston by presenting to the harbor a frontage of pleasing residences. In all these cities were mansions which still remain and are prized today for their charm. Some were already in 1830 over a hundred years old. The majority, however, had been built since Independence. From city to city there was some variation in type. In New England the fashion was a square built, three-storied structure, with a "captain's walk" railed in upon the roof, generally built of wood, and with a wealth of craftsmanship lavished upon doorway, fireplaces and stairs. In the Middle Atlantic states, stone or brick, with trimmings of wood or marble, and with suggestions of the Georgian period of English architecture, was more common. In Charleston graceful vine-clad galleries had developed to keep out the too insistent sun, while in New Orleans the Mediterranean tradition faced the house toward a courtyard or enclosed garden. In New York, Philadelphia, Baltimore and some other cities rows of connected houses lined many of the best blocks.

Notable buildings had come only after the merchants had established themselves in dignity. In Boston, however, Faneuil Hall and Market, and in Philadelphia, Independence Hall, were already storied edifices, and about the college buildings at Harvard, Brown, Yale, Columbia, Princeton and William and Mary clustered tales of the Revolution. Since that date ambition had grown, and Bulfinch's state houses at Boston and Hartford were well worthy of what they represented. In New York the city hall was at once beautiful and imposing. Spanish rule, however, had given to New Orleans what were perhaps the most impressive relics of the past. Curiously, the deep and widespread interest in religion had not manifested itself in churches corresponding to residences and public buildings. But there were churches everywhere; and the traveler might have noticed that they fell into architectural types, such as the delightful square brick and marble parish churches of Virginia, and the long, high-windowed meeting-houses of New England, with their fine tapering spires, often modeled on those of Wren.   The dominant note was the Protestant desire to worship God "in purity and truth," rather than in costly temples.   From an architectural point of view the most important ecclesiastical edifices were the Catholic cathedrals in New Orleans and Baltimore.

Even before the Revolution the rearing of statues had begun, and now monuments were rising, which still in our day befit the dignity of what they commemorate. Baltimore deserved her title of "the Monumental City," with her memorials to Washington and her Battle Monument in memory of her famous victory over the British fleet in 1814.   Boston was carrying out a great conception in her Bunker Hill Monument, and Richmond had paid her respects to Washington with an excellent statue by Houdon.   Such undertakings illustrated civic pride as well as gratitude.

Here was what the Americans chose to have when they had wealth and leisure.   On any well selected site in the West, the best the East possessed might have been reproduced; and some of it was.   This simple architecture, however, held a charm which vitally affected the form of what the Americans had to have, as dwelling houses, banks and stores.   This charm lay in simplicity and   good workmanship.   The first impression an American city gave was of its whiteness.   In some red brick was used, in some native stone, but the decoration was in marble, or wood painted white; the ideal of Americans was the new white capitol rising on the Potomac.   In form there was little that was American. Jefferson and Bulfinch were great architects, but they brought over to America the current styles of Western Europe, the one the French Revolutionary return to the Greek, and the other, Roman themes as adapted in England. For the most part, however, American edifices were not built by architects, or by owners who made their own plans, but by skilled masons and carpenters working from books of drawings produced in England and France. Architecture, therefore, was American by selection rather than by creation; it was indicative of taste rather than of thought. In this respect the United States was still colonial and the West was a colony of the East.

What is still more significant is the unquestionable fact that this architecture had a symbolic quality. The taste which made the selection was not that of "the people" but of "the others." Mansions possessed in their simplicity a certain aloofness. By instinct each builder got an effect of dignity which, either by design or by reason of the spirit of the times, the architects even of the very rich rarely attain today. In these mansions and in those of the country estates that dotted the interior from Maine to Georgia, there was evidently lived a life at once orderly and refined.

Philadelphia, New York and Charleston were perhaps the only cities where, when you were invited to dine, you knew exactly when to go and what to wear. Yet an American gentleman would not feel awkward as a guest in any cultured home from that of the Dearborns of Maine to that of the Livingstons of New Orleans. Families like the Winthrops of Massachusetts, the Carrolls of Maryland and the Lees of Virginia had been gentry and had lived as gentry for hundreds of years. The founders of other families had migrated in the seventeenth century with the definite intention of making their descendants gentry, and many had succeeded. These groups had intermarried with the successful administrators of plantations, the great merchants of the eighteenth century and the war profiteers of the Revolution.   They had intermarried from city to city, and in any house party, no matter how far from home, one was apt to meet some dowager who would ask if one were a Smith of Smithtown, Maryland, or one of the Smiths of Boston, or alas! merely a Smith.   To some extent, then, there was an American Society.   In 1830 it was considering what its attitude should be toward very successful lawyers such as Daniel Webster, and incredibly wealthy post-Revolutionary families such as the Astors.   Soon it admitted both.

Like architecture, society was colonial in that it was not only derived from Europe but looked to Europe for standards of manners and taste.   In molding its standards of morals and habits, however, American experience had been more creative.   Its outstanding feature was that its women controlled it.   Not even Andrew Jackson could cause the wife of one of his cabinet members to be received in Washington.   Feminine control at that time meant a more than Victorian censorship of art, literature and the stage.   It created an atmosphere that welcomed poetry and tragedy, but did not encourage humor.   Such control, however, stopped at the driveway gate.

Society required a certain standard of living, but not an extravagant one.   It averaged about what one could attain today, according to the locality, for from twenty to fifty thousand dollars a year.   Few individuals, however, handled anything approaching that amount of money.   In Boston successful men had on the whole more than they knew how to spend.   In Virginia a single plantation seldom produced enough to maintain one's place, and the balance was made up by interest on investments saved from more prosperous times.   In South Carolina, on the other hand, the plantation society was in 1830 rising toward the crest of its economic efficiency, and supported the most complete and self-confident aristocracy of the land.

The American aristocracy of this period was distinguished from contemporary foreign aristocracies by its insistence that all its members engage in some form of labor economically productive; it was distinguished from the later nonaristocratic money kings of the United States by its refusal to immerse itself in such labors, and by its aim to reach in middle life a position where such employment might be foregone, and politics, reading and other occupations of leisure take its place.   This universality of practical activity is nowhere better illustrated than in the daily round of the mistress of a Southern plantation, whom one met at dinner, charming, lanquid, pleasingly unable to sway her fan, but who, during the day, had performed all the tasks necessary in the executive head of an establishment of twenty or thirty operatives which ran the house, supplied the table and made the clothes of several hundred Negroes, sometimes from the wool to the finished article; who furnished all ordinary medical attention to the whole community; and who besides was expected to be an expert in such arts as fine sewing and an amateur in literature and music.[1]

This society, with some local variations, danced and attended horse races; it read solid and sentimental literature but not that which was too highly sophisticated; it followed in dress, slowly and with discretion, the European fashions; the men hunted and the women rode; it went to church on Sunday, attending, generally, in New England Congregational or Unitarian services, in New York the Dutch Reformed, in Baltimore and New Orleans the Catholic, in Philadelphia Quaker meeting, in South Carolina the Presbyterian, in Virginia

[1] V. R. Gearhart, *The Southern Lady, 1840-1850* (unpublished thesis, Univ. of Wis.).

and also to some extent in all the states the Episcopal.[1]
Its members dined each other, but more frequently enter-
tained at house parties. It had begun to move somewhat
with the season; in South Carolina, from the plantation
to Charleston, in Virginia, for a holiday at the Hot
Springs, in New York, to country places up the Hudson
or to Saratoga. Honeymoons were spent in leisured
journeys by carriage or canal boat to Niagara Falls.
Europe was an experience which came to but few, and
to them as the event of a lifetime.

American aristocracy was not a closed caste, and it
was everywhere firmly linked with the mass. Like the
presidency and a fortune, it was theoretically within
everyone's reach. It had, of course, lost the colonial
protection of entail and primogeniture, and had not yet
caught the idea of race suicide. Its sons and daughters
swarmed out, carrying inbred ideals that they sought to
realize in new regions. It was, therefore, pervasive, and
few of the towns or countrysides of the West were
without its representatives. Its mode of life thus presented a model toward which most Americans had always
looked with desire, and now could look with confidence.
Thus Henry Clay became Mr. Clay of Ashland, Andrew
Jackson made the Hermitage a country seat fit to rank
with Mount Vernon; even the young Andrew Johnson,
who hated this aristocracy, dressed and formed his
manners to its standards. So during the riotous generation of the thirties and forties, despite the advent of
new industrial classes who might talk of socialism and
other novelties and despite the unchecked individualism
of the Western pioneer, there remained on the surface
some of the decorum of colonial life. In architecture,
in costume, in the form of oratory, in the conduct and
the content of education, there was sufficient uniformity

---

[1] M. L. Edwards, "Religious Forces in the United States, 1815-1830,"
Miss. Valley Hist. Rev., V, 434-449.

of aim and method to make it possible to judge whether one had or had not "arrived."

As our story begins, the economic control by this aristocracy was limited, and affected life only at certain points. Of the natural resources of the land, in so far as they were used at the time, they controlled very little; they were distinctly an aristocracy by prestige based on the service of their fathers or themselves. In the years following, however, they became to some extent amalgamated with a rising moneyed class. By 1850 the two together practically monopolized the very good land of the South, and by organization they acquired some control of iron ore, coal and water power in the North.

In 1830, international trade, shipping and fishing were open everywhere to the enterprising. Internal trade was absolutely open. Skilled trades were pursued by independent workmen, who, like the farmers, were generally their own capitalists. It was exceptional for the aristocracy to control labor, save in the case of Negro slaves in the South.[1] There would indeed have been little economic ground for class feeling, had it not been for finance. The number of banks was small, and to be upon their directorates was a distinction. Most of them were conservatively managed, and were in friendly relations with the great United States Bank which had branches in every state and headquarters at Philadelphia, where resided its president, Nicholas Biddle, the archpriest of American aristocracy. The banks were supplemented by more venturesome private bankers; but they too belonged to the inner circle. A philosophic observer might well have marked that finance was controlled by but a small element of the American people, while it was daily more vitally affecting the lives of all.

Still more striking, and to the typical American of

[1] For exceptions see J. R. Commons, "American Shoemakers, 1648-1895," *Quart. Journ. of Econ.*, XXIV, 39-84.

In the basin of the Great Lakes men worked in the forest;

*In the East, as at the Catskill Mountain House, it was now a playground
for the rich.*

1830 more galling, was the relationship of the aristocracy to politics. As politically minded as that of England, the American aristocracy had for many years maintained a monopoly of officeholding almost complete.[1] It dominated both parties, and while elections made fundamental changes in political policy, much more fundamental than are made today, they did not change the fact that most offices were filled by gentlemen. These gentlemen, moreover, failed to share to the full the exuberant optimism of the majority of their fellow countrymen, and they quite failed to accept its belief in equality. With old John Winthrop, they believed that of the whole the good are the fewer, and of the good the wisest are the fewest. It is true that, unlike the High Federalists of 1800, the greater number believed in popular government, but they did not believe in popular administration.[2]

This was a spirit and a monopoly which the optimistic equalitarians of the new generation set out first to break. Between 1815 and 1829 they had dented it seriously in such states as New York and Pennsylvania. In 1829 the new spirit swept into national power with Andrew Jackson. His election, however, was not a final settlement, but the beginning of the most bitter struggle.

It was not the aristocracy alone which had an inheritance of standards. When, however, one steps from the city mansions to the smaller homes nearby or to the farmhouses beyond, it is less safe to generalize. The middle classes, who made up the great body of the Americans, were provincial, with characteristics and habits as yet unblended. Most significant of all American elements for their generation were the middle-class

[1] D. R. Fox, *Decline of Aristocracy in the Politics of New York* (Columbia Univ., *Studies*, LXXXVI), chaps. xii-xiv.
[2] George Ticknor, *Life, Letters and Journals* (G. S. Hillard, ed., Boston, 1876), II, 1-21, 240-241.

New Englanders.   Like bees they lived in many communities, but the laws of the different hives were much the same—penetrating laws affecting deeply the individual in the innermost recesses of his soul.   Perhaps two thousand such communities, villages, towns or small cities, each complete with its own social gradations, and to a large extent economically independent also, dotted New England, western New York and northeastern Ohio— the "Western Reserve."   To those formed to meet it, nothing could be more stimulating than the earnest conformity to community standards of plain living and high thinking, which characterized these places.   Many individuals failed, and constituted a degenerate and often wandering class to be found in certain quarters of the villages and on the remoter farms.   Others revolted, and hived new communities which, once formed, it required a metaphysician to differentiate from those they swarmed from.

The standards which they maintained represented one of the highest community achievements in history. They were lacking, however, in cheer and emotional outlet.   Games were few in 1830, though faint shadows of English rustic dances remained.   Muster day in May afforded some general merrymaking.   Boys went to sea, men almost universally drank, occasionally heavily.   The women gossiped, with each other and with the peddlers who brought news and wares from town to town. Occasionally bills flared on the sides of barns, a premonitory clown sported on the common, a bugler blew his trumpet, and the less pious gathered in the open air for a circus.

To such a people the new impulses of the period opened a world of light and happiness.   More important than the economic opportunities which they were called to share was the change in spiritual outlook, a change which only gradually showed itself in creeds, a growing, happy, moving conviction that all men were equal, not as they had thought of it, in sin, but in possibilities of good. This changed point of view rushed many off their feet into the excesses of religious revivals. Others, however, were too firmly grounded in the practice of a life based on reason to be overwhelmed. New England was like a well-made engine into which an electric current was newly turned, increasing its power of production.

Perhaps the most notable factor in this change, which escaped being a revolution, was the continuity of leadership. As two centuries of close intellectual training in the manses of Scotland fitted the minds of their sons for the great outburst of intellectual activity which in the eighteenth century made the Scotch the bankers and engineers of the world, and as the German parsonages bred the great leaders of German thought in the nineteenth century, so the New England ministerial families furnished a most unusual proportion of the leaders of her new activities. Hundreds of the radicals of the thirties and forties possessed the bone and sinew and the moral earnestness and mental habits of six or seven generations of ministers who would have regarded their aims and views as conceptions of the devil. With trained minds and steady habits, with economic resources adequate to its measured needs, with a high consciousness of its relative merits, and now thrilled by the enthusiasm of the hour into a belief that the great experiment of 1630 had finally succeeded and that its light should now shine penetratingly abroad for the regeneration of the world, the New England dominant, but not always ruling, middle class was prepared to do its duty.

From the sober, commodious, fairly comfortable, clean, white-painted houses and red barns of New England, one passed over the Berkshires to find a different countryside. The Dutch in the Valley of the Hudson, the Quakers in that of the Delaware, and the Germans in those of the Susquehanna and the Mohawk built their farmhouses somewhat more substantially than those of New England, often indeed of stone. Their farms, too, spread about them somewhat more graciously, there were generally more farm laborers, and the villages were farther apart. There was, too, more distinction between country and town or city. A New England village, except for its common with church, town hall and academy, consisted of houses much like those of the farms, and with good-sized "yards." Even in the cities the same mode prevailed, and long streets stretched out with the small white cottages, green-shuttered and with long receding outhouses, of small tradesmen and mechanics. In New York state and Pennsylvania, the towns were more closely built, with double houses, or houses in blocks, whose contribution to the passerby was an austere front and a doorstep, often of white marble, whose cleanliness was the measure of respectability. Here as in New England, however, practically every house was independent in its sewage arrangements and in its water supply. Infant mortality was high and serious epidemics not uncommon.

The civilization of the middle region was not in so forward a state as that of New England. None of its three dominant strains possessed so isolated a habitat. From the first many mingling currents had flowed into the land with them, and now they were rapidly losing their individuality, while the time had not yet come when the blend should be complete. Dutch habits had received a serious blow from Washington Irving's *Knickerbocker History of New York*. Before the Dutch traditions came back into high estimation, the Dutch element had lost its individual distinctiveness. In 1830 few spoke Dutch, and only the unimportant spoke Dutch alone. Dutch blood, solidity, business ability and political common sense persisted, and extended through intermarriage; but Dutch brasses and long clay pipes, and types of dress were becoming comic symbols of the very rustic.

Quaker discipline, that extraordinarily effective controller of lives and habits based on the doctrine of extreme individualism, was in full vigor. The members of its meetings were aristocrats, merchants and farmers. Their dress was, decade by decade, becoming more distinctive as its fixed style came to be farther and farther from the fashions of the day. More and more it became a hallmark of industry, real sobriety, philanthropy, and of an honesty which was no foe to shrewdness. · This success, however, had not been gained without loss. The uncompromising maintenance of a rigid standard frightened the weak, and, in the absence of persecution, the meetings ceased to attract many of revolutionary temper. More and more the children of Quakers left the meetings and became "worldly," some joining other religious bodies, and some remaining in sympathy though not connected with the faith of their parents. Of new converts there were practically none. The Quakers, as had been the Spartans, were a carefully trained and diminishing stock.

The German settlements were in an intermediate position. Coming to America with the least capital of any of the community groups they had had a severe struggle. Now they were economically on their feet, but the effort which had been necessary to bring their farms to a point of comfortable productiveness had absorbed the energies of several generations, and much of the culture brought over by men like Pastorius had been lost. In the districts which they occupied, German was still the dominant language, but it was in the mouths of most of them an impoverished tongue. The opportunities of those speaking it only were limited. The ambitious youth were amalgamating with the population about them. By the close of the period this element had reached about the stage of absorption that the Dutch had reached in 1830, except for a few communities, such as those of the Mennonites of Pennsylvania, which were held together by a strong bond of religious particularity. While, however, they were in the process of group dissolution, they contributed, like the Dutch and the Quakers, some of those qualities of strength and distinction that seem to be best developed in small and isolated societies.[1]

On the whole, through this middle region, people drank as heavily as in New England, but more regularly; they generally drank whisky instead of rum. There was not much more playing of games, but there was less disapproval of amusement. Through these rich farming districts traveled not only more peddlers but more circuses. More than one ambitious boy of speculative genius started climbing to fortune by amusing the rustic with curiosities, stunts and fakes. Daniel Drew made such enterprises the foundation of more questionable successes in other lines. P. T. Barnum capped sensation with sensation until he made his circus his fortune.[2]

South of the Potomac the social organization of the middle classes was less significant. Poor boys of the piedmont made their way in the world, but the one standard of life that seemed worth emulation was that of their rich planter neighbors. Sturdy mountaineers descended to the plain, numerous among them the virile inheritors of the education established by John Knox and the disputations that he started; but they had no memory of an attractive social order, and sought to achieve the like of what they found. The reasonably

---

[1] Martha B. Lambert, "A Dictionary of Non-English Words of the Pennsylvania German Dialect," Pa. German Soc., *Proceeds. for 1924,* *appendix.*
[2] Bouck White, *The Book of Daniel Drew* (N. Y., 1911), chaps. ii-iv, vi-xi; P. T. Barnum, *Struggle and Triumph* (Buffalo, 1874), 40, 50, 66-67, 70, 86; M. R. Werner, *Barnum* (N. Y., 1925), chaps. i-ii.

successful in the South, then, formed themselves on the aristocracy. It took but a few slaves and a slight dwelling to make the imaginative eyes of that generation visualize their farms as ancestral plantations. When, however, they failed to secure enough to feed their fertile imaginations, they left the plantation country, or sank into a habit of slovenliness. A traveler coming southward noticed quickly the change from the kempt landscape of the Middle states to one of charming estates, cheek by jowl with ragged, ill-farmed holdings.[1]

In the South more time was given to relaxation than elsewhere. In this social life there was somewhat more of a distinction between the sexes than in other regions, though such separation was everywhere marked. There was a double standard of morals for men and women, which, in so far as it was a restriction upon the latter, both sexes sternly enforced. The result of this limitation of what was "proper" for "females" was that the social activities of women were largely conditioned upon wealth and position, and the life of those of the poorer classes was drab indeed. To their comfort came religion. Revivals, *colporteurs*, circuit riders in the remoter regions and yearly campmeetings, lasting one or two weeks, established religion in the hearts of millions by meeting a crying human need.

The men had a wider range. Like those elsewhere, they drank whisky, and more generally than elsewhere they hunted and rode. Nor were the Negroes left without amusement. The week of Christmas to New Year's was their festival, and they found ready response to their greeting of "Christmas gif', Miss Sally." So widely scattered a population felt the need of occasionally coming together, and politics, like religion, endeared itself to all by its thrilling barbecues where roasted oxen

[1] P. H. Buck, "The Poor Whites of the Ante-Bellum South," *Am. Hist. Rev.*, XXXI, 41-54.

and punch were followed by the fluent and emotional orators whom every Southern county produced.

The mountain area of 1830 had changed little since Revolutionary days.   Such change as had taken place was a subtle one.   Its more ambitious blood had been drained away to the southeastern piedmont and the West.   It waited strong and unyielding until the sixties and seventies should send it a new influx to tap its concealed treasures of iron and coal and oil.   Beyond the mountains, however, from Lakes to Gulf and from the mountains to beyond the Mississippi, all was change. The explorer and hunter had passed on, or fretted derelict amid a life they did not understand.   The brief day of romantic adventure, of the fine code of men always in danger, of perilous and lawless dreams, when empires seemed to depend on personal encounters in the forest, had vanished.   The West was in its awkward age. Nothing that man had yet done there compensated for the ugly slashings he had made in primeval woods. Steamboats with their white two-and-three-storied colonnades were the most impressive evidence of man's handiwork.   St. Louis, indeed, was an old town; Cincinnati, though the emporium of the West, was little more than a river market-town; and across the stream in the "blue grass" of Kentucky were rising some comfortable mansions.   But most people lived in log cabins as yet unboarded, surrounded by a few roughly cleared acres, and inaccessible to neighbors except by river, to one of which most farms were close.

There was in 1830 no separate and distinctive Western life.   Here and there, to the north, were communities which had transported themselves entire from the East. To the south were often whole organized plantations transferred bodily from Virginia.   For the most part, the movement into the region, and in 1830 it was still chiefly populated by those who themselves made the movement, was, like that into the Ark, two by two. Though many men and boys came individually, the great valley was occupied principally by families.[1]

These families were germs for the diffusion of all the cultures which had been bred in America. They brought furniture, seeds, fashions and recipes, they brought the gayety and the charm of South Carolina, the stern New England belief in persistent education, the steadiness of the Dutch, the thoroughness of the Germans, the political wisdom of Virginia. Notable in numbers were those whose ancestors had carried the sinewy tradition of Scotch intellectual life through the disappointments of Ireland. Such family movements were among the forces that made the section colonial to the East. The better educated kept in touch, in spite of the infrequent and expensive mail, with home. Younger brothers and sisters, nephews and nieces were brought out, and as mothers grew old they nourished in their descendants the traditions of the past, so that into the third and fourth generations there were passed on, and still flourish, habits and phrases developed before the time to which the memory of man runneth not to the contrary.

The great majority, moreover, had no such desire to create a new thing in the world as had the Puritans and the Quakers. Many indeed came because change attracted them, and others, who were to be much more potent for change, were of those who saw visions which they hoped to realize in a flexible society. The greater number, however, wished and expected, before middle age should be upon them, to reside in a community such as that from which they came, with a few improvements, and in which they themselves would occupy a better position and be able to live as the top men lived at home.

[1] A good account of a family migration is in A. W. Kellogg, "Recollections of Life in Early Wisconsin," *Wis. Mag. of Hist.*, VII, 473-498.

These dreams, whether of new utopias or of a renewed and regenerated environment of their youth, had small chance of realization. There were too many dreams. On the whole, the settlement of the coast had been by communities, and a community, however small and isolated, may and often does progagate its conceptions of life. Individuals and families may pass on traditions, but no one of them can shape a civilization. Diversity was the leading social feature of the region in 1830, and chaos, or a blending into one or more social orders more purely American than anything which had previously existed, was the prospect for the future.

Towards the latter outcome signs were already pointing. Intermarriage of the different elements was common though not yet usual. Common problems brought the divergent into coöperation. Particularly, divisions on national policy arose between the inhabitants of this new region and their brothers of the East, which developed a local self-consciousness in the West and gave to Andrew Jackson, its representative, its almost solid support for the presidency in 1828.

Already there was characteristic of the region a certain spirit of youth, of confidence and of willingness to discard the tried. In fact, Westerners thought themselves freer from the past than they were. Nowhere in the country were the new impulses of the time so strongly felt. They believed in equality because to such a high degree equality was a fact among them. Any man might hope for anything more reasonably here than elsewhere. The great tasks required courage, ingenuity and endurance, not trained skill. According to their native abilities and character they might succeed, and they were largely of the stripe who believed in themselves. The optimism of the period heard everywhere sounded its loudest, and not altogether lovely, note among the four and a half million inhabitants of the frontier, who constituted one third the population of the country. Not by numbers alone, however, but by their crude embodiment of the spirit of the age, they prepared to lead the country. Their partial success marks the first case in history of a nation dominated by a frontier population.

On the whole, the developed material inheritance of this generation was not a remarkable tribute to the two centuries that preceded. Greek colonies came much more rapidly to wealth and the power to foster art. Australia and New Zealand advanced with quicker economic strides. Considering the amount of European capital brought to America, its increase had been but slow.[1] The greatest material accomplishment had been in the soil brought into cultivation; the next was the accumulation and the acclimatization of animal stocks, fruits, vegetables and grain. This new generation, in its efficiency, could in ten years' time have duplicated the houses, furniture, roads and bridges that it found, but its tastes and standards had not much improved; indeed it is quite possible that such a restoration would have lost much in form and soundness of workmanship. A greater legacy was that of social organizations, the fruits of millenniums of European development, now adapted to American conditions. These they could not have created, nor could they break away from them save by development. It was a legacy which their ancestors had been able to give them only by devoting an unusual proportion of their lives to the things of the spirit at the cost of material accumulations.

[1] See L. H. Jenks, *The Migration of British Capital* (N. Y., 1927), chaps. iii-iv, for the part played by London money in developing American industry and public works in the thirties and forties.

CHAPTER III

AIMS AND METHODS

WITH such an inheritance this generation set itself to the accomplishment of gigantic tasks. It aimed to fix its civilization upon the great central plain of the Lakes, the Mississippi and the Gulf, and to secure for itself the Pacific Coast, and possibly other areas. This was an undertaking similar to that in which Englishmen were engaging at about the same time in Australia and New Zealand, Russians in Siberia, and French in Algeria, but there was little comparison and mutual exchange of experimentation, and different methods led in all cases to success, though with significant differences in the character of the results.[1]

Americans aspired, however, not merely to carry on the civilization that they inherited, but to transform their life while they were transplanting it. In this, too, they were not alone, for all European civilization was in the throes of transformation, social, political and economic. Of this Americans were not totally unaware and there was some conscious and more instinctive interplay of ideas. Emerson read and imported the doctrine of German philosophers; Calhoun studied and utilized the writings of such Englishmen as Austin, Cobden and Bright; William Lloyd Garrison brought to America English abolitionists; Father Matthew preached temperance in America and Ireland; and foreign travelers, such as de Tocqueville, studied American conditions for indications of the future. Waves of popular excitement,

[1] C. R. Fish, "The Frontier, a World Problem," *Wis. Mag. of Hist.*, I, 121-141.

such as that of 1830, generated in popular discontent, and that of 1848 in the will to nationalism, ignored the Atlantic;[1] the former was reflected in labor's demands for better living standards and education, and in the many-sided movements for humane reforms, the latter in the great enterprises of expansion into Mexico and Oregon. On the other hand, different individuals, but particularly different sections and provincial cultures, had their own views of the transformation that should take place. All hurried with their millenarian optimism to the early accomplishment of their ideals. Protected by our federal system, many different ambitions found realization, and there was in certain respects greater diversity in the nation when the generation was old than there had been in its youth.

For the rapid materialization of these vast purposes, there were needed transportation more effective than had ever been known, and means of communication that could connect a people scattered over immense spaces. It was necessary that invention be quickened and that its results be made immediately available. To do this, capital must be secured and encouraged to plunge boldly into unheard-of enterprises. To facilitate its accumulation there were never enough hands at work, and, except by the craftsmen, labor-saving devices were welcomed as in no other part of the world. Still, accumulation was too slow in the areas that needed most, and the savings of other sections and countries were sought.

On its first entrance into national power, in 1815, this generation had seemed inclined to pursue these ends by the agency of the national government. It was the view that Hamilton would have taken, and it represented the natural attitude of that part of any people, at any time,

---

[1] See, for example, E. N. Curtis, "American Opinion of the French Nineteenth-Century Revolutions," *Am. Hist. Rev.*, XXIX, 249-270; also J. G. Gazley, *American Opinion of German Unification, 1848-1871* (Columbia Univ., *Studies*, CXXI), esp. chaps. i, vii, ix.

who believe that progress comes as the result of joint action and leadership.   It was obviously the natural inclination of three of the greatest political leaders of the period, Clay, Calhoun and Webster.

The individualistic attitude, however, with its ideal of restricting the government to the preservation of order among individuals, and of leaving the impulse to advance to individual initiative, had been well developed in America by Thomas Jefferson, and was bound up with an interpretation of the Constitution which was common and which he had made popular.   The conflict between these two ideas might have been close in any event, but it was sharpened by the entrance of another element into the situation.   In the competition of sectional interests, the South came gradually to find itself in a minority which it believed would be permanent.   In that region, therefore, the Jeffersonians, who disbelieved in governmental guidance, were joined by the faction that preferred strong government but feared that under existing circumstances the national government would lead in the wrong direction.   By 1830 Calhoun had changed sides.

The consequence was that throughout this period the agency of the national government was reduced to a minimum.   Although a protective tariff was maintained during most of the time, it was so much the result of sectional compromises that it scarcely meant a comprehensive plan for the development of industry.   In 1846 it was abandoned in theory, and was not revived until 1861.   In 1836 the charter of the United States Bank was allowed to expire, in 1840 a "Divorce" bill, as it was not incorrectly called by John Quincy Adams, attempted to separate the money transactions of the government from those of the community, and while money questions were discussed in politics, the actual currency function of the national government was reduced to the minting of coins. In 1830 President Jackson vetoed the Maysville Road bill, and by so doing placed an effective stop to the development of transportation under national auspices. National aid in the form of land grants was from time to time extended to transportation enterprises, but construction and management were left to other agencies.[1]

The next agency at the disposal of the people was that of the state governments. In 1825 New York state had completed an undertaking of truly national importance: the Erie Canal. That state, taking advantage of a great natural opportunity and of the fact that it could borrow at a lower rate of interest than individuals, opened the first cheap transportation route between the East and the West. This gave a great impulse to similar action by other states. It rallied the believers in governmental guidance who were balked in their hopes of national leadership. Even in the South, there being in the case of state activities no danger of outside dictation, the natural adherents of active government were able to carry out many of their designs. Congress from time to time, as in 1836 when it distributed the national surplus among the states, encouraged them. The rivalry of the port and other trading cities of the different states stimulated their activity. To the states in addition was left, by the policy of the national government, all such regulation of banking and of currency as the people chose to exercise.

Still a third function of the states was that of social regulation, and through them many sought to give universality to the changes they hoped to create in the character of American civilization. Opposed to such uses of state authority were not only those who disliked each change, but also those who disapproved of reform

---

[1] T. H. Haney, *Congressional History of Railroads* (Univ. of Wis., *Bull.*, III, no. 2), 8, 15-263.

by legislative means.   In the ultra-individualistic South, therefore, such proposals were rarely made.   In the North such schemes as could be carried out only by state approval and assistance, as universal free education, were often successful.   Laws to supplement the dictates of conscience by police compulsion, on the other hand, though frequently urged in the later days of the period, were rarely found, except in states where there was a strong New England element bred to the idea of community responsibility for individual conduct.

State legislatures were, therefore, throughout this period the scene of great activity and debate.   State interest in transportation was manifested in every conceivable way, from full responsibility, as in the case of the Georgia railroad from Atlanta to Chattanooga, to the buying of stock, or to the mere authorization to counties or towns to take stocks or bonds.   The capacity of the state governments to fill the gap left by the national government was, however, limited in various ways.   No other state possessed within itself a complete smoothed path from East to West as did New York.   Most states confined attention to a more local policy and sought to bring trade to their own chief ports; particularly in the South the first improvements ran fan-like from ports like Charleston, with small attention to national necessities.   Jealousy often created artificial obstacles, as when Pennsylvania fixed the standard gauge for railroads rather with reference to preventing those of New York from connecting with those of Ohio than with engineering advice.   It was not only difficult for the states to devise a national system but even a sectional one.   The sections which were business units had no political organization.   Toward the end of the period agreements between state governments were sought by conventions and by men like Calhoun to meet sectional needs, and some progress was made in developing a southern system of state-assisted roads.[1]

More important in determining the scope of state control of the means of transportation was the fact that the states were simultaneously responsible for the supply of money and the regulation of banking. The story of how the different states experimented with different systems, ranging from a state-owned bank in Mississippi to a system of no banks in Wisconsin, how one state copied another, how they were all tested by the great Panic of 1837, and how a store of experience was accumulated and the people gradually educated, is one of the most complete examples of how a federal system of government works towards constructive accomplishment. To live through such a period, however, is far from comfortable. One result was that this generation never attained banks that could be relied upon or an adequate currency.

The states in which transportation was especially needed were precisely those of the frontier where capital was least. The temptation was, therefore, strong to take advantage of the freedom of action allowed the states to create it. During the flush times of the middle thirties, when the generation was in the vigor of its exuberant youth, unable to coin its dreams, many states printed them and then discounted them in the money markets of the East and of Europe. Brought to earth by the Panic of 1837, ground down by four years and the subsidiary panic of 1841, some failed of payment, and such states as Mississippi, Louisiana, Indiana, Maryland, Pennsylvania and Michigan repudiated their obligations, though some of them afterwards paid in part or in whole. State credit received a staggering blow, and

[1] U. B. Phillips, "Transportation in the Ante-Bellum South: an Economic Analysis," *Quart. Journ. of Econ.*, XIX, 431-451; same author, "An American State-owned Railroad," *Yale Rev.*, XV, 259-282.

the states were to a large extent prevented from thereafter undertaking such work upon a large scale, however willing.[1]

Dissatisfaction with American political institutions was almost unknown, yet in two important particulars the agencies above described were deemed unsatisfactory. In the first place, Americans were not content to leave the decisions on the various points of dispute to a system purely representative. Pure democracy of the Greek and Roman pattern, on the other hand, was physically impossible for a population so widely scattered. There was a demand, amounting to insistence, that questions be brought directly to the people, and that their decisions on major controversies be carried to the various legislatures by men instructed, rather than by men elected for their general qualities and acting on their individual judgment. In the second place, the wish of the people, and added to it the force of circumstances, removed many important matters from the province of the legislatures. It was the philosophy of the time that they could best be dealt with by individual initiative, but many of them were beyond the capacities and resources of individuals. The inevitable result was nonpolitical organization, which was so necessary that it was encouraged.

Basic tasks, then, were the building up of an extra-legal system of political discussion and management, with the purpose of bringing the representative government more closely under popular control, and the development of nonpolitical bodies, capable of handling such problems as money, banking and transportation. In neither case was creation necessary; such organizations did actually exist. Yet so much was accomplished in the way of shaping inherited institutions to the new Amer-

[1] W. A. Scott, *The Repudiation of State Debts* (R. T. Ely, ed., N. Y., 1893), chaps. ii-v; C. F. Dunbar, *Economic Essays* (O. M. W. Sprague, ed., N. Y., 1917), 17-18, 168-171, 177-180.

ican conditions that political organization and business corporations in the modern sense may be regarded as actual contributions made by this generation, and among its contributions as important as any in influencing the future.   Both played so large a part at the time that the molding of these new agencies for larger use must be discussed as a preliminary to the study of the forces which operated through them, and of how far the aims of the generation were accomplished.

The development of political organization was closely connected with the attacks upon the aristocracy of office-holding.   One such attack began in the abduction in 1826 of William Morgan, a Free Mason, who, having become dissatisfied with the order, resolved to expose its secrets.   The facts of this particular case have never been satisfactorily ascertained and are unimportant.   Its results are significant.   The Masonic order had been popular in America and had received the patronage of men like Washington.   Naturally large numbers of office-holders of both parties were Masons.   In the investigation into the death of Morgan, it was claimed that use was made of this influence to prevent the discovery of truth.   Such a charge did not need precise evidences of soundness.   It appealed instinctively to the fears of the suspicious, especially of the rural classes of New York, New England and Pennsylvania.

A number of exceptionally clever young men seized upon this popular sentiment, and organized it into a political party.   Perhaps the most brilliant, suave and subtle was Thurlow Weed, who began at Rochester the *Anti-Masonic Enquirer*.   Conventions were held at which delegates gathered from groups of neighboring counties, adopted resolutions and nominated candidates for office.   Under able leadership sentiment was organized, and this organization became less a medium for turning sentiment into action than for capitalizing this particular sentiment and turning it to other purposes. How the Anti-Masonic party was steered by its leaders into the arms of the Whig party, and how its leaders stepped into the larger organization on a secure footing, is a story full of interest and of value for the study of political management.[1]

The larger significance of the movement was that it correctly expressed the fear and dislike of this generation for secret organization, and that however its adroit managers may have taken advantage of their supporters, they did secure for them their main object. The new political organizations that the time called for would not be in the nature of societies, secret or otherwise. Never since, in American history, have social and secret organizations played so small a part. Even college fraternities were attacked, and John Quincy Adams and a number of the ablest men of the time spent several days at Cambridge, deciding that Phi Beta Kappa should reveal its secrets to the world.[2] Almost alone of political clubs, Tammany Hall survived. The spirit of the time was, if not always for free speech, at least for open discussion and for political machines at least ostensibly in the light.

The positive movement had been preparing for some time in various states. In New York a number of factions, such as the Albany Regency, headed by the dapper and adroit Martin Van Buren, and the Clintonians who had held together for fifty years by the use of patronage, had long divided the people, formulated the issues for elections, and selected candidates. In Pennsylvania, a majority, and in many states as Massachusetts and Rhode Island, a minority, had maintained permanent political organizations charged with the

[1] Charles McCarthy, "The Anti-Masonic Party, 1827-1840," Am. Hist. Assoc., Report for 1902, I, 366-574.
[2] J. Q. Adams, Diary from 1795 to 1848 (C. F. Adams, ed., Phila., 1874-1877), VIII, 382-386, 389-392, 394-396.

Such movements as Antimasonry and Antislavery were carried forward by literary propaganda and conventions.

William Morgan writing his book against Masonry

Captured by the Masons, 1826

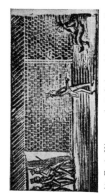

At Fort Niagara, just before his final disappearance

fighting of elections and with keeping a wary eye on those selected while in office. To make national such organizations had been the ambition of many leaders ever since the generation began to count. Failing to win Monroe or Adams, they had thrown their weight to Andrew Jackson, and, confident of his support, they flocked in 1829 to his inauguration.

Never was there a more striking symbol of change than this inauguration. From North and West his supporters gathered by the thousands, and the quiet and decorous little Southern city of Washington was taxed beyond its resources and its tolerance by a nightmare of crowds without manners or with ill manners. Many had made the journey at great sacrifice, some supplied chiefly with the coin of hope. On one point all were united. As expressed by one New York politician, an old friend of Aaron Burr, Samuel Swartwout, it was to turn out the "damned rascals." In the more philosophic language of William L. Marcy, a member of the Regency, "To the victors belong the spoils." Jackson, now, as so frequently, the authentic voice of the people, endorsed these views with the further purpose of destroying the idea of permanence in office. It was not an idea entirely new or American that officeholders should change with the changing party. The innovation was that, regardless of party, men should not hold office long. Rotation in the holding of offices from the most important to the least was to destroy the hold of the aristocracy on the machinery of government.

The revolution of 1829 was not a proletarian movement, and the new officers appointed by Jackson came from all classes. Nor must one imagine that all officers before Jackson's day came from the gentry. One change was that formerly officers had in fact regarded their positions as permanent, and had gradually assimilated their manners and their views to those of the governing

classes. Now they felt an insecurity which kept them
more alert to popular sentiment, and they tended to
affect the manners of the majority rather than of the
few. Thus Francis Preston Blair, a well-educated young
fellow of good family, came to Washington, acquired the
confidence of Jackson, and became in December, 1830,
the editor of the administration paper, the *Globe*.
Instinctively a quiet, conservative man, endued with a
powerful strain of canny Scotch wisdom, he affected as
editor a style vociferous and blatant, which he believed
was called for by the people and because of which he
has been written down in American history in colors
which were certainly not native.

To secure appointment, the first requisite was proof
of service in the election of 1828. Most numerous of
the successful were the editors, whose crude, ill-supported
sheets had spread broadcast the charges that Adams had
won his election by a corrupt bargain with Henry Clay,
and that the House of Representatives in 1825, in
electing Adams, had gone against the expressed preference of the people for Jackson. Major J. H. Eaton,
the new secretary of war, had written a campaign biography of Jackson. For these and similar reasons was
favor given.

Past service was, however, not all that was considered.
The new appointees were expected not only to perform
the functions of their offices—it was rather taken for
granted that anyone could do a thing so simple. The
point of investigation was, how the new appointment
would affect the party, and what further political service could be expected of the appointee. William B.
Lewis, Jackson's enthusiastic neighbor whom he had
brought from Tennessee to Washington, wrote to one of
the New York appointees in 1834: "Tell Swartwout to
peel off his coat and roll up his sleeves also; but, perhaps,
as he has to go through the 'glorious Senate,' it would

not be prudent for him to do so. Price, as his nomination will be certainly confirmed before the 8th, must do his own and Swartwout's part too." [1]

It was the combination of these three elements—political removal, appointment as a reward for past service, and an assurance of continued support in the future—that constituted the "spoils system." Jackson undoubtedly introduced this into national American politics, although it had existed in several states, and was still flourishing in Great Britain. Its evils have been too deeply impressed upon the present generation to need recapitulation. At the moment it meant a greater geniality in public service, which foreign travelers remarked with pleasure though they often commented upon the informality and boisterousness of American officials. In estimating the effects of the spoils system on internal conditions, one must consider also the fact that public services, both state and national, were during this period reduced to a minimum, and inefficiency, which would under an active government have been intolerable, actually caused little inconvenience.

The evil consequences of such a method of selecting public officers were brought out by the Panic of 1837. When it became impossible easily to obtain cash, it was discovered that some officials had been looting the government, and that a majority had used the government funds in their possession for private speculations, the failure of which left them defaulters. It cannot be said, however, that the government was left in much worse position than private business; for appointments by favoritism, absence of careful supervision and loose methods were characteristic of the period. When in 1840 the party of Jackson was at length defeated, their opponents the Whigs could think of no better method of

[1] C. R. Fish, *Civil Service and the Patronage* (*Harvard Hist. Studies,* XI), 124.

reform than that of turning out the men he had put in office, and no better criteria for appointment than those which he had sanctioned. The spoils system had become established for this generation at least; but some of its evils had been discovered, and there was during its latter years some improvement in administrative methods.[1]

The effects of the introduction of the spoils system were not merely on administration and in breaking the hold of aristocracy upon the public service; still more important was its connection with the development of party organization. The work that these new postmasters, land officers and custom-house officials were expected to do was to organize the party in their own localities. Committees gradually came into existence in all voting districts. In country towns the fortunate contender was sometimes the editor but more often the storekeeper. In either case he made his place of business popular by official prestige, and generally by whisky. In the coast cities organization was elaborate, and the chief officials used as party workers the employees in the government navy yards, custom houses and mail service. Some of those in the more important positions were expected to maintain newspapers, which were part of the party equipment and which rarely paid for themselves. Besides such personal service, all were expected to pay assessments, often amounting to one tenth of their salaries, for party expenses. The greatest political job was that of the printing for the United States government, and those who held it were expected to contribute heavily to the general funds of the party, and also to publish at Washington a paper which should be the mouthpiece of the administration. The organ of the Democrats, after a brief experiment with Duff Green's *Telegraph*, was the *Globe* of Blair and Rives, which was sold out in 1845 to the *Union* edited by Thomas Ritchie

[1] Fish, *Civil Service and the Patronage*, 124.

of Virginia. The Whigs gave such patronage as they controlled, generally the special printing of the Senate, to Gales and Seaton, whose *National Intelligencer*, founded as early as 1801, was for over fifty years the most quoted paper in the country.

The object of these local organizations was in the first place to hold and control party caucuses. This was done by calling such meetings at strategic times, and if necessary, in unexpected places, by arranging their business beforehand, and by breaking them up if they proved restive. At the caucuses, candidates for local offices were selected, and, still more important, delegates to county, congressional-district and state conventions.

Before 1830 conventions were unusual. During the thirties it became increasingly easy for people to get about, conventions were endorsed as democratic by Jackson, and in particular the system was advertised by its use in national politics. Although there had been some slight anticipation, it is substantially true that the first national convention was that of the Anti-Masons in 1830. In 1831 they again met, and this time nominated candidates for the presidency and vice-presidency. In 1831 the National Republicans met in convention at Baltimore, nominated Henry Clay, and called a second convention which met in 1832 and adopted a party platform. The Democrats had at this time no doubts about their candidate, the overwhelming majority favoring the "Old General." The latter, however, differed, it seemed, from a majority of his party in wishing Martin Van Buren as a running mate. To accomplish this purpose he favored a national convention. As he said, "I am no politician"—about which opinions may differ—"but if I were I would be a New York politician." [1] All the influence which the spoils system had given the administration was exerted to

[1] C. T. Brady, *The True Andrew Jackson* (Phila., 1906), 316.

secure delegates who would vote for Mr. Van Buren, and in spite of the adoption of a rule, which has become historic in the Democratic national system, that candidates must receive a two-thirds vote to be nominated, Van Buren was chosen on the first ballot.

This use of the convention to override the popular will influenced many to oppose the convention system. Such men, however, as Daniel Webster and Calhoun, struggled against it in vain, and the more worldly-wise Henry Clay adhered to it even when it repeatedly disappointed his dearest hopes. By 1840 it had become the recognized method of presenting candidates for office to the people, and in most cases of framing the political issues by the presentation of platforms.[1]

Superficially this system seemed to thwart rather than to facilitate the popular will. The majority of the delegates owed their selection to the manipulation of the basic caucuses. The conventions themselves were apt to be managed by shrewd men with a capacity for intrigue, such as Thurlow Weed, who in 1840 secured the nomination of Harrison when a majority of the Whigs probably preferred Clay. On the other hand Weed's object was not fundamentally hostility to Clay but the selection of a candidate who, while less pleasing to the majority of the party, would be less displeasing to a minority and to the independent voters who must be won over. Again, while Van Buren was nominated as vice-president contrary to the wish of a majority of the Democrats in 1832, in 1844 the will of the majority broke through and defeated his renomination for the presidency.

It is still more important that the rules of the conventions soon became as well known to the mass of the people as those of the Constitution, that their conduct

---

[1] Edward Stanwood, *History of the Presidency* (Boston, 1898), 166-177.

was under an increasing glare of publicity, and that consequently the convention system of party management was but an extension of the old Anglo-Saxon method of playing politics as a game with recognized rules of fair play, rules not perhaps always reaching to the heart of the matter but at least strictly enforced in so far as they went.

It was an interesting circumstance that in the United States the party organizations were at this time governed by the holders of public office and not by the party officers. Each convention, county, state or national, elected a committee charged with calling the next convention. The national committee consisted of one member from each state, chosen by the delegates of that state. These committees, by passing upon the credentials of the delegates for the succeeding convention, often exerted great influence. On the other hand they exerted little influence between elections. The head of the victorious party was the governor or president elected, and the minority party, though there was never so direct a leadership as in England, was held to speak through various legislative leaders, who indeed maintained their own separate congressional committees to look after their election interests.

The convention system, moreover, appears out of true focus when considered only in relation to the well-established major parties. It was during this period that it began to be a characteristic phase of American life. Legislative bodies of state and church, and the practice of law in circuit courts, state and national, had been almost the only means of bringing people from different localities into personal contact. Almost the only national reputations had been those of political leaders and clergy, lawyers and military heroes. Now all kinds of the like-minded began to flock together. It is significant that the first national party convention was that of the Anti-Masons, for conventions were especially desirable in the crystallization and advertisement of third parties.   To those established, they afforded merely means of stabilization and effective control.   The abolitionists began to meet early in the thirties.   In 1839 a section of them in convention organized the Liberty party, and a year later cast votes in twelve states.[1]   Under stress of great emotion, in 1854, independent conventions were held in almost all congressional districts in the North, and successful popular revolt swept the Whig party out of existence.

It was not alone to produce political action, however, that people met in conventions.   The abolitionists in fact met first to hearten each other and to organize nonpolitical agitation.   About the same time the advocates of temperance in the use of intoxicating beverages began to assemble.   Such conventions were not so closely organized as those of political parties.   Delegates were not apportioned, but all who chose could come—at least all men.   The arrival of women stirred discussion, but in most cases they took their seats, cast their votes, and became increasingly talkative.   Such conventions rallied the support of the lukewarm.   They were demonstrations of the public opinion behind their proposals.

When such conventions represented a movement of some permanence, they rested generally on local organizations.   In most cases, as in that of the abolitionists and the peace advocates, some such local organizations antedated the first convention.[2]   The convention then took measures to organize the movement widely over the country.   Delegates ceased to attend as individuals, but came to represent local bodies which sometimes paid

[1] T. C. Smith, *The Liberty and Free Soil Parties in the Northwest* (*Harvard Historical Studies*, VI), chap. v.

[2] See *post*, chap. xii.

their expenses. The conventions also generally provided a permanent set of officers, who counted far more than the national committees of the parties, for they had no officeholding rivals. The least important maintained a paid secretary, those more amply supported had several secretaries and also traveling agents. Each movement came soon to have a press, either by individual effort as in the case of Garrison's *Liberator,* which was the organ of the abolitionists, or by corporate effort, of which the most striking manifestation was the publishing activity of the Methodist Church. In these nonpolitical or semi-political organizations there was no protection against secession. Soon most causes were being urged on the public by several bodies, standing for varying degrees of intensity. In the forties and fifties they very generally ceased to be national and came to be organized on sectional lines.

It is characteristic of the trend of American civilization that the system of representative meetings for government and propaganda should have begun in matters of church and state, then expanded to the organization of public opinion, and later reached the business world. In the thirties conventions of business men, particularly those of the South interested in providing railroad development, directing it to the advantage of various cities and districts and mobilizing influence to bring about legislative assistance, became common. In the early fifties national conventions of passenger agents began to meet, which discussed common problems, and introduced several agreements which facilitated the whole process of getting together for others as well as for themselves.

The Americans of the thirties and forties, therefore, may be said to have devised in the convention system a new method, based roughly on their inherited political and religious institutions, of coöperating by representation for any purpose which seemed to them important—

a system which has ever since grown, and whose scope has been extended to administration, research, sport and pleasure. One immediate result was to give to minorities a means of presenting their causes to the public, and an influence before unprecedented. Another result was to increase the importance of sectional division in the United States. Of fundamental importance through the economic and social differences that they represented, the sections had been restricted in their activity by the fact that they were without organization. By, or shortly after, the end of this period, North and South each formed various organizations that expressed sectional opinion, policy and aspiration without the modifications that came from meeting together, and more completely than did the several state organizations. Whatever, therefore, may have been the undemocratic elements in the conventions of the political parties, the net result of the convention system as a whole was to make the organization of American life more flexible and give all who had anything to say a more effective mode of expression. It blended in some degree the element of pure democracy with that of representation.

The aristocracy of finance was as distasteful to Jackson as that of officeholding. His antagonism was not to wealth, but to the monopoly upon which the financial system of 1830 was supposed to, and to some degree did, rest. The chief attention was directed against the outstanding illustration of privilege and power: the United States Bank. In legal form this institution possessed certain rights which were monopolistic. It was the authorized financial agent of the government, and it held practically, though not absolutely in law, the right to receive on deposit all government funds. The question of the Bank was the more momentous because it was not only an institution for the ordinary purpose of banking, but it also possessed a complete monopoly of issuing all the legal-tender money of the United States, except that coined by the government. State banks, private banks and individuals did indeed issue notes that were used as currency, but they were without legal-tender quality. In exercising this function the policy of the Bank pleased neither Jackson and his protagonist in the Senate, "Old Bullion" Benton of Missouri, who distrusted all money except gold and silver, nor the more optimistic members of the party who wished abundant, if not unlimited, issues resting upon the future riches of the country. The magnitude of the Bank gave it the power to enforce its policy upon smaller institutions which were legally independent of it.[1]

The attack on the Bank was the stronger because that organization was merely the conspicuous example of a common, growing method of doing business, which all along the line aroused an opposition resting on innate ideas. The increasing importance of corporation privileges was enough to fire the indignation of a generation more violently antimonopolistic than any since the English of the early seventeenth century. Daniel Raymond in *Thoughts on Political Economy,* published in 1820, one of the first American textbooks on the subject, says, "A money corporation should be created with as few exclusive privileges as possible." This feeling had come into existence partly because of a flood of acts passed by the various legislatures. An article in the *North American Review* in 1827 complained that acts of incorporation "granted to any set of men, who ask it . . . almost any powers which they are pleased to have inserted in their bill." [2] The antagonism was increased by the decision of the United States in the fam-

---

[1] A good account of such influence by one who was both politician and reformer is in Neal Dow, *Reminiscences* (Portland, Me., 1898), 128-139.

[2] A book review by W. H. Gardiner in *N. Am. Rev.*, XXIV (1827), 199.

ous case of Dartmouth College *v.* Woodward in 1819, in which Chief Justice Marshall laid down the opinion, not entirely new in America but contrary to general practice, that corporation charters might not be amended by the power that granted them.

Opposition to monopoly generally rests not only upon the question of privilege and mortmain but also upon the character of the granting power. In part the hostility of the English Puritans had arisen from the fact that the king granted the charters. In the United States the authority lay in the legislatures. This was indeed less offensive to the democratic sense, but it meant that each charter was the offspring of politics. This was in itself disturbing, but particularly so when a political revolution brought a new party into power which found vested interests created by, and in general sympathetic with, its defeated opponents, left immune in the possession of rights important and remunerative. Thus Jackson exclaimed against the Bank because its stock was held by Easterners and Europeans; he waxed to anger at the sight of its destinies directed by Nicholas Biddle, whose personal manner and philosophy no less than his family connection stamped him as of the aristocracy.

Linked in his mind, then, were the assaults upon life interest in office and upon privilege in the instance of the United States Bank. Against the advice of his associates and insubordination even in his cabinet, he pushed his attack, his anger rising with the opposition. In the presidential campaign of 1832, and the congressional elections of 1834, this was the leading issue, and Jackson won not only his reasoned point, that the banking monopoly must go, by defeating the recharter of the Bank, but also his personal duel with Biddle, by bringing practical ruin to the Bank as a financial institution. In his specie circular of 1836, Jackson ordered that the United States receive only gold and silver in payment for public lands, a blow to banks in general. After another election turning largely on this latter issue, that of 1838, Jackson's chosen successor Van Buren secured in 1840 the passage of the independent treasury act, which made the United States its own financial agent. Thus the great national corporation had been slain by the American Saint George, and the national government was officially immured from contact with lesser corporations.[1]

One phase of antimonopolistic thought admits that monopoly is in some respects inevitable, but in such cases it should be a function of the state. It was perhaps in accord with this idea that Roger B. Taney, appointed by Jackson as chief justice, laid down in 1837 in the case of Briscoe *v.* the Bank of the Commonwealth of Kentucky the remarkable doctrine that, although forbidden by the United States Constitution to "emit bills of credit," states could nevertheless establish and own banks which could exercise the privilege. Such bills could not, of course, be made legal tender, but at least they would not now come into competition with such bills, for after the fall of the United States Bank and the passage of the independent treasury act, the only currency possessing that quality was gold and silver coin.[2]

The financial aristocracy of 1830 was defeated, its financial monopoly was disestablished, and for the time being at least, its policy was reversed. On the one side the government had become bullionist; on the other, the

[1] Nicholas Biddle, *Correspondence* (R. C. McGrane, ed., Boston, 1919), 192-269, 282-290, 318; R. C. H. Catterall, *Second Bank of the United States* (Chicago, 1903), chaps. xii-xv; W. G. Sumner, *Andrew Jackson* (J. T. Morse, jr., ed., *American Statesmen*, Boston, 1882), chaps. ix-xi.

[2] Charles Warren, *History of the American Bar* (Boston, 1911); same author, *The Supreme Court in United States History* (Boston, 1922), II, 301-303; T. G. Gronert, *The Development of Corporations in the United States during the Jacksonian Period* (unpublished thesis, Univ. of Wis.).

note-issuing agencies of the country became inflationist. Freedom had triumphed with regard to money and banking, except freedom from the natural laws of trade; and before these laws all were equal. Thus Gresham's law of currency remained—that the bad drives out the good; and American bullion began to flow across the Atlantic.

Public opinion, however, was not fully satisfied. Hostility was merely keenest against banks; it existed against all corporations. Senator McDuffie of South Carolina said in 1828: "Individuals are always open to impressions of generosity. But classes of the community, and sections of the country, when united and stimulated by the hope of gain, being destitute like corporations, of individual responsibility, are, like them, destitute of hearts and souls to feel for the wrongs and sufferings they inflict upon others." [1] A story in *Niles' Register* tells of a farmer who called on the trustees of a certain religious corporation with respect to a request he had to make. Each was friendly, one giving him "brandy, another beer, a third wine, a fourth Hollands." Next day sitting together as a corporation they refused his request, and he said, "Gentlemen, I can compare you to nothing but the good cheer I received at your houses yesterday; taken separately, you are excellent, but mix you together and you are a mess for the d—l." Niles comments: "The conduct of corporate bodies sometimes would incline one to suspect that criminality is, with them, a matter of calculation rather than of conscience." [2]

In the Pennsylvania constitutional convention of 1837 it was proposed that no charter should be granted for the accomplishment of a project which individual ac-

[1] George McDuffie, *Speech . . . against the Prohibitory System; Delivered in the House of Representatives, April, 1828* (Wash., 1828), 16.
[2] *Niles' Register,* XXX, 427.

tivity could accomplish, and in 1851, in Ohio, there was discussion of the possibility of substituting partnerships for corporations. This feeling was naturally strongest in the West. Constitutional conventions in both Iowa and Wisconsin presented to the people constitutions prohibiting banks, and while these were rejected, the constitutions adopted in 1846 and 1848 provided that the question of "banks" or "no banks" be left to popular referendum.

The corporations, however, were too well established to be overthrown. In 1831 appeared the first American treatise on the subject: Angell and Ames, *Law of Private Corporations.* The *American Jurist*, reviewing this publication in an issue in 1832, declares: "Not only have corporations multiplied among us during the last thirty years to an extent without parallel in any other country, but they have been created for a great variety of purposes, to which in England they have seldom or never applied. . . . We have corporations for banking, insurance, building bridges, turn-pikes, railroads and canals, for building and occupying wharves and holding and improving buildings, for manufacturing, and for owning and employing vessels; besides a great variety of charitable purposes and the promotion of learning, religion, agriculture, and the arts." It was estimated that scarcely an individual of respectable character could be found not a member of some incorporated body.

These statements must be judged by comparisons with the earlier paucity of such organizations rather than with modern conditions. Individual initiative and partnerships still in 1830 handled most of the nation's business. The corporation type dominated only in the fields of religious organizations, banking and road building. Their greatest bulwark against attack was the fact that the call for them was increasing. When the national government rejected the functions of credit and transportation improvement, when the limitations of state action became increasingly obvious, and when the subsidiary panic of 1841 and the repudiation of their debts by several states destroyed the capacity of the states to borrow cheaply, there remained the alternative of the promotion of the private organization of capital or stagnation.   The tasks the generation insisted upon were beyond the power of any individual or of partnerships.

Increasingly, therefore, legislatures and constitutional conventions turned their attention to making corporations safe for democracy, and to a lesser extent, making them safe for investors.   Attention was first turned to the question of mortmain, raised by the Dartmouth College case.   In 1827 the New York government reserved by constitutional change the right to "suspend, alter, or repeal" any charter thereafter granted by the legislature.   In 1831 the new constitution of Delaware provided for the power of revocation, and that no charter continue in force longer than twenty years except those of corporations for public improvement. Such provisions were widely discussed and frequently adopted.

A second characteristic of corporations that was a focus of attack was the limitation of the stockholders' liability.   The Jeffersonian democracy had been almost as sensitive to the responsibilities of individualism as to its rights.   The idea of bankruptcy, whereby a man could legally escape his debtor, was so repugnant to them that in the few intervals when national bankruptcy laws were in force, as 1801-1802 and 1841-1842, hundreds of humble and unsung Americans did what Sir Walter Scott was so praised for doing, and refused legal release from their creditors.   To the Jacksonians the exemption of a shareholder in a corporation from its debts was one of those privileges which were to be swept away by the flood tide of equality.

Here, however, the people experienced an illuminating illustration of the fact that one cannot eat one's cake and still possess it. The restriction of the functions of government made corporations necessary; investors were not ready to put their money into corporations whose mismanagement might threaten the loss of all they had. Limited liability was a necessary characteristic of corporations. Throughout the period this was a subject of controversy in legislatures and constitutional conventions. As early as 1822 even staid Massachusetts partially nullified the established legal doctrine of limited liability. Maine changed its mind five times between 1821 and 1856. The New York constitutional convention of 1846, finding the question too difficult, left it to the legislature. The net result, however, was that the generation recognized facts and accepted the corporations with a limited liability of their stockholders in preference to no corporations.

The recognition that corporations must have privileges was a painful lesson which this generation learned. In the reconciliation of this fact with democratic practice it made a real constructive contribution. In 1811 New York had allowed the formation of corporations for certain manufacturing purposes, under a general law, without a charter granted specifically in each case. This law was merely temporary, but it seems to have furnished an idea to Theodore Hinsdale and others in Connecticut, who wished to incorporate but were confronted by a hostile Jacksonian legislature. At any rate they succeeded in persuading the legislature of that state in 1836 to pass the first important general incorporation law in the United States. This allowed corporations with not less than $2,000 or more than $200,000 capital to incorporate for certain manufacturing purposes, by filing certain documents with the secretary of state and receiving his license, and on condition of conforming to certain regulations of management and control.[1]

The next year, 1837, the whole subject of corporations was threshed out in the Pennsylvania constitutional convention. C. J. Ingersoll pointed out that in the last forty-five years one hundred and sixty millions had become "locked up" in that state alone. J. M. Scott stated: "Our great canals, many of them have been made by corporations, our bridges have been erected by corporations, and our turnpikes through almost every county in the state, have been made by corporations."[2] It was characteristic of Pennsylvania, poised in its opinions between Jacksonianism and industrialism, that it took no action.

In 1845, however, Louisiana adopted a constitutional provision for general incorporation, and in 1846 the New York constitutional convention worked out what amounted to this generation's solution of this difficult problem. Section I of Article VIII of that constitution provided that corporations be created only under general statutes, unless the legislature concluded that the object desired could be obtained only by special act. This was speedily followed by Wisconsin in 1848, Illinois in 1848, and Maryland in 1851. California in 1849, and Michigan in 1850, made general incorporation absolutely mandatory. Other states accepted the idea, and the legislatures of many states that did not revise their constitutions began to frame general acts standardizing incorporation for this purpose or that.

Here then was a case of clear if unwilling thinking

---

[1] F. Morgan, ed., *Conn. as a Colony, and as a State* (Hartford, 1904), IV, 266. The North Carolina law of 1795 applied only to canals.

[2] *Proceedings and Debates of the* [*Constitutional*] *Convention of the Commonwealth of Pennsylvania. . . . Commenced at Harrisburg, May 2, 1837* (Harrisburg, 1838-1839), XIV, 15; VI, 190.

pushed through to a conclusion, by a generation which was so much more inclined to believe and feel than to think. It followed characteristic lines in that, accepting the fact that corporations must have privileges, it made their privileges equal under laws applying to all. It followed also the Jacksonian precept of separating business from politics, and from this time, although many corporations became involved in politics, at least the majority were not born in them.

Of positive legislation rendering corporation investments attractive to the investors by protecting their interests against mismanagement, there was little at this time. Massachusetts framed statutes that might well have been copied, but this generation followed the "Old Bay State" less freely than it did New York. Massachusetts also developed, at the end of the period, a plan of supervising its corporations, though it fell short in carrying it out. Such ideas, however, democratic as they appear today, were not democratic to the mind of the thirties and forties. To the Jacksonians, their corporations, if allowed at all, should be as free as themselves. The very thought of supervision was inharmonious with the spirit of the age, and not even a corporate individuality, bloated to superhuman size, however much it might anger, could really frighten the self-confident American.

Corporations were less an invention of the generation than the convention system. Their adaptation to the philosophy of the time, however, was striking, and still more was the amount of business thrust upon them by the restriction of government functions and by the growing complexity of life. Already in 1850 an American business corporation differed from those of Elizabethan England and of the colonial period, not only in its origin and its subjection to regulations uniform with other corporations, but in the multiplicity of its small stockholders, who attended its annual meetings only by proxy and had no real share in its management. In form pure democracies, the tendency was for control to be concentrated in the hands of directors. Annual reports were indeed more intimate than at present, but most investors were more influenced by the reputation and standing of those responsible than by a study of conditions. Some invested because they had confidence in the sobriety, judgment and honesty of men like J. Murray Forbes of Boston. Some speculated in shares because they trusted the shrewd unscrupulousness of men like Daniel Drew to draw their chestnuts if mixed with his. Some bought shares in any new project because of their belief in the new and that there would be enough profit to go around.

The hold of the old aristocracy over banking had been broken, but by 1850 a new class of moneyed men were in control of far more of the life interests of the community than in 1830. Wall Street was already denounced as the center of this money power, although it was far less concentrated there than it is today, and Boston, Philadelphia, Baltimore and New Orleans were independent rival capitals. The whole was connected with the buying, selling and loaning centers of Europe by such Americans as George Peabody and Joshua Bates, who maintained their chief offices in London. On the whole there was much more popular admiration for such men than denunciation, for entrance into this new class was still easy, and it was after all engaged in doing what the people had definitely refused to do collectively.[1]

[1] Boston City Council, *A Memorial of Joshua Bates* (Boston, 1865), 15-16 (in London, 1826-1869, Baring Bros.); Phebe A. Hanaford, *Life of George Peabody* (Boston, 1870), 70-71, 77 (George Peabody and Co., throughout the period); John Murray Forbes, *Letters and Recollections* (Sarah Forbes Hughes, ed., Boston, 1900), I, chaps. iii-v (Michigan Central 1845, later Chicago, Burlington and Quincy); Carl

Corporations must be regarded rather as an addition made by the generation to its armory of weapons than as a revolutionary change. In business methods, as in other activities, many things were introduced but few discarded, and so individual enterprises and partnerships continued to flourish, while the newly equipped corporations were actually more significant for the future than potent for the generation that forced their formation.

Hovey, *Life Study of J. Pierpont Morgan* (N. Y., 1911), 1-35 (on financial background). See also W. P. Stearns, "Foreign Trade, 1820 to 1840," *Journ. of Pol. Econ.*, VIII, 34 ff, 452 ff.

CHAPTER IV

F A R M , P L A N T A T I O N A N D H I G H W A Y

A LIVING—that is, what was generally conceded in 1830 to be the minimum which an American should secure—was decidedly above what was actually necessary to existence. Food was to be unlimited in quantity, and on festive occasions, choice in quality. Drink was to be ordinarily limited by a liberal conception of hygienic consequences, and on festive occasions, unlimited. Dress was to be adequate for protection and was to include a "best" for Sunday use, but was not expected to respond to the demands of fashion. Every family was to own its home, which was to include, beyond the demands of necessity, a "parlor" and at least half a bedroom for each member of the family. On the frontier many lived much less commodiously, but this was considered to be merely a temporary condition. With each home there was to be a "yard," with some flowers and summer vegetables. A fundamental element of a living was liberty, and all Americans were expected to look forward to becoming their own masters. A chance to educate one's children in the elements was considered a just demand. On the other hand little heed was paid to hours of labor. People expected to work long hours and to work while the power to do so held out. The poor farm was not such a horror as the workhouse in England, and less often pressed the mind, because it was a contingency so much more remote. One was not expected to provide in health complete support for old age or for one's widow, but was expected to accumulate something which would compensate children, relatives or others for a few years' care at the end of life.

It is plain that in a period so rich in opportunity, a comparatively large number would, as they worked, cherish dreams of exceeding a mere "living." Such dreams in youth were fabricated far more from the tangible material at hand than from literature. The process by which energy and imagination realized such ambitions was constantly developed before their eyes in the lives of neighbors. Eager youth looked forward to the manner of life and acquirements of the aristocracies of the several sections which have been described. The more sober ideal of middle age was comfort. Lincoln thought that a house and twenty thousand dollars would be a substantial attainment. Ten thousand dollars was a modest fortune, twenty was success, fifty was reasonable affluence.

A very large majority of the people of the United States made their living by agriculture. There were two long-established systems of agricultural organization, one in the North and one in the South, each employing approximately one third of the agricultural population. The agricultural methods of the remaining third had not been systematized in 1830.[1] In New England, New York, New Jersey, Pennsylvania and the earlier settled portions of Ohio, the primary unit was the farm and the secondary unit the village. The farm was generally owned by its occupier, though it was frequently mortgaged. Along the Hudson many farms were rented, but even here the farmer was, in most respects, his own manager. Conditions varied with facility of transportation and with fertility, but a basic similarity existed.

[1] E. L. Bogart, *Economic History of American Agriculture* (N. Y., 1923), 17-29, 32-50, 61-100; L. B. Schmidt and E. D. Ross, eds., *Readings in the Economic History of American Agriculture* (N. Y., 1923), chaps. xii-xiv.

A New England farm was more apt to consist of over than under a hundred acres, picturesquely varied with pasture, arable and woodland. On it were raised practically all food products needed for home use, and small quantities of wheat and corn, together with a few cattle and horses, for sale. It was generally cultivated by the farmer and his sons with frequently a hired man who lived and ate with the family. Seasonal stress of harvest work was generally met by exchange of services with neighbors. During the winter, "chores" could be attended to in a short time, and left long hours during which most farmers employed their time at some mechanical work, as the making of hats or harness or furniture, for use or for sale.

The farmer's wife and daughters were equally producers. Except for the killing of the pig, the milling of flour and the making of cider, the products of the field were fitted for the table by their hands. They made their own yeast and soap, they dried meat and fruits, they hulled corn, they gathered and prepared medicinal herbs, and they tended the poultry and churned butter. In the hill districts they still, in 1830, spun the wool of the farm sheep, in anticipation of the itinerant weaver on his rounds. Where factory-made cloth was bought, they made their own and their husband's clothes, except perhaps his "Sunday suit." Children from the time they could walk were expected to assist. Such tasks as hunting the eggs, unscientifically laid all about the barn yard, belonged particularly to the girls. Keeping up the wood supply for the kitchen fire, habitually "the" fire, was boys' work.

The connection of the farm with the outside world was slight. What it needed was sugar, except in the maple region, salt, and generally tea; then small quantities of cloth, linen, shoes, and well-made, long-treasured tableware and tools; then certain services, as religion, education, the milling of flour and meal, and occasional medical attendance.

For the first time, the wife was beginning to play a part in these exchanges. She had no money, but exchanged rags and the products of her own handicraft, with the tin peddler, who with his glittering wagon, his glib tongue and his gossip of distant towns was reaping fat profits from these unaccustomed bargainers. Otherwise the exchanges of a hundred farms were gathered together in the village to which the farmer hauled his surplus behind his oxen, his solitary nag, or, if he were prosperous, his pair of "Morgans," over the rutty roads, in the maintenance of which he and his neighbors worked out a good portion of their taxes. Few dollars passed in these transactions. The miller received a proportion of the wheat and corn, the general storekeeper, the cobbler and the minister were paid in large part by produce; balances on the storekeeper's books were carried from year to year. Agents from the larger towns, however, with leather wallets, paid for cattle and horses in coin, which went home to fill a carefully concealed stocking, or, in the case of the more shrewd, to be loaned on mortgage to less successful neighbors.

The village craftsmen generally included the miller, frequently the tanner, the cobbler, who made as well as repaired carpenters and masons, the tailor, the seamstress, the cabinet and furniture maker, most of them, it will be seen, owning a small stock of materials. Trade was represented by one or two storekeepers who performed some of the functions of bankers; the professions by two or three ministers, several lawyers, a physician and a school-teacher. It was the function of the village also to collect the surplus products of the farms and to dispose of such of them as it did not need for the foreign and manufactured products which have been enumerated. Periodically the mail arrived over the highway, generally a fairly well-built toll road running to a seaport or to one of the distributing centers of the interior, such as Worcester or Hartford. At seasons, droves of cattle, increasing in numbers though not in succulence as village after village passed, leisurely progressed over the same roads; at other seasons wagons, heavy with products on their way to town, lighter when they returned with the less bulky goods the village needed.

Between 1830 and 1850 this life was in New England slowly breaking down under the influence of changed conditions elsewhere. In 1830 it just about supplied its cities and its merchant fleet. By 1850 wheat from the West, butter and cheese from New York and other agricultural products were being sold at lower prices than those produced at home, while farm and village handicrafts were being supplanted by factory-made goods. Some farms in Vermont and the Berkshires were united and turned into grazing pastures for sheep, but, for the most part, there was a gradual decay rather than adaptation. Farm boys and girls in increasing numbers left their home communities and sought their fortunes in the West, or in the nearer factories of their own regions. Agricultural New England simply became less important and less self-sustaining than previously.[1]

The adaptation of this system to changing conditions was taking place during these years in New York, Pennsylvania and Ohio. In these states farmers were remarkably alert to the new methods that were presented to them in agricultural periodicals which nearly all of them took,[2] and at county fairs which many of them

[1] W. V. Pooley, *The Settlement of Illinois, 1830-1850* (Univ. of Wis., *Bull.*, no. 220, I, 1908), 335-346.

[2] A good example of agricultural literature is T. G. Fessenden, *The Complete Farmer and Rural Economist* (Boston, 1834), which in 1850 was in its tenth edition.

attended. There was no dramatic reconstruction of their life, but they gradually came to give more attention to selling crops, to buy more of the things they used; in response the village merchants stocked their stores with goods brought from the East or from Europe, while the village craftsmen drifted away. Here and there were men of larger means, such as Nicholas Longworth of Cincinnati, who experimented with new crops and methods. Increasing numbers bought the farm machinery which began to be marketed in the forties, but not enough seriously to affect agriculture as a national industry.

West of Ohio agriculture was in 1830 in a preparatory stage, and the most important change of these decades was in extending the area of land broken to cultivation. By 1850 it was apparent that the Northwest would become organized on the basis existing in the Ohio region, that of small owner-worked farms, with villages spaced eight or ten miles apart, whose importance would rest more upon their distributing function, and less upon craft production, than in New England. Every year there were more farms. Between 1830 and 1850 the number of new farms each summer in the region north of the Ohio and the Missouri averaged about twenty thousand. Each farm, with its dependence on buying and selling, meant an increased demand upon transportation. Even when some of the grain was reduced in bulk by turning it into whisky, and corn was fed to hogs which at Cincinnati, the "Porkopolis," were converted into salt pork, the pressure upon transportation facilities was only lessened, not eliminated.

The question as to whether the migrating farmer would be able to realize his dream depended as much upon the development of transportation as it did upon his energy. In 1830 this question was practically

unanswered; in 1850 it had been answered in the affirm-
ative, in that roads and carriage had been provided
or were in prospect.   The equally vital problem of a
reliable system of exchange and marketing had made far
less progress.   The farmer was hardly as certain in 1850
as he had been in 1830 that money received would
maintain its value.   By means of the telegraph he was
better able to insist on standard prices, but on the other
hand, he had little more protection against dishonest
agents.   Western farming was still a speculative undertaking, and of two equally deserving neighbors one
might secure a sound return and the other have his
crop rot on his hands.

In the South there was in 1830 a greater variety of
method.[1]   The greatest change during these years was
in the extension and increasing dominance of the plantation system.   As compared with the North, the farming
units were larger, they were both more highly organized
and less independent, and the profits, probably less in
proportion to those engaged, were concentrated in fewer
hands, so that the agricultural leaders were more wealthy
and powerful and cultured.   The unit of the Southern
system was the plantation.   A plantation consisted of
from a dozen to several hundred persons, occupied an
ample area, and was generally separated from its neighbors by woods and streams.   Economically it existed for
the production of some staple crop—in Maryland and
Virginia, tobacco; in the Carolinas and westward, cotton; in Kentucky, horses: along the South Carolina seacoast, rice; in Louisiana, sugar.

For production it was organized with the owner as

[1] M. B. Hammond, *The Cotton Industry* (Am. Econ. Assoc., *Publs.*,
new ser. 1, pt. 1); U. B. Phillips, "The Economic Cost of Slaveholding in the Cotton Belt," *Pol. Sci. Quart.*, XX, 257-275; same
author, "Plantations as a Civilizing Factor," *Sewanee Rev.*, XII,
257-267; same author, "Origin and Growth of the Southern Black
Belts," *Am. Hist. Rev.*, XI, 798-816; same author, *American Negro
Slavery* (N. Y., 1918), chaps. xiii, xvi-xvii.

merchant and supervisor, generally with an overseer of labor, and with "hands," who were divided into gangs. In marked contrast to colonial times, practically all laborers were slaves belonging to the owner. The bulk of plantation necessities were home raised. Garden vegetables and poultry were abundant, hunting and fishing brought variety to the diet. Corn was a standard crop; in the form of meal and hominy it furnished one chief item of food and, intermediately, in the form of bacon the other. The plantation force also did many of the necessary odd jobs of carpentering, blacksmithing and the cruder crafts. The amount of these varied occupations, however, was growing less. Salt pork, cattle and flour were increasingly imported from the Northwest, and, more and more, imported implements and manufactured materials, even to doors and window sashes, took the place of those produced at home.

The mansion with its dependent village, where all the community lived, was the center of much activity. Corn was made into hominy, and clothes were prepared for all the laborers, chiefly from cotton and other cloths brought from New England or old. Its occupations were less varied than those of a New England village, but more attention was given to the conduct of the rather elaborate life of the owner's family, with its frequent entertainment of large numbers of guests. Not only did the mere process of living require more time and effort than in the Northern farm home, but there was much more demand for things brought from the outside. Practically no portion of the mansion-house equipment was of local origin, and many choice articles, even of food, came from far away.

This was a much more developed organization than that of the North. The very life of the plantation depended on the sale of its products in far distant markets. Commerce and credit, therefore, were its breath of life.   In such staple-producing communities there is generally a tendency to concentrate business and wealth in some one dominant city such as Babylon, Alexandria, Sydney or Buenos Ayres.   That this was not the case in the South was due in part to the strong social prestige attaching to plantation ownership and the strong credit position which slavery gave the planters, and in part to the political division of the plantation area into states.

At intervals, irregular and farther apart than in the North, were centers where were necessary craftsmen and a general store.   The real economic divisions corresponded to those of nature, the goods of an entire valley being brought to the town at the river mouth, where the real exchange for the commodities needed took place. This natural economy had been somewhat modified by canals connecting the mouths of several rivers with the principal port of a state, and still more by the fact that where this had not been done, agents from the chief state port generally collected the produce from those which were smaller and shipped it home in coasting vessels.   In this way Baltimore, Norfolk, Wilmington, Charleston, Savannah, Mobile and New Orleans were coming to be the real marketing points for the whole South, though important districts spread out from interior cities such as Richmond, Augusta, Memphis, Nashville, Louisville and St. Louis.[1]   The New England seaports ate the products of the farms, the Southern seaports exchanged them.   As many of these exchanges were with distant points, and the exchanges simple, there was a tendency for them to fall into a few hands, and mer-

---

[1] The comparative insignificance of such interior centers is indicated by their population.   In 1830 Richmond had 16,060 inhabitants, Nashville, 5,566, and St. Louis, 5,582.   They grew respectively in twenty years to 27,570, 10,478, and 77,860.   J. D. De Bow, comp., *Statistical View of the United States* . . . *Being a Compendium of the Seventh Census* (Wash., 1854), 192.

chants were generally wealthy. The larger planters, however, with their credit basis resting on the ownership of their laborers, were not dependent, and could, and often did, deal over the heads of the native merchants with those at the point of consumption, as Liverpool or Boston. To a degree rarely found, the economic control of Southern agriculture, in spite of its highly organized and dependent character, was distributed in the hands of a hundred thousand plantation owners; the country, not the city, was dominant.

Next to agriculture as a means of earning a living in 1830 stood shipping.[1] Four fleets—that engaged in foreign trade, the coasters, the river boats and the fishing fleet—employed, directly, well over a hundred thousand men, and indirectly many more. How much more water transportation counted in 1830 than now may be appreciated by noting the work of these groups of vessels. The river and canal boats, crafts of every size and type, did practically all the inland work now done by railroads, sharing it only with the slow and cumbersome wagons on the few practicable highways.[2] The coasters performed most of the work of our coastline railroads, collecting products from many harbors for final shipment at an export port, and bringing back imported goods. Increasingly, this latter function required two voyages, one from New York which had already become the great importing port, to, let us say,

---

[1] There are histories of the American merchant marine which cover these years by W. W. Bates, *American Marine* (Boston, 1897), 127-149, 166-173; W. L. Marvin, *The American Merchant Marine from 1620 to 1920* (N. Y., 1902), chaps. xi-xii; J. R. Spears, *The Story of the American Merchant Marine* (N. Y., 1910), 173-176, 201-268, 277-284.

[2] A. B. Hulbert, *Historic Highways of America* (Cleveland, 1902-1915), I, VIII-XI; H. M. Chittenden, *History of Early Steamboat Navigation on the Missouri River* (N. Y., 1903), and other studies; G. B. Merrick, *Genesis of Steamboating on Western Rivers* (Madison, 1912); and same author, *Old Times on the Upper Mississippi* (Cleveland, 1909).

Savannah, and then a reshipment to a smaller port such as Brunswick, Georgia. Such vessels were distributed fairly evenly among the states in use and ownership, for everywhere transport was primarily water transport.[1]

From the ports of New England in the thirties a hundred thousand tons of little fishing vessels fared forth for the cod and mackerel, of which they brought back all the fish Americans cared to eat, and two and a half million dollars' worth for export.[2] Chiefly from New Bedford, about ninety thousand tons of somewhat larger craft sailed forth on voyages adventurous and three years long, to bring back from the Pacific the whale oil, whose use in the better American homes was the first step in the transition from the candle to the electric light.[3]

The high sea fleet of foreign traders was the largest and most dignified. It carried over two thirds of our foreign commerce, and in addition imported goods from the Far East for redistribution to other countries, notably those of South America. Competition was keen, and rivalry between masters and men and ports from Eastport, Maine, to Baltimore was causing a constant improvement in models and seamanship.[4] All these vessels were American built, and a few were still built for sale to foreigners. The merchant marine, there-

[1] See *Annual Reports on Commerce and Navigation* (Wash.), which began publication in 1821.

[2] Raymond MacFarland, *New England Fisheries* (N. Y., 1911), chaps. ix-x.

[3] Obed Macy, *The History of Nantucket . . . Rise and Progress of the Whale Fishery* (Boston, 1835), I, 210-214; Alexander Starbuck, *History of American Whale Fishery* (Waltham, 1878), 95-104, 110; J. R. Spears, *The Story of the New England Whalers* (N. Y., 1910), chaps. xi-xii; A. H. Verrill, *The Real Story of the Whaler* (N. Y., 1916), a popular treatment.

[4] S. E. Morison, *Maritime History of Massachusetts, 1783-1860* (Boston, 1921), chaps. vi, viii, xvi-xviii, xx, xxii; State Street Trust Company, *Old Shipping Days in Boston* (Boston, 1918), profusely illustrated.

fore, not only performed the national services required of it, but earned money by performing services for others.

The organization of the merchant marine was highly individualistic. Ships seldom represented an investment of more than thirty thousand dollars. Some were owned by partners, some by individuals, and some individuals and partners owned many. One out of each four or five of the ship's company was an officer, and in many cases he was permitted to have a share in the cargo. In the fishing fleet the catch was generally divided on fixed shares among all. This meant that there was individual opportunity. It was also primarily a young man's, or rather a boy's and young man's, occupation. Boys were enrolled by the consent of their parents, or as runaways, frequently at twelve; they rarely stayed after thirty unless they had begun to rise to the top. Employment in the merchant marine was, therefore, a stage in the career of many who devoted their maturity to other things.

The conditions of the ocean marine in 1830 were not substantially changed by 1850. The American fleet increased its proportion of the growing trade. The Baltimore clipper and the ocean steamship improved facilities, and Cornelius Vanderbilt developed organization. These changes, however, were small compared with those in inland transportation, which was attracting the interest and the genius of the country.

In 1830 inland transportation was based on water transit and on toll roads and bridges. In some districts the road system was reasonably satisfactory, but few cared to invest in such undertakings far from home, and these roads were rather an evidence of civilization achieved than an aid to its accomplishment. Federal aid had stretched the National Road into the heart of the Northwest, and built military roads in Florida and to

the outskirts of settlement across the upper Mississippi.[1] Jackson's Maysville Road veto of 1830, however, put an end to hopes of a comprehensive national
system.

More important than the roads were the waterways
which in 1830 were rapidly becoming equipped with
steamboats.   Their use ideally fitted the needs of this
individualistic generation.   In the beginning each boat
was a separate investment, so that no large capital was
required, and competition stimulated hundreds of ingen-
ious-minded mechanics to devote themselves to improvement.[2]

Many travelers considered the clean-cut, swift Hudson
River liners, turned out at such works as those of the
Stevenses at Hoboken, as the finest products of American
material civilization.   On the Mississippi and southern
rivers, the raftlike hulls with their fairylike superstruc-
tures, pushed forward by their high rear wheels or by
their separately driven side-wheels, did everything human
ingenuity could do to take their cargoes over the sand
bars, up and down the rapids, and across the snags.
Sturdy wide side-wheelers carried on the trade of the
coast and the lakes; screw propellers shot long slim hulls
through canals and the narrower streams.

The range of action of the steamboat was fairly clearly
determined by the extent of navigable water.   This
might, however, be increased by reasonably moderate
expenditures for the cleaning of streams and for short
canals about obstacles.   It was characteristic, however,
that little was done in this direction.   The most successful of such pieces of work constructed during these
years were a system of slack-water navigation on the
Kentucky rivers, which was created by that state, and

[1] A. B. Hulbert, *The Cumberland Road* (*Historic Highways*, X, Cleveland, 1904), chaps. ii-iii, v, appendix A.
[2] Note Lincoln's attempt.   J. G. Nicolay and John Hay, *Abraham
Lincoln* (N. Y., 1890), I, 70-71.

a three-mile canal to escape the rapids of the Ohio at Louisville, which was a private enterprise.[1]

During this generation one generally traveled where one could by water, which came to mean, in most instances, by steamboat. There were few long journeys part of which could not be so taken. One would ordinarily travel from the interior of Georgia to Savannah or Charleston to take steamer for New York, in spite of the storms off Hatteras, rather than go up the coast inland. Going west, one sought Pittsburgh or Buffalo and then took steamer. Steamers ran their noses up streams west of the Mississippi where no captain would think of going today. More important was their carrying of merchandise to the interior, and of its products to Eastern and seaport markets. Steamboats doubled or tripled the commercially profitable areas of the United States. They made civilization possible, and quickly possible, in large sections. They served directly or indirectly practically every American. They were, however, subject to serious defects, the most important perhaps being that they drew the trade of all the Southwest and Middle West to New Orleans, whereas there seemed to be many advantages, and a decided instinct to be served, by concentrating imports and exports on the Atlantic Coast.

The idea of supplementing the natural watercourse system of the country by canals was one which the United States shared with Western Europe. The preceding generation was impressed by the Duke of Bridgewater's famous Liverpool canal and was not unaware of the Napoleonic development in France. The difficulties of canal construction were not particularly those of engineering but of finance. Each represented a unified investment, instead of large numbers of small ones as in

[1] Lewis Collins, *History of Kentucky* (Covington, 1874), 542-553; anon., *History of the Ohio Falls Cities* (Cleveland, 1882), 42-56.

the case of steamboats, and they were infinitely more expensive than roads. To the solution of this problem the earlier generation left the idea that the work be made governmental. In 1830 it seemed that the development of transportation by canals might well become a national function.

In the meantime, under the lead of her great governor, DeWitt Clinton, New York had accomplished the simple but imposing task of making a waterway between the Hudson and Buffalo. This success caused bitter rivalry on the part of other Eastern cities which saw New York absorbing the trade of the country. Boston, Philadelphia, Baltimore, Charleston, even Portland, Maine, and Portsmouth, New Hampshire, formed visions of tapping the golden stream and sought aid of their state governments.

Three classes of canal projects were undertaken. First were short canals to connect near-by rivers and feed the trade of a wider neighborhood into such ports as Boston and Charleston. These were built generally by private enterprise. One of the most important was that connecting Philadelphia with the anthracite coal region of the Lehigh and the Lackawanna. A second class were the canals connecting the water system of the Ohio with that of the Great Lakes, and so through the Erie Canal to New York. Here private capital was quite inadequate, and these developments came only after 1830 when Jackson had put his foot on national enterprise. These canals, therefore, were state affairs. Frontier urgency found methods of evading Jackson's prohibition. State activity was stimulated by the surplus revenue act of 1836, whereby the federal government, having abnegated all projection or control of transportation, proposed to divide its surplus revenue among the states. There was a surplus, in the intent of the bill, for only three quarters of one year; but already frontier imaginations had conceived a Venetian West. More substantial assistance was given by land grants from the national government to the states, and such canals were actually constructed through Ohio, Indiana and Illinois, but it remained true that there was no national policy. The national government merely aided the states.

The third class of canals, upon which depended the efficiency of the whole system, were those designed, like the Erie, to connect East and West. Most favorably situated for such an enterprise, after New York, was Pennsylvania. Here the financial problem was undertaken by the state, but the engineering problem was of peculiar difficulty. It is hard to conceive a geographical formation more aggravating than that afforded by the successive ranges of the Alleghany Mountains, rising in obstinate placidity, one after the other, up and down, for nearly a hundred and fifty miles. The idea of making water run over them was preposterous. This was precisely the kind of problem with which the thirties and forties were at their best. The canal was brought to the foot of one range, and then, by a stationary engine at the top, boat, cargo and passengers were hauled up and let down on the other side, to resume the slow monotony of canal life until another range interrupted. With five such interruptions, one arrived at Pittsburgh with its choice of the National Road or the Ohio for the further journey. In 1834 this system was complete, at a cost of $10,038,133, and the route was used for a dozen years to the extent of its physical capacity—that is, at the seasonal peak of trade.[1] Philadelphia thus maintained herself against New York. Baltimore's attempt, by the Chesapeake and Ohio canal, in spite of national help, never reached a satisfactory western terminus.

[1] Charles Dickens, *American Notes* (Phila., 1859), 61-71, describes a journey on this canal in 1842.

To have provided itself with steamboat and canal transportation was no mean achievement for any generation. The main obstacles of nature had been overcome and the development of the continent might conceivably have gone forward satisfactorily, if somewhat slowly, with no new innovation, but by gradual improvement and extension. "Somewhat slowly," however, did not appeal to the men of the period, and while this system was still far from complete, the generation was expending more thought and capital upon the development of a system quite different, that of the railroad.

The railroad involved two separate ideas. First was that of the economy of friction in transportation by the use of fixed rails. Later, but very soon, came the idea of using steam power to draw vehicles over the rails, and, after very little experimentation, it was found that this should be done by locomotives and not by stationary engines drawing the cars to them. The moving cable was a later idea. To build such railroads involved problems of finance similar to those of the canals, but it was soon discovered, somewhat bitterly, that it involved also another point of public policy quite contrary to the spirit of the age. In 1828 a committee of Congress recommended that monopoly of use should no more be granted to railroad companies than to companies building roads or canals; they should all be open to the use of all, on paying proper tolls. Even in 1839 Governor Seward of New York clung to this hope. It was soon realized, however, and by the power of ratiocination of which this generation was not devoid, without experiment, that steam locomotives, running on a single track, must be under a single control. One must, therefore, accept railroads with this monopolistic feature or do without them.

The first center of railroad interest was in Baltimore, whose hopes of surmounting the mountains by water

Three of the types of transportation in use in the thirties: scenes at Northumberland, Pennsylvania, and at Little Falls, New York.

were proving so chimerical. In 1826 the Baltimore and Ohio Railroad was incorporated. The best brains of the city were put upon the subject. In 1831 steam was finally chosen for motive power. A locomotive, the "Tom Thumb," was built by Peter Cooper, which ran thirteen miles in an hour and surmounted grades which had been pronounced impossible. Soon Ross Winans established engineering shops which were laboratories of practical experiment and from which year by year came forth improvements by the dozen.

From this time for thirty years the ablest mechanical talent of the country was devoted to the perfecting of a railroad system. Of course railroads were not an American invention, but equally of course they were not an invention of any country. A railroad system required ten thousand new ideas and applications of ideas. Simultaneously European engineers were at work, but there was very little exchange of ideas, and when the American system developed, it was an American product and quite different from that developed elsewhere.[1]

The American railroads had for many years the reputation of cheap and shoddy construction, reckless management and wild speculative finance. This reputation was undeserved to the extent that the careless and the cheap were not actually more prevalent than their opposites. Particularly in the very earliest stage of devel-

---

[1] E. R. Johnson, *American Railway Transportation* (N. Y., 1910), is a pathfinding work. The most recent edition of this book is E. R. Johnson and T. W. Van Metre, *Principles of Railroad Transportation* (N. Y., 1921). Seymour Dunbar, *History of Travel in America* (Indianapolis, 1915), describes the conditions of every mode of travel in the thirties and forties. B. H. Meyer, *History of Transportation in the United States before 1860* (Carnegie Inst., *Contribs. to Am. Econ. Hist.*, Wash., 1911), 306-608; U. B. Phillips, *A History of Transportation in the Eastern Cotton Belt to 1860* (N. Y., 1908), chaps. iii-viii; and F. L. Paxson, "Railroads of the 'Old Northwest' before the Civil War," Wis. Acad. of Sciences, Arts and Letters, *Trans.*, XVII, 243-274, are also of value.

opment the eighteenth-century tradition of painstaking workmanship still persisted; and workers with these standards were now quickened by the confidence that they could find new methods and thus new possibilities of achievement. With these two characteristics, but not trained in scientific research or by technological study, there grew into being a class of railroad men as brilliant and original as any group of mechanics America has ever produced, and who laid the foundations of railroad development not only in the United States but in South America and even in Russia.

The first roadbeds were probably the most substantial we have ever had, solidly built of granite and ballasted with rock. They were unsatisfactory, however, because they lacked elasticity. Not only was each new line an experiment, but the directors of the longer roads freely laid a few miles of one kind, and a few of another, kept careful reports of each, and studied with care the reports of other roads. By 1840 they had pretty generally become convinced that the roadbed was not a final investment but a continual expense, and construction became generally less costly; but it had been learned how long rails should be, how they should be joined together, and how fastened to the ties.

There was longer experimentation with the rails because there was a keen desire to use the timber which was so abundant and cheap rather than iron which in the beginning had to be brought for the most part from abroad. The iron-capped wooden rails were in fact so well made that, where used with care, they were really sufficient for the light traffic of early years, and remained on many roads throughout the period. Most people, however, soon realized that they were doomed, and when the tariff of 1842 gave impetus to the domestic manufacture of iron rails, wooden ones ceased to be newly laid. American iron rails did not indeed.decrease costs, but it was claimed in the forties that they were of superior durability; and they were modeled on the American designed T pattern, which experiment had convinced American managers was the most desirable. When this generation passed on their tasks to their successors, the chief uncertainty was as to the weight of rail which would prove most efficient, and development was in the direction of greater and greater weight.

Bridges in the beginning were, on poor lines, of wood, on rich lines, of stone. The first, however, proved unsafe, and the second too costly. Engineers, therefore, began to experiment with iron, which had already been used here and there for ordinary bridge building, and during this period developed the suspension type and also built up movable iron trusses to span fifty or sixty feet between stone piers. In the fifties the American bridges began to attract world attention. Until then, broad rivers still interrupted one's journey, and one crossed on ferries to take new cars on the other side. Journeys were interrupted as frequently by the differences in gauge, a matter which was one of the leading subjects of controversy. Not only did engineers differ as to the desirable gauge between wide limits—chiefly between the four feet, eight and a quarter inches, which has become standard, and six feet—but companies and states, such as Pennsylvania, used these differences to thwart the plans of rivals. Even where two roads of the same gauge met in the same town, the rights of hack drivers and lunch vendors became vested interests, often riotous and obstinate, preventing the continuous routing of cars. Thus in the forties seven changes were necessary between Albany and Buffalo.

After brief experiment with horses, sails, mules, stationary engines and "atmosphere," steam locomotives were shown to be most desirable, and American manufacturers, such as Peter Cooper, the Baldwins and Ross

Winans, speedily made them effective. The long life of the earlier of the engines, some of which served forty years, is a tribute to their makers, but for years scarcely a new one was put out which did not represent an improvement on those that went before.[1] They grew gradually heavier. When in the thirties a locomotive collided with a cow, the locomotive had to be sent to the repair shop; in the forties, the company had to pay for the cow.[2] The losses in both cases caused the development of the elaborate "cow catchers," and finally to the fencing of the railway, so that at the end of the period the ratio of such accidents was much reduced.

Except in the coal regions the fuel was wood, although its scarcity was already apprehended. Cinders were not merely an inconvenience but a danger. In 1845 a spark arrester was generally introduced, which netted its inventors what seems now the very modest reward of $45,000.[3] Speed tests were often impressive, but few roads maintained a speed as good as the Hudson River steamer *Oregon* which made twenty-five miles an hour, Some lines made thirty miles, but from ten to twenty was more characteristic.[4]

The cars began like the English, resembling stagecoaches, at first separate, then joined together, and finally with a running board along which the conductor perilously made his way. This type, however, gave way to the long car, with two double seats divided by an aisle. Just why this change was made it is difficult to say, but it is significant that when it was complete, the American traveled everywhere, whether by canal boat, steamer or train, in a long narrow saloon, in close association with

[1] The *Report* of the Philadelphia and Reading Railroad for 1857 showed four locomotives constructed in 1838 still in use without rebuilding.

[2] Phila. & Reading Railroad, *Report for 1857.*

[3] Anon., "Baird's Spark Arrester," *Scientific American,* VI (1850), 9.

[4] H. G. Richey, *Railroad Improvements, 1845-1857* (unpublished thesis, Univ. of Wis.).

his fellow travelers, and with the opportunity for general conversation or for the expression of his opinion before an audience, willing or unwilling.

In 1840 such cars bore a not very remote resemblance to those of today. Of course, they were constructed of wood; they were connected by chains, which took up none of the slack on starting and stopping; and their ventilation and heating were of that variety of the primitive which is unsatisfactory. Cars were of first and second class. The first seated about forty people, on double benches covered with horsehair. The Eastern (Massachusetts) road in 1845 put on a chair car, with seventy seats on pivots, and walls of inlaid wood. In 1836 a sleeping car was introduced by the Cumberland Valley Railroad with twenty-four berths which resembled the bunks of canal boats; but the type convertible for day use was a later development. Frequent stops made restaurant cars unnecessary, and the usual absence of toilet facilities less inconvenient.

Gentlemen traveling alone were expected to use gentlemen's cars, and, in regions where they were numerous, Negroes used "Jim Crow" cars. Heavy luggage in most instances was handed over to the company in return for a check, but the generation never arrived at a decision as to whether the company was responsible for damage. Originally passengers were "booked" as on stagecoaches, but by 1840 tickets were coming into use, and passengers were encouraged to purchase them by some slight reduction in fare. Tickets over connecting lines, however, could not be bought until the fifties. They were collected by the conductor, who, in contrast with the European system where the engineer was chief officer, ruled the train. On the main lines he was a lordly personage, dressed in top hat and with a medal proclaiming his number, but contemning both uniform and tips.

While the railroad companies carried the baggage of

their passengers and, of course, freight shipments, they would not undertake the expedition of small parcels for people not traveling. There was, however, an increasing demand for this kind of service, which had been performed by the stagecoach drivers or by regular carriers with their wagons. In 1839 William F. Harnden of Boston undertook such an express service, traveling with a carpetbag between Boston and New York. Soon the Adams Express Company, which ultimately swallowed that of Harnden, came into existence, and Wells and Fargo extended the system to the West. Contracts with such companies and mail contracts with the United States government became part of the regular revenues of most lines.[1]

Railroads were generally undertaken by corporations, though, in the case of the first, the Baltimore and Ohio, Maryland and Baltimore subscribed half the stock. They needed very special powers, as that of securing their right of way, of crossing turnpikes and canals, and, especially, a monopoly of transportation on their rails. The Baltimore and Ohio charter was modeled on that of a turnpike, with power to condemn land whose value was to be fixed by a jury. Rates were fixed, and shares exempted from taxation. Early Massachusetts charters reserved to the legislature the right of fixing charges conditional upon not reducing profits below a fixed percentage. No charters, however, provided, as did some of those of toll roads, for ultimate reversion to the state; but Massachusetts in some cases reserved the right to purchase.

As has been usual in America, less attention was given than in England to the relation of this newly rising institution to that which it was to supplant, the canal. In New York, however, the state, as proprietor of the Erie Canal, made efforts to protect the latter. The new

[1] A. L. Stimson, *History of Express Companies and the Origin of American Railroads* (N. Y., 1858), 13-25.

carriers were likewise ardently opposed by the stage-coach interests and the tavern keepers. In New Jersey in 1832, the Delaware and Raritan and the Camden and Amboy railroads were given a practical monopoly of trade between Philadelphia and New York, but their interests were united with those of the preëxisting canals.[1] These tendencies were summed up in a general railroad incorporation law of New York of 1847, which provided in some degree for the protection of stock-holders and the general public, and retained legislative control of rates, with the provision that profits be kept within ten per cent. As the thirties merged into the forties, and as the poorer portions of the country began to see golden futures if they could but secure railroad communication, the terms of the charters, and particularly their enforcement, began to grow more lax. *Hunt's Merchants' Magazine* said of that given by Maine to the Atlantic and St. Lawrence: "Taken all in all, since the days of Charles II, a charter of broader privileges, and of more valuable exemptions, has not been granted by any government touching any interest within the boundary of any old or new state of this Union."[2] Here was a perpetual charter to hold unlimited funds and to exact any tolls the corporation itself deemed rea-sonable. The road was exempted from all taxation, but profits over ten per cent were to be divided with the state.

Not only did charters grow more liberal but public assistance was more and more successfully invoked. Georgia undertook as a public work the building of a strategic road from Atlanta to Chattanooga. In most cases, however, the states simply took shares in the cor-poration. In the South these state shares usually

---

[1] J. O. Raum, *History of New Jersey from Its Earliest Settlement to the Present Time* (Phila., 1877), II, 339.
[2] Anon., "Legislative Policy of Maine," *Hunt's Merchants' Magazine,* XVI (1847), 262.

amounted to a third of the whole, and in Virginia and North Carolina a board managed the interests of the state in all roads.   In the West, not only was little or nothing said about rates in railroad charters, but every encouragement was given in towns and counties to bond themselves to secure funds with which to promote railroad construction; and at the end of the period the local politics of those states centered largely in the efforts of the local communities to persuade prospective railroads to pass through them, and of railroad agents to induce the communities to grant as large sums as possible on the easiest of terms.   Meantime investors in the East and in England had the choice of buying bonds of the railroad companies themselves or bonds of localities which assumed the risks of the venture.   The mania for railroads and the acceptance of the fact that they should be built by corporations led in 1850 to the successful tapping of the resources of the national government in a grant of land to the state of Illinois, to be turned over by the state to a railroad company.

The working through of preliminary railroad problems by 1850 was actually more important than the services performed.   By 1840 there was a broken line of railroads from Portsmouth, New Hampshire, to Wilmington, North Carolina.   Between 1840 and 1850 the greatest development was in New England.   Boston was connected with Albany, New York and Montreal. Elsewhere railroads were serving useful purposes as connecting links between rivers and canals.   Only in one case, however, did they actually cross from the East to West, and that merely duplicated the route of the Erie Canal.   They were, however, nosing westward along many other routes, the completion of which was assured. In 1850 the Erie was two thirds of the way to its goal at Dunkirk.   The Pennsylvania had reached Johnstown and was confronting its Horseshoe Curve; the Baltimore

and Ohio had passed Cumberland; Charleston and
Savannah were both reaching westward.[1]

More important was the fact that real difficulties had
actually been mastered, and that American engineers
were unafraid and investors willing to back them. Asa
Whitney was agitating for the building of a railroad to
the Pacific within our territory, hoping in part to realize
the dreams of Columbus for a western passage to the
riches of the Orient. Military and naval officers reviewing the defenses of the United States were suggesting
that the national government undertake the construction
of railroads for military purposes, as one to the Pacific
and one along the coast. William Wheelwright was
projecting a transcontinental line from Buenos Ayres to
Valparaiso, and soon engineers and managers trained by
American experience were swarming over South America
and surveying the expanses of Russia.

[1] A good account of the situation in 1850 is to be found in Dionysius
Lardner, *Railway Economy* (N. Y., 1850), 387-414.

CHAPTER V

INDUSTRY, INVENTION AND TRADE

AGRICULTURE and transportation employed most Americans. Both were self-sustaining occupations, supplying the nation and earning the wherewithal for improvement and purchases abroad. But most Americans of the day were unwilling to be dependent upon foreign nations for their manufactured goods. While, therefore, manufacturing employed a much smaller part of the population, and never during these years reached the adequacy of the two major occupations, it attracted an interest quite as deep.

The most discussed of its problems was that of protecting it from foreign competition.[1] That of the greatest industrial significance was the struggle between individual and factory production.[2] The relation in the factories between labor and capital was far from satisfactory, but during these years the subject was one which attracted interest only to a minor degree.[3] Of labor it may be said that throughout this period no Americans intended to remain laborers in the sense of living all their

[1] This controversy may be followed through the period in Edward Stanwood, *American Tariff Controversies in the Nineteenth Century* (Boston, 1903), I, chaps. viii-x, and F. W. Taussig, *Tariff History of the United States* (N. Y., 1914), chap. iii.

[2] These twenty years are most important in the industrial revolution in the United States, but the movement has not been adequately studied. See, however, R. M. Tryon, *Household Manufactures in the United States, 1640-1860* (Chicago, 1917).

[3] This subject has been admirably presented in J. R. Commons, "Labor Organization and Labor Politics, 1827-1837," *Quart. Journ. of Econ.*, XXI, 323-329, and J. R. Commons and Associates, *History of Labour in the United States* (N. Y., 1918), I, 71-88, 153-184, 215, 322.

lives dependent on wages.   The only fixed laboring class was in the South in agriculture, and there capital owned it.   Moreover, in 1830 the total number of wage-earners in America was relatively very small, and the amount of organized gang labor was slight.   The first great piece of pick-and-shovel work had been the digging of the Erie Canal, for which much of the labor had been drawn from abroad.

Factories were generally small and the industries were in that condition where even unlettered mechanics often contributed new ideas which gave them standing, and ingenious and industrious youths not infrequently rose to partnership.   The New England textile mills were scattered up and down the valleys to make use of the river water power.   Their labor they drew from the farms around them.   The farmers' daughters did not mind long hours or hard work, they knew little of the hygiene of congestion, and any money seemed to them a great deal.   They did, however, demand conditions clean and moral.   If they did not find them, they could return home.   Most of them thought their factory experience, as boys did sailoring, an episode introductory to life.   For all factory people was the possibility, daily made easier, of migration westward.   It was not entirely with an undue devotion to vested interests that orators of the forties dwelt more on protecting the labor supply for manufacturing than on the dangers of capitalism.

In fact, laboring conditions during this period were generally satisfactory except for the long hours.   Foreign travelers were usually taken to see the Lowell mills, and all were enthusiastic over what they found.   Dickens waxed lyric in describing the girls he found there and their life.   Factories were generally located in villages rather than in cities, at waterfalls and mines, and most laborers lived in separated cottages with gardens or, if unmarried, in boarding houses.   It was with the employment, toward the end of the period, of foreign immigrants, who had no country homes to which to return and who could less easily seek the West, that the pressure of the industrial system began to express itself in unwholesome conditions.[1]

The struggle between factory and individual production was a complicated one.   A clear illustration is found in the textile industry.   Here factory cottons and woolens had already by 1830 almost driven the spinning wheel from the New England kitchen to the attic.   From the mountain area they never quite drove it away, and today fashion is reviving its use.   In many cases it is impossible to draw a line between the factory and the nonfactory unit, as in the production of the innumerable novelties that Connecticut inventiveness was turning out.   In the boot-and-shoe industry of eastern Massachusetts, work was done in homes, but was so tied by agreements with finishers and agents that the essentials of factory conditions existed.   The fundamental conditions of change seem to have been that craft education by apprenticeship was not as good as it had been, that the imagination of the best minds of young Americans devoted to such things was fired rather by the desire to invent and use machines than by the eighteenth-century zeal for expert mastership, that factory-made goods were displacing individual-made goods first in one line, then in another, and that consequently the career of the independent craftsman rising from apprentice to master was becoming less attractive.   The shoemaker's apprentice was no match in the city streets for sailors off the high seas, with their trim dress, black silk kerchiefs about the throat,

[1] The condition of women is discussed somewhat unfavorably by Edith Abbott, *Women in Industry* (N. Y., 1910), chaps. vii-viii, x-xi.   The universally favorable comments of travelers capable of making contemporary comparisons seem more important, as Harriet Martineau, *Society in America* (London, 1837), II, 242-255.   See also G. S. White, *Memoir of Samuel Slater* . . *History of Cotton Manufacture* (Phila., 1836), 125-140, 165-169.

Above: First sewing-machine.

Below: Sky line of Lowell, Massachusetts, 1845.

Printing—a handicraft shop.

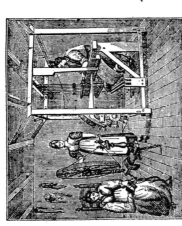

Cloth making as a household industry.

belled trousers, and their pockets full of the wages of a three months' voyage, nor in prospect with the city mechanic from the Stevens engineering works at Hoboken, who might by an inspiration followed with patience become a millionaire. Such craftsmen were the only actively dissatisfied class in the country.

Less thought was given to the problems of labor and the industrial revolution than to the widespread national ambition to make the nation entirely self-supporting. Therefore in its youth this generation was generally protectionist. Some, however, like the Southern gentry and even Webster on his first entrance into public life, preferred that foreigners do what they considered the "dirty" work of preparing raw materials for consumption, and to their opposition was added that of the consumers of such products, who found foreign imports cheaper. There was consequently a steady development of free-trade doctrine and policy which in the old age of the generation triumphed. Between 1830 and 1850, during which years the population more than doubled, imports, which varied from year to year, increased at a lesser rate. Since imports of totally noncompetitive products, such as coffee, greatly increased, it is plain that American manufacturing was coming more nearly to perform its allotted task. This was the result of the development of machine production.[1]

The chief products of the factories in 1830 were the textiles of New England, the iron goods of Pennsylvania, and the specialties, such as clocks and firearms, of Connecticut. In all these lines the progress during the period seems to the student of today steady; to the manufacturer of the time, it seemed a road of romance and peril, with

[1] Imports in 1830 amounted to $70,876,920, in 1837 to $140,-989,217 and in 1850 to $178,138,318. J. D. De Bow, comp., *Statistical View of the United States . . . Being a Compendium of the Seventh Census* (Wash., 1854), 185.

prospects constantly dependent on the varying prices of raw materials and the variations of the tariff. From 1833 to 1842, under the terms of the compromise tariff, there was a period when government policy was fixed, but this condition of stability was broken by the business panic of 1837. Relatively, textiles throve more than iron, until the last years of the forties, and men like the Lowells and Lawrences were able to make large benefactions.

Of more interest than this steady growth of established industries was the diversification of products by the introduction into America of the manufacture of things previously made abroad, but still more of things newly invented to meet or to tempt American demand.[1] It was to an outstanding degree an age of invention. There was almost no department of life which the inventors left untouched. So universal was their scope that their work defies classification; but it is interesting to distinguish those things which were of the period generally from those which were American by origin, and then those whose purpose was to change the conditions of labor from those that affected chiefly the home.[2]

One of the simplest and most complete was an American contribution, the telegraph. Here, as in the case of the railroad, were two distinct features: the means of signaling, and the code of signals. While signaling by fire and by smoke and mirrors is as old as history, the times began to call for something more flexible and far-reaching before inventors discovered new principles for dealing with the problem. The semaphoric tele-

[1] V. S. Clark, *History of Manufactures in the United States, 1607 to 1860* (Carnegie Inst., *Contribs. to Am. Econ. Hist.*, Wash., 1916), 245, 262, 314, 401-492, 509-576; C. S. Boucher, "The Ante-Bellum Attitude of South Carolina towards Manufacturing and Agriculture," Washington Univ., *Studies*, III, 243-270.

[2] E. W. Byrn, *The Progress of Invention in the Nineteenth Century* (N. Y., 1900), chap. ii.

graph, introduced during the first days of the French Revolution and used by Dumas as one of the leading features of his *Count of Monte Cristo*, was something that, so far as scientific principles or mechanical ingenuity are concerned, might have prevailed during the Roman Empire. Its adoption is indicative of the new zest for rapid communication which set brains at work on the problem of some better method.

For seventy-five years electricity had been a problem to the scientist and a toy to the public. Its habits had become fairly well understood, and the possibility of its application to communication intrigued many. It was the American, Samuel F. B. Morse, a characteristic son of the time, with many gifts from portrait painting and literature to medicine, who made the successful combination. Morse was an inventor by dint of ingenuity and general information. He was fortunate in attracting the interest of Amos Kendall, who having contributed more perhaps than anyone else to such administrative success as the Jackson régime attained, was now at loose ends looking for a fortune. Working together they secured the support of Congress, and in 1844 a line was laid between Washington and Baltimore. Comparatively inexpensive to construct and meeting so obvious a demand of the time and particularly of the vast spaces of America, its use was extended with such rapidity that by 1850 the daily receipt of news from one end of the country to the other, excepting the Far West, was an accepted fact of life, and people were confidently expecting the system to be extended across the Atlantic.[1]

Perhaps the most important of all the inventions and the most characteristically American was that of the reaper. For many generations at least the amount of

[1] S. F. B. Morse, *Letters and Journals* (E. L. Morse, ed., N. Y., 1914), II, chaps. xxix, xxx-xxxiii.

agricultural products in Western Europe had been chiefly limited by the amount of land.   Agricultural improvement consisted in intensive cultivation.   In America, on the other hand, the obvious limitation was the number of hands employed; land was supposed to be unlimited to the thousandth generation.   The result was naturally a concentration of interest upon devices saving agricultural labor, and this was stimulated by the epoch-making changes plainly traceable to Eli Whitney's simple cotton gin.   The peak of agricultural employment came at harvest time, and the amount which could be handled at that time determined the crop.   To this problem, therefore, the ingenious bent their minds, and hundreds of patents were issued for machines to assist in the harvesting.

The successful experiment was in this case undoubtedly the one best deserving.   The father of Cyrus H. McCormick was an active-minded farmer, whose home in the Virginia piedmont exhibited all that variety of occupation which has been described as more particularly characteristic of New England.   He was interested in the problem of a harvesting machine, and made some progress toward its solution.   In 1834 young McCormick patented an automatic reaper which contained essential new principles.   Unlike the majority of inventors, he was remarkable for his business ability as well.   Delayed by the Panic of 1837, he continued active in exhibiting his reaper at agricultural fairs and in seeking capital and a strategic location for manufacture.   At first he selected a position on the Erie Canal, where one hundred machines were turned out, and some profit accumulated.   He then moved to Cincinnati, the capital of the West, where German immigration was supplying a population of skilled and unexacting mechanics.   In 1847, however, he saw the promise of the future in Chicago, and reëstablished himself in that muddy and scattered frontier station, which nevertheless soon proved to be near the center of his developing market.[1]

The reaper was merely the most important of the agricultural inventions of the period. Plows were continually improved, and practically every agricultural process was attacked by some inventor with the hope of performing it by mechanical means. Even a milking machine was patented. Nevertheless, taken together, they did not constitute a system, as did those in transportation. It was not until the next generation that the supplementary inventions lightening the work of planting were put in satisfactory shape, and the population of agricultural regions began actually to decrease while production increased. Moreover, the generation which produced the reaper did not to any large extent use it. Only three thousand machines were manufactured in 1850, and, indeed, only twenty thousand in 1860. Such numbers had no real effect on production, and they affected life on but an infinitesimal proportion of the farms. Why, in spite of the demand for them, and the increasing demand for agricultural products caused by the greater ease of transportation and the growth of the European market as industrial life developed there, agriculture was so much slower to change than transportation, it is difficult to see. Not much can be attributed to the natural conservatism of the farmer, for the proportion of progressives among the immigrant farmers of the West was large. More was perhaps due to sheer poverty. Probably most important was the enormous swell of immigration which began to roll in by the middle forties and which temporarily met the labor problem. The reaper was bequeathed to the next generation, but mechanical agriculture had yet to be developed,

[1] H. N. Casson, *Cyrus Hall McCormick* (Chicago, 1909), chaps. iii-v.

both as to some fundamental principles and as to application.[1]

It was, indeed, generally true that the leading labor-saving devices produced by this generation were put on the market too late to have much effect on its life; yet they resulted directly from popular demands based on a recognition of a need.   One of these was Richard M. Hoe's rotary printing press.   Still more important was the sewing machine patented by Elias Howe in 1846. It was invented, however, rather in time to be perfected for use in the Civil War than to profit the generation that produced it.   Countless little short cuts, new tricks introduced in factory, foundry and machine shop, tended to produce more textiles in New England, more iron ware in Pennsylvania, and more novelties in Connecticut. The Colt revolver, patented in 1835, Americans generally recognized much more quickly as a necessity than they did the reaper or the sewing machine.   It was generally characteristic of these innumerable little changes that more goods were produced by each laborer; the resulting products were in some cases things never produced before, at least in America, and in other cases things not quite so good as the more expensive articles which the mothers and fathers of the generation had possessed and had been forced to cherish with such care because of their scarcity and price.   Cheapness and waste were more in evidence in 1850 than in 1830, but had reached nothing like subsequent proportions.

When John Winthrop in the early years of the seventeenth century was putting aside bad habits, among others he repudiated that of making inventions, which he found to waste his time to no end except that he should have things which his ancestors did without and which might, therefore, be presumed to be unnecessary.   But,

[1] B. H. Hibbard, *History of Agriculture in Dane County, Wisconsin* (Univ. of Wis., *Bull.* no. 101), 67-214.

among other things, it may be observed that Winthrop lived after the spacious days of Queen Elizabeth had evolved a technique of life which, with gradual adjustment, fitted the requirements of living until this generation of the forties. Now it was beginning to prove unsatisfactory in two particulars. In the first place, the new speed of life and other changes outside the home called for adjustments within it, and in the second place, the dominant ideal of equality demanded less, or at least less obvious, differences in standards of living between rich and poor. New methods of living were received with more applause than new ideas, and their rewards of fame and fortune were greater. Immense effort, therefore, was put into the mere attempt to change the mechanics of life, regardless of the solving of the essential problems of the time. The attitude toward innovation had undergone a complete revolution from that expressed by Winthrop.

A characteristic series of inventions were those for the taking of likenesses. The desire to transmit one's appearance to posterity is a human trait that has always pressed hard upon the resources available. As soon as wealth accumulated in the colonies those who could afford it began to employ painters to pass on their countenances. This demand gave employment to many youths with artistic talent all over America. Several, such as Benjamin West, John Singleton Copley and Gilbert Stuart, found means of training their talent abroad, and ranked as creative artists. Many more became portrait painters by force of will power and continued experiment, and, as in the case of Robert Fulton and S. F. B. Morse, accumulated funds to carry out other undertakings.

Portrait painting, however, was a costly process, and the rise of democracy called for something less expensive. Early in the century the silhouette afforded a new method, cheaper but inadequate.   More satisfactory was the process discovered in France by L. J. M. Daguerre. Introduced into America by S. F. B. Morse, it was rapidly developed; and by 1850 as good likenesses were thus taken as have ever been printed, but at a cost in the long holding of a fixed expression which our generation would find it hard to pay.   Late in 1849 Daniel Webster, on his way to Washington to consider the dread problems raised by the question of the extension of slavery into the territories, stopped in Boston for such a portrait. It remains today a convincing document, refuting the charge that his part in that controversy was actuated by personal ambition, a searching picture of a disturbed and earnest mind.   Daguerreotypes became common in a large proportion of American homes, and Americans set themselves to the further cheapening of the process.

A more basic change was with regard to domestic heating.   This was a development peculiarly American, perhaps because of the driving power of our cold winters. Franklin had made a practical contribution in his open-grate stove.   Still more was accomplished by Benjamin Thompson, Count Rumford, whose study of the physics of heat lie at the foundation of all subsequent development.   On the basis of these principles great numbers of American inventors set to work during this period to make more practical stoves for both heating and cooking. All through the Northeast this was the period when kitchen fireplaces were closed up and iron ranges took their places, the first step in a long procession of such changes, each one of which has been regarded by the older housewives as destructive of real delicacy in cooking, but has been welcomed by their daughters, because of increase in the speed of living and cleanliness and the saving of household labor.

Fireplaces elsewhere in the house were at the same time being sporadically supplanted by stoves for heating, of which there were many kinds, some justifying the outcry that they were dangerous to health. Such stoves in railroad cars made traveling possible in winter, which in the stagecoaches had only been endured by heavy wraps, rugs, hand and foot warmers, and by crowding. In churches and public buildings large stoves were employed, and soon these began to be dropped to the cellars and to heat the auditoriums indirectly. By 1850 practicable furnaces were on the market. Some of the enterprising and wealthy began to install them in their houses, to warm the halls and upper rooms which before had generally been left without heat.

In the South the fireplace survived, and in the West iron stoves were too expensive for general use, though their adoption was a matter of time only. The heating system, like the railroads, existed, and remained only to be generally adopted. A new American characteristic, the love of heat, was on the way to development, and a new strain was about to be placed upon the American constitution. Still, in 1850, Fredrika Bremer found the cold bedroom as yet more usual, and complained bitterly of its discomfort.[1] The fuel used depended largely upon locality, though coal, with the aid of vigorous advertising, was driving out wood. Smoke consumption was in its infancy, and the streets still resounded with the calls of the chimney sweep.

A second change of similar character toward which important, though not so great, strides were made was in lighting. The desire for brilliancy was as marked as that for heat though the need for it was less obvious. In general, it may be said that this generation was born by candlelight, and died by the light of oil lamps. Here again were no fundamental inventions but a continual succession of adjustments. The real interest was less

[1] On heating see Fredrika Bremer, *Homes of the New World* (N. Y., 1853), I, 66, 71-72 and *passim*.

in the container than in the fuel.   The best by far was whale oil, but the supply was limited in quantity and the oil expensive.   Lard and many other sources were sought, but the petroleum supply, lying just below the surface, was not discovered, and lamps consequently remained a mark of moderate prosperity.   When used, they were, in spite of the attention they required of the housewife, another saving of labor in the home; for candles had been generally one of the many products of each household.   Whether lamps or candles were used, however, they had come by 1850 to be in most instances lighted by the friction match invented in Europe and first patented in America in 1836.   It very soon reached an almost universal use because of its outstanding superiority to the flint or steel and tinder which it supplanted.   In the meantime lighting by gas, which had been introduced in the preceding generation, was spreading from city to city and from public uses to private. Gas companies were naturally dependent on a closely populated area, and consequently this illuminant was among the things making for an increasing difference between life in the city and on the farm.

The kitchen, which was not beyond—or below— the ken of practically every American woman, was being transformed not merely by the cook stove but by new kitchen ware.   In place of the copper of the Dutch countryside and the iron ware of New England were coming the new tin goods.   The tin had to be imported, but American cleverness shaped it into so many useful forms that its vendors not only tempted American housewives but exported some of their products.   Less substantial than what they replaced, tin goods were so much cheaper that they could be purchased in relative abundance, and so much lighter that they reduced drudgery.   They formed the stock in trade of the peddler who frequented all the closely settled portions of the country and who not only rapidly distributed the new wares but was an agent for collecting the rags from which to make paper for which there was an increased demand. Such peddlers carried with them, also, all sorts of novelties of a less useful character, as well as forerunners of direct labor-saving devices for the kitchen, such as hand mills to grind coffee which was rapidly becoming a new national drink.[1]

The dining room was less changed. It, as well as other rooms in the house, was more frequently papered, now that the making of wallpaper had been brought to America and made cheaper, though imported French papers were preferred and constituted a mark of distinction. The service of the table began to be enriched by new implements such as fruit knives,[2] and the whole house from kitchen to attic began to creak with the restless rocking-chair, which of all such American-conceived trivialities penetrated perhaps most speedily and widely. More and more in the public rooms carpets were substituted for the earlier rag rugs—carpets, the cheap manufacture of which was in part an American invention and the manufacture of which throve with the tariff; carpets tacked down snugly against the wall and presenting problems of sanitation which were not to be solved even by the next generation; carpets blossoming with roses of fantastic size and brilliancy and which flashed not only from the floors but on street and railroad from the sides of the carpetbags in which the ever growing number of travelers carried their few necessities. More and more generally, entrance to the house was sought by ringing the modish bell, instead of the knocker, which was becoming vulgar but not yet old fashioned.

Another striking illustration of the fertility of Ameri-

[1] In 1850 the United States imported tin plate and bars valued at $2,868,190.

[2] See such books as *Laws of Etiquette by a Gentleman* (Phila., 1839), and Mrs. Kate C. Maberly, *Art of Conversation* (N. Y., 1846).

can inventive genius began to accompany some from the home into the street.   Raw rubber, like raw tin, must be imported, yet this did not discourage the American experimenter.   In 1822 an India Rubber Company was organized at Roxbury in Massachusetts which produced overshoes, hot-water bottles and such articles.   This attempt and others failed, but out of them came Charles Goodyear's invention of the vulcanizing process, which was patented in 1844.   This gave a substantial basis to an industry built on American brains rather than material resources, but it attained importance only with the Civil War.   Most men relied for protection upon high and heavy leather boots, for which in the homes they often substituted carpet slippers; women in rainy weather experimented with "gums."

Meantime the structure of the home was changing. The houses of the rich reflected a greater variety of influences in their architectural styles—all foreign influences though with American adaptations.   The building of houses in continuous blocks extended little beyond Boston, New York, Philadelphia, Baltimore and St. Louis.   Here and there over the country the influence of Washington Irving and Scott was seen in the many-gabled cottages which were a distant echo of a growing interest in the Gothic.   Toward the end of the period the cult of Italy, which began among the esoteric and throve chiefly among the aristocratic, produced some rather beautiful studies in window spacing and iron grill work.   A plan which appealed more to the innovating reformer was that reflecting the teaching of Fourier, and which resulted in many localities in octagonal houses, which were supposed to afford an economy in heating, and the interior treatment of which was managed with some cleverness.   These houses served to give a more varied appearance to the cities of 1850 than those of 1830 had possessed; they were somewhat more complicated by the elementary beginnings of plumbing, and occasionally possessed bathrooms. They seldom equaled in dignity or size those of the preceding generation.[1]

What amazes is their cheapness of construction, even when the subsequent rise of general values is considered. One could build a six-room house, with some evidence of taste, for eight hundred dollars; fifteen hundred would give a seven-room house with architectural pretensions. Twenty-five hundred secured a town mansion or a country villa of Greek, Gothic or Italian style. With such prices it is apparent how easily the general housing of the population could improve.

With regard to public buildings, the greatest change was in the churches, where the Gothic was more in evidence, Trinity Church in New York representing a really creditable example of that ecclesiastical type. More common, however, were rather awkward combinations of dome and portico. In church and public buildings the Italian influence also was in evidence. One of the most artistic effects of the period, or rather just following it, was the railroad entrance to Providence, Rhode Island, with a graceful structure in red brick with cloisters and campaniles edged against a round cove, bordered by a double row of elms. In this case the age of individuality had given the control to culture, but lack of taste and indifference had equal rights, and cities lost rather than gained attraction.[2]

Business had not yet generally realized the advantages of display. Banks were impressive, properly advertising their conservative tendencies by using the standard Greek

[1] A. J. Downing, *Cottage Residences* (N. Y., 1847) ; J. R. Ritch, *The American Architect* (N. Y., 1852) ; Samuel Sloan, *The Model Architect* (Phila., 1852) ; Gervase Wheeler, *Rural Homes* (N. Y., 1852).

[2] G. M. Davison, *The Traveller's Guide* (8th edn., Saratoga, 1840), gives a good account of all public buildings existing and in process of construction. See also Sir Charles Lyell, *Travels in North America* (N. Y., 1845), I, 88-92.

forms.   Shops were generally inconvenient and small, but their error in psychology was becoming apparent, and the more successful merchants, as Jordan and Marsh at Boston and A. T. Stewart at New York, were increasing their frontage and window space.   The most advanced were the hotel builders.   Perhaps the most admired structure of the period was the white granite Astor House on Broadway, New York.[1]   It is fairly evident that the majority of Americans were too busy with other things to change their artistic conceptions; to them white was still the essence of good taste and marble the material *de luxe*,[2] though private homes were affecting variations running from cream brick to brown stucco.

Not an invention but a tribute to the capacity for large design and the successful completion of complex undertakings was the water system of New York.   Here water was brought about forty miles, over hill and dale and river, finally crossing the Harlem River, on a bridge equal in strength and beauty to the finest of Roman aqueducts.   It was stored in an artificial reservoir of gigantic size, where the New York Public Library now stands, and distributed through the city in pipes laid and joined by the rising trade of plumbers, who indeed brought over much of their information and skill from abroad but freely adapted, unhesitatingly invented, and began a change in the character of home life, which as it extended outward from the large cities was destined to be greater than that made by heat and light.   Other cities such as Boston rivaled or followed New York, and new varieties of pumps reached many farms.   Yet during this period water systems and sewage systems affected

[1] On the leading hotels, see Hiram Hitchcock, "The Hotels of America," C. M. Depew, ed., *One Hundred Years of American Commerce* (N. Y., 1895), I, 151-152.
[2] See John Finch, *Travels in the United States of America* (London, 1833), 17, 42-43, 126 and *passim*, on local building material.

Architectural Design in the Forties.

the lives of but a small proportion of the population, and the absence of the water trap made a house plumbed for sewerage almost as liable to disease as one with the primitive well and cistern.[1]

On the whole, the contrast in life between 1830 and 1850 exhibits an astonishing fertility of resource and willingness to change. One cannot say that the technique of living was occupying more attention than previously, but whereas Washington devoted his attention to bringing his gardens to an exquisite perfection, the men of the thirties and forties sought novelty rather than perfection. In some respects, as in the use of carpets, ease of heating, cherishing of personality by daguerreotypes, and cheapening of kitchen supplies, these changes decreased, except in the case of the frontier, the differences between the homes of rich and poor. On the other hand, the close of the generation saw greater contrasts between city and country than had previously existed, and a wider variation due to the scattered use of the new inventions. This, of course, was chiefly an accident of time, and the rising generation might expect to see the use of such things practically universal. Taking these changes altogether, they cannot be said, economically or socially, to have produced a satisfactory new scheme of life. They did not accomplish for the home what the railroad did for transportation. Many more inventions and developments were needed to complete the revolution in living which this generation began in America and the continuance of which they rendered inevitable.

It is plain that the amount of business was increasing during these years. As farmers produced more for sale and bought more of what they needed, the number of

---

[1] In 1850 there were 83 cities in the United States with public water supplies, for the most part privately owned and managed. M. N. Baker, ed., *The Manual of American Water-Works* (N. Y., 1892), ix.

exchanges increased, and, of necessity, the number of people who made a living by handling such exchanges. On the whole, the organization of this trade was less systematic at the end of the period than at the beginning, owing to the destruction of the United States Bank and the Panic of 1837.   Experimentation was in progress, but results were negligible in 1850.   Bankers and merchants were of all types, and there was little sifting to separate the sheep from the goats.   Except that the stronger, whether good or bad, found more extensive opportunity, and began to accumulate larger fortunes, there was comparatively small change of conditions.[1]

One general aspect of American commerce which caused some friction was that foreign exchanges followed a triangular course.   Our imports were chiefly paid for by the exports of the South.   These imports were, for the most part, received at New York and only a portion of them were ever forwarded to the South, for many were retained to pay for the textiles and novelties of New England, the iron goods of Pennsylvania, the food of the West, and the services of the merchant marine which the South required.   Actually this was an indication of a closely interlocking national life, but to the Southern planter it seemed to indicate that he was paying the national bills.

In 1830 only a very few like Washington Irving and James Fenimore Cooper were making a living from literature.   Even the indispensable newspapers rarely supported their editors without the assistance of political patronage.   Art supported no one, except a few portrait painters, church musicians and theatrical families.   By 1850 a good-sized corps of writers earned their living, many taking recourse also to lecturing; a dozen newspaper men, such as Horace Greeley and James Gordon

---

[1] In the absence of any reliable statistics, the best picture of this development is in the advertisements of the newspapers.

Bennett, were rich.[1] Sculptors were obtaining contracts for decorating public buildings, foreign artists were coming to America to secure fat fees, and writers and singers of popular songs were enjoying large incomes. Pure science was in 1830 frequently the pursuit of men of fortune; by 1850 wealth was beginning to endow chairs for such studies in colleges.

The nation carelessly supported, as a nation in its experimental condition should, an incredible number of cranks of all calibers and varieties, who wandered over the land, prying into secrets, keen-eyed for new things, many no more efficient than Mr. Micawber, but generally unlike him in that, instead of waiting for something to turn up, they expected to turn something up. Floating like wind-blown seeds over the land, perhaps no larger proportion met fructifying conditions, but their undirected efforts were part of the process by which the nation secured some of the new hybrid conceptions and organizations it needed. It was a time for experiment, even if undirected and controlled only by natural forces.

These various activities came reasonably near producing the living that Americans believed they must have, and more nearly so in 1850 than had been the case in 1830. They allowed, also, an increasing production of capital. There was not, however, enough capital to realize the plans which this large-minded generation conceived, nor was the machinery for accumulating small savings and applying them to distant undertakings yet developed. Most capital was invested near home, and many small amounts were laid away in a "napkin." In 1830 the idea that this capital needed, as did the rivers, damming and dredging and ditching for the use of the whole country interested few. The great majority be-

[1] The *New York Tribune* was made a corporation in 1850, with a capital of $100,000. Thereafter for twenty-four years its dividends averaged $50,000. W. A. Linn, *Horace Greeley* (N. Y., 1903), 56-70.

lieved that natural resources were in themselves sufficient. The same feeling that made people accept the idea that endowments of unoccupied land would create a school system caused people to believe that the mere peopling of fertile land would establish civilization.   By 1850 there was among some a better realization of such things, but they were still a minority.

CHAPTER VI

NEW AMERICANS AND NEW HOMES

THE outstanding indication of change in this civilization was movement. To settle America had required determination to make the great leap across the Atlantic. The majority, once landed, had, however, again settled into their European habit of fixed residence, and for generations the New England Thanksgiving and the Southern house party had gathered tribes of cousins to the new ancestral home. On the other hand, the modern flux of life in travel and business had not in 1830 become possible. The distinguishing characteristic in the movement of this generation was the impulse to shift the home from one part of America to another.

Judging from the census figures it would seem to be a liberal estimate to suppose that, of the thirteen million Americans of 1830, four hundred thousand were foreign-born.[1] But the United States government was less interested in origin than in citizenship; and the census of that year reported 107,882 unnaturalized foreigners. This not very striking number was highly localized. The only great industry in which they played an important part was shipping. Hardly a seagoing vessel of the merchant fleet was without foreign sailors, and often they formed a large part of the crew. On land, aliens were most numerous on the seacoast, and chiefly on the commercial seacoast of the Northeast. New York had 52,488, Pennsylvania, 15,435, Massachusetts, 8,787, and Maryland, 4,786.

[1] The annual statistics of immigration, 1830-1850, are summarized in W. J. Bromwell, *History of Immigration to the United States . . . from 1819 to 1855* (N. Y., 1856), 61-152.

109

The distribution of those in New York was characteristic. Twenty-nine thousand lived in or about New York City. The majority of the remainder were to be found in the northern counties where their presence merely indicated that the Canadian boundary was not a very important barrier. The rest were nearly all found along the Erie Canal, to whose building their brawn had made no small contribution. With new arrivals so concentrated, there were vast areas with no foreign-born element. Many of this generation in old age could relate the sensation with which they saw their first foreigner, or when the first Irishman came to their village. It is not surprising that, more than in earlier times, assimilation was not generally taken for granted, and people of foreign birth were generally regarded as foreigners even after they became resident voters.[1]

Between 1830 and 1850 nearly two and a half million foreign immigrants were added to a population that increased altogether from a little less than thirteen million to a little over twenty-three million. Of these newcomers, nearly half arrived in the last five years of the period. It is evident that immigration was an important feature in the life of the time. The attention that it attracted was due not merely to its magnitude, but to its distribution and character, and in part to its relative novelty. It was inevitable that during this period the New England conception of a selected population should sink into obscurity.

The dominant and simple belief in equality, the vast demand for labor and the individualistic conception of government, all reënforced the sentiment that the United States was a refuge for the oppressed as well as

---

[1] S. F. B. Morse, *Imminent Danger to the Free Institutions of the United States through Foreign Immigration* (N. Y., 1854), first printed in 1835.

an example to the world. Often, and by many, the immigrants were disliked. No serious proposal, however, was made for their exclusion or for a limitation of their number or character.[1] Dislike, moreover, never during this period offset their utility as unskilled and inexpensive laborers in the East, and as prospective settlers, land buyers and taxpayers in the West. Never were their privileges curtailed. Rather, increasingly were they welcomed in so far as the laws were concerned. In the West they could generally vote on the same terms as migrants from the older states, often after one year's residence. The national government gave them the privileges of the preëmption act. Truly the door was open.[2]

A steady stream, already started and continuing to grow, brought English, Welsh and Scotch. They were of varied classes and occupations, many had family connections in America, and with their similarity of language they quickly found a place in American life, which made it unnecessary, if not impossible, to maintain a group life. Thus the Scotchman Alexander Mitchell, establishing himself in Wisconsin in 1839, speedily inspired perhaps the greatest confidence of any banker of the Northwest. As farmers they were to be found throughout the Northwest, but perhaps the largest number were those who continued in the new country to be factory operatives as they had been in the old. These latter naturally belonged at home to the dissatisfied classes, and they contributed something to American

[1] Proposals were mainly directed against speedy naturalization and equal participation in the benefits of the national land system. C. L. Bouvé, *A Treatise on the Laws Governing the Exclusion and Expulsion of Aliens from the United States* (Wash., 1912).

[2] For the movement in general see Jesse Chickering, *Immigration into the United States* (Boston, 1848), as well as such later studies as J. R. Commons, *Races and Immigrants in America* (N. Y., 1920), 188-197; J. W. Jenks and W. J. Lauck, *The Immigration Problem* (N. Y., 1912), 290-293, 324, 351-356, 427-432, 451; Richmond Mayo-Smith, *Emigration and Immigration* (N. Y., 1890), chaps. iv-v, vii.

sympathy for the Chartist movement at the end of the period.[1]

Much more attention was attracted by the Irish, whose number steadily grew until at the end of the period they taxed the rapidly increasing means of ocean transit. This influx was novel rather because of its rapid increase than its newness, for the Irish had always come; it was chiefly to be attributed to the greater ease in reaching America; for the causes of emigration had long existed. In the late forties, however, it received an enormous impetus from the famine that for several years devastated Ireland. The Irish immigrants consisted of all classes but not all occupations. Few were mechanics, and such as were came from Ulster and properly are to be joined with the Scotch. Some were gentry, with a little money, who sought, often with success, to build up country estates in the West. More were of the intellectual proletariat at home, and with their national adaptability rapidly found their way into newspaper offices and the innumerable new jobs created by the changing life of America. The great majority, however, had been peasant farmers working under an abominable land system, whose effort reached its limit when they paid their fare to America. They arrived at Boston, New York, Philadelphia, Baltimore or New Orleans, but chiefly at New York, equipped with the knowledge of a simple tillage, but with no money to secure the land to till or even to journey to the place where land was.[2]

They constituted, therefore, what the new life of America was demanding and what America did not possess—a laboring class with no choice but to accept such

[1] S. C. Johnson, *History of Emigration from the United Kingdom to North America, 1763-1912* (London, 1913), 39-67, 80-81, 158-159, 176-196, 316; S. H. Collins, *The Emigrant Guide to and Description of the United States of America* (Hull, Eng., 1830).

[2] Stephen Byrne, *Irish Emigration to the United States* (N. Y., 1874), chaps. iii-v, x; J. F. Maguire, *The Irish in America* (London, 1868), chaps. xi-xiii, xvii.

jobs as were offered. Fortunately for them such jobs were numerous. Pick-and-shovel work was new in America. Few of the native stock cared to or were forced to engage in it, for nearly all could scratch together a living on some family farm, even if they could not gather the cash to migrate. The Irish, therefore, were welcomed by the new corporations, and stayed in the coast cities to excavate ditches for gas and water mains, or were taken in gangs to dig canals or prepare the track of new railroads, or served as engine crews in the omnipresent steamboats. Throughout the period their brawn was laying the foundation for the new material civilization of America.

While so employed they stepped on no economic toes and were regarded with general indifference. A second economic stage appeared, however, before the period was over. The railroad gangs, when the work was completed, were apt to settle down in some near-by manufacturing town and to enter the factories on terms which began to drive the natives from their posts. They won the hatred not only of those whom they displaced, but also of the independent skilled mechanics, the demand for whose services was slackening not really because of the Irish but because of the increased use of factory-made goods. In the cities, too, the Irish girls, who began to come over in almost as great numbers as the men, not only permitted many Americans for the first time to indulge in the luxury of a maid-of-all-work but took the place of native "help."

In addition to this competition, the Irish movement was characterized by several features differentiating it from that of the English and Scotch. The Irish laborers generally settled in groups, whether in the cities or in the factory villages. While they spoke the language of the majority, they were distinguished at this time by their poverty, and secondly by their religion. American tolerance was not a simple trait, and during this period the Roman Catholic Church was becoming more distasteful to the majority as it became more important. The feeling toward it was not merely religious but political, for it was considered as an extension of the great established church of Europe, monarchical in its own organization and the chief prop of civil monarchy as well. When, therefore, the first Catholic church arose in the Irish quarter of city or town, the combination was regarded as a menace.

The cohesion of the Irish extended to politics. The Irish had played a part in American politics since the end of the eighteenth century; Tammany Hall attracted them in the early twenties and in time they came to control that institution. As New York City grew and the public services increased, they showed a capacity for securing appointments and contracts; the typical policeman came to be an Irishman, and policemen were growing more numerous and powerful.

In this period Irish allegiance went primarily to Andrew Jackson and the Democracy. Their leaders from New York City were increasingly able to swing the vote of the smaller groups in up-state cities, and outside the state they became a factor in elections in Philadelphia, Baltimore and particularly in Boston. No other group was at this time so organized and so united. They came to be, therefore, a factor more important than their numerical strength would have made them, unless at the very end of the period. The chief interest of their leaders at this time, aside from securing the victory of the Democratic party and the spoils of victory, was in the newly arising question of tax-supported education. In general, they stood for a division of school funds among the schools of the various denominations, and, failing that, the exclusion of religious teaching and of the use of the King James version of the Bible from the public schools.

The reaction of the native population to these conditions varied. The combination of religious, political and economic rivalry became at times intense. In 1834 an Ursuline convent was burned in Charlestown in Massachusetts.[1] The following year S. F. B. Morse returned from Austria deeply suspicious of Catholic enterprise in the United States as propaganda for monarchy and published his small but influential book on *Foreign Conspiracy*.[2] Rioting, particularly at election time, was a feature of the life in the more crowded districts of New York and Baltimore. In Philadelphia from time to time during the forties there were attempts to organize an American Protestant party with the idea that the foreigner was the leading problem of the day;[3] nativist mayors were elected in that city and in New York. When in 1844 Clay was defeated for the presidency by a narrow margin in an election in which the Irish were against him, the Whigs consoled themselves, or at least their pride, by saying that the nation that England governed, governed America. Wiser leaders, however, including Clay himself, came to the conclusion that if the Irish were so powerful, they must be won over, or divided. Particularly young William H. Seward of New York made a point of his thoughtfulness for the Irish in general, and with his talent for friendship cultivated the Reverend John Hughes.[4]

[1] G. R. Curtis, *Documents Relating to the Ursuline Convent in Charlestown, Mass.* (Boston, 1842); same author, *The Rights of Conscience and of Property. . . . The Ursuline Convent Question* (Boston, 1842); Patrick Donahue, comp., *The Charlestown Convent: Its Destruction by a Mob on the Night of August 11, 1834* (Boston, 1870).

[2] S. F. B. Morse, *Foreign Conspiracy against the Liberties of the United States* (N. Y., 1835), first published in the *New York Observer* for 1834.

[3] Joseph Schafer, "Know-Nothingism in Wisconsin," *Wis. Mag. of Hist.*, VII, 3-21.

[4] F. W. Seward, ed., *William H. Seward* (N. Y., 1891), I, 471, 502, 586, 593 and *passim*.

In the crucial matter of foreign affairs, moreover, the Whigs would seem to have expressed the dominant desire of the Irish better than did the Democrats, by twisting more vigorously the tail of the British lion.   Jackson came to an agreement with Great Britain on the subject of West Indian trade which John Quincy Adams had rejected.   In the election of 1840 Martin Van Buren on the basis of his rigid enforcement of neutrality in the case of the Canadian rebellion was attacked as pro-British and his recently published autobiography shows that he certainly found Englishmen and English public life congenial.   During the forties the outstanding anti-British leader was the Democrat, Lewis Cass, who made himself a national figure by opposing British plans for extinguishing the slave trade by extending the right of search.   But so far as his position was affected by politics it was to the South that he was looking, and not the Irish, and in 1848 he was defeated for the presidency. It is plain that the influence of the Irish in determining national policies was not so great as many supposed. Throughout the period, moreover, the great bulk of the Irish continued to adhere to the Democratic party, in spite of the smiles for them and the somewhat stagy bluster against the English, which Seward and the other Whigs employed.

More novel than the Irish immigration was that of the Germans.   Germans were indeed known and numerous in America from the earliest days.   There was, however, a virtual cessation of immigration at the Revolution, and a revival about 1830, which separated the population of that stock into two elements.   During this period the immigration was of varied classes and types. From a political point of view it represented, as had the Puritan emigration to New England, practically all phases of liberal opinion.   From an economic point of view, and this was what influenced the larger number,

Bishop Hughes, of New York.   *The Charlestown Convent, 1834.*

Irish immigration made the "Catholic question" more prominent;

The Germania Musical Society, about 1850.

Among other things the Germans brought a taste for music.

it brought over the more conservative, who were out of harmony with the rising industrialism of modern Germany.[1]

The first notable movement was a consequence of the revolutions of 1830 and their failure. Political leaders and their followers came in great numbers, and continued to come as opportunity offered and as the liberal reforms aimed at in those revolutions seemed farther and farther from attainment. Each year there arrived greater and greater numbers of the skilled mechanics whose places were being taken by the factories, and of peasant farmers. They were from all parts of Germany, but in the beginning the Rhine was their great highway, and the larger number were from the south. Increasing rapidly, this flow had already reached very large proportions when in 1848 it received an immense impulse from the failure of the renewed revolutions of that year. This new wave brought over particularly great numbers of young men, with their families, who had for some years been associated in the movement for a liberal and united Germany, and who arrived knowing each other personally or by reputation. Many had been through the German universities, then at their prime, and their names were known to thousands less conspicuous who looked upon them as leaders and martyrs. Here then were the reasonably complete elements of a cultured colony.

In many more instances than in the case of the Irish, these immigrants arrived with some money. A large number prepared carefully for the move and had read emigrant guidebooks, such as those of von Gerstner and

---

[1] A. B. Faust, *The German Element in the United States* (Boston, 1909), I, 581-588, II, 59-74; Gustave Koerner, *Memoirs* (J. T. McCormack, ed., Cedar Rapids, Iowa, 1909), I, chaps. xiii-xiv, xvi-xvii. Frederick von Raumer, *America and the American People* (N. Y., 1846), says in his preface, "If we are forced to despair of the future progress of the Germanic race in America whither could we turn our eyes for deliverance, except to a new and direct creation from the hand of God."

of Bromme.[1] As time went on, the greater number came over to join friends and relatives from whom they heard intimate accounts, and sought to reëstablish in America family and village groups. Few, consequently, stayed in the coast cities or in the older portions of the country, where it was difficult to break into American life, socially and economically, except at the bottom. Some, such as musicians, mechanics with some special skill as watchmakers, or merchants interested in developing an import trade in German goods, scattered about the country, and Germans were as familiar as Irish in cities and along routes of trade. The great bulk, however, sought the first and easiest road across the mountains. Like the Irish, they generally eschewed the South, and consequently the majority were to be found in the Ohio Valley and the Lake region.

During the first part of the period they went particularly to the Ohio. Here most of the farming land had been taken up, and they sought the cities: Cincinnati, Louisville and St. Louis. In Cincinnati, the largest city of the West, they were well received. They pushed out the city to the north, and by 1840 owned five thousand houses and cast one third of the votes. The native population seems to have realized in an unusual degree the opportunity of uniting their capital with the skill of the new immigrants. Protected by its distance and with its markets easily available, the city soon became a center for small factories, turning out an unusual variety of wares. Lard oil was a natural product of the "Porkopolis" of the West, but jewelry, stoves and musical instruments were the contributions of its inhabitants rather than of its site. Nicholas Longworth took advantage of the combination of a native grape

[1] F. A. von Gerstner, *Berichte aus den Vereinigten Staaten von Nord Amerika* (Leipzig, 1839); T. Bromme, *Gemälde von Nord Amerika* (Stuttgart, 1842).

susceptible of development, with a population of wine drinkers and growers, and a local wine was produced which many professed to prefer to that imported. A Horticultural Society interested men of means, and the Germans contributed a gardening skill and patience unfamiliar in America.

The two groups remained, however, apart. The Germans published and read their own newspapers; they met at their beer gardens; they opposed the public schools and organized their own, in which in 1830 they obtained permission to teach German. Nevertheless there seems at this period to have been no hostility—Germans and natives belonged to the same societies; and Professor Calvin E. Stowe was sent to Germany to study its educational system. In Louisville and St. Louis the Germans performed much the same functions, but there was less congeniality between the two populations, owing, probably, to the German hostility to slavery, which, while not so acrimonious as that developed in New England, was nevertheless deep and widespread. In Indianapolis the German colony was not so large, but its circumstances more resembled those of Cincinnati.

Meanwhile the Germans were coming in larger and larger numbers to the Lake region. Here they began to form similar groups in the rising new cities, and in particular to make Milwaukee for a time almost their own. More important, however, was the farming element. In this opening region they took their place with the pioneers, and showed themselves capable of breaking new land and maintaining themselves until their land became productive. In general they kept somewhat to themselves, and settled in congenial groups. In a new state, such as Wisconsin, the first population was not indiscriminately mixed together, but there would be a community of German Lutherans, a community of Belgians, one of Swiss, one of German Catholics, one of Welsh, and others of native Americans.   The latter, however, settled with less particular reference to their origin, and scattered more generally over the new territory.[1]

These German farming communities were to be found in northern Indiana and Michigan.   They were numerous in northern and central Illinois.   In Wisconsin they came to constitute a large element in the new state, which some among them hoped to make a German settlement, representative of the ideals of the liberals who were balked of realizing their dreams at home.   Here they occupied predominantly the shore of Lake Michigan from Milwaukee northward and for fifty miles inland. In Iowa they were less numerous, but formed some of the idealistic community groups which were characteristic of the time, as the Amana Society.   Speculators were keenly alive to the possibilities that lay in directing this growing stream, and while most such plans failed financially, one of them resulted in the establishment of a not inconsiderable colony in Texas.[2]

In general the Germans, like the Irish, adhered to the Democratic party, but during this period they were by no means so powerful an element.   The arrival of so many intellectual and political leaders just at the close of the period began a change.   These men were not only concerned with politics but were keenly interested in particular questions of state and national policy.   They had ideals in accordance with which they wished to mold the United States.   By 1852 they were in the thick of affairs and it was believed that they could swing their fellow countrymen as easily as did the Irish leaders of the East. At the same time they were placed even more stragetically in the balanced Northwest which was to be the po-

[1] Joseph Schafer, "The Yankee and the Teuton in Wisconsin," *Wis. Mag. of Hist.*, VI, 125-145, 261-279, 386-402, VII, 3-19, 148-171.

[2] G. G. Benjamin, *The Germans in Texas* (Phila., 1909) ; M. Tiling, *History of the German Element in Texas from 1820 to 1850* (Houston, 1913).

litical battle ground of the next ten years; soon Abraham Lincoln was studying German.

In the case of both Irish and Germans there continued to be for many years a cultural contact with the home country. With the Irish it consisted chiefly in the fact that the church kept them well supplied with priests, who in the beginning were Irish-trained. Economically, from a very early time, Ireland drew more money from the Irish Americans than it gave. Sons came to America to help support father and mother at home and to earn passage money for brothers and sisters and sweethearts. While this was true to some extent of the Germans, the latter received more from home. Various missionary organizations helped in the establishment of schools and churches, and the United States remained a missionary field for German and Austrian contributions.

While the Irish and the Germans were the most important in number and in the interest they attracted, other elements were of some significance at the time or promised to be in the future. Of the first type were the French whose number was very small but whose influence on the native population was decided. These newcomers occupied themselves to a large extent with the arts affecting manners and customs. It was a period when French etiquette was supplanting British, and while this was chiefly due to the dazzling influence of Paris, it was assisted by French dancing masters and chefs. During the same years the French Canadians began to drop down from their rural homes to garner in the cash wages of the New England mills. Dutch, emigrating for commercial reasons or distressed at home by fine shades of religious differences, founded towns in Michigan, Iowa and Wisconsin. Belgians settled in the Lake region of the last state, and Swiss about its hills. Curiously like the Israelites, Norwegian communities sent men and families to spy out the land, and while their numbers were few, the reports returned were being read on many a breakneck farm. On the whole, the impression created by the United States, however contrary to the reports of their consuls who investigated their settlements,[1] was so favorable that in a few years Norwegians, Danes and Swedes would be coming by their tens of thousands.[2]

The native Americans increased rapidly. The large families of colonial times continued to be the rule, and the easier conditions of life allowed more to reach maturity. All settled areas produced a surplus population urgent to move. Cities drew ambitious boys from their neighborhood, but their attraction was small in comparison with that of the new West. From New England there still emerged occasionally complete towns, each with some new idea to germinate. Most emigration, however, was of families and individuals. The greater part came from the outer edges of New England settlements, the Berkshires, the Green Mountains of Vermont, and the hilly country of New Hampshire and Maine. Here the new woolen manufacture was causing the farmers to develop sheep culture with its lessening of the demand for agricultural labor. Moreover, with every new Western farm and every improvement which decreased the price of farm products in transportation, the struggle for existence on rocky New England farms was rendered more difficult. The census showed that much of this region was sending out not only its increase, but that population was actually declining from that reported in 1790.

This population sought the West chiefly by way of Albany and the Erie Canal, passing through the earlier

[1] Report of Consul General Adam Løvenskjold, October 15, 1847, *Wis. Mag. of Hist.*, VIII, 77-88.
[2] R. B. Anderson, *The First Chapter of Norwegian Immigration (1821-1840)* (Madison, 1895); G. T. Flom, *A History of Norwegian Immigration to the United States . . . to 1848* (Iowa City, 1909).

New England settlements of central New York, which soon began to add their young men to the gathering stream. From Buffalo it dispersed over the southern shores of the Great Lakes, settling northern Ohio, southern Michigan, northern Illinois, southern Wisconsin, northern Iowa and Minnesota. Individuals and groups drifted southward into the Ohio Valley, and small but powerful communities were established at Cincinnati and St. Louis.[1]

The impulse for migration was less strong in the Middle States, but was reënforced as time went on by the increasing flow of foreign immigration. From New York most followed the natural watercourse of the Hudson and joined the New Englanders at Albany, whose newspapers they continued for many years to read. The highways of Pennsylvania, and the Ohio and Chesapeake Canal, gathered other thousands at Pittsburgh and Wheeling. From these ports some took boat down the Ohio, landing nearly always on the northern bank, while others set out on the National Road, which took them to the interior of Ohio, and later into Indiana and Illinois.

From the older South two streams flowed with increasing strength. The growing monopoly of the best land by the plantations caused a constant exodus of the poorer farmers to the northern bank of the Ohio where slavery did not exist. To these were added many who were affected by slavery not so much economically as in their consciences. They reënforced the earlier Southern elements all along the northern Ohio Valley, but contained fewer representatives of the plantation aristocracy than had settled there in the preceding generation when shoots of so many families, like the Harrisons, had

[1] F. L. Paxson, *History of the American Frontier, 1763-1893* (Boston, 1924), chaps. ii, viii-ix, xiii-xv, xxi-xxii, xxx-xxxiii, xlii-l; W. V. Pooley, *The Settlement of Illinois from 1830 to 1850* (Univ. of Wis., *Bull.*, no. 220).

taken root. More and more in this region the element of Northern origin gained on that from the South. When legislatures and constitutional conventions met, an increasing proportion of their members were of Vermont and New York birth, and when laws were needed, those of New York came to be examined and to be copied as had been those of Virginia at an earlier time.

The second stream was impelled to move by the declining profits of plantation culture. Some planters, such as the Chestnuts of South Carolina, fortified themselves by investing the profits of past years in the bonds of the rising corporations. Others, like the Hamptons of the same state, opened investment plantations to the West. Many sought new fields where they could refound their plantations on a virgin soil. They moved with their establishments and their slaves, southwesterly, leisurely, over the rough valley roads, into Alabama and Mississippi, Louisiana, Arkansas, Missouri and even Texas. This movement received a great accession of strength from the virile population of the Southern mountains, a large portion of whose ambitious youth saw the great possibilities of cotton culture, and emerged between 1810 and 1840 on the "Black Belt" with a capacity and energy which enabled them soon to rise from the position of farmers to that of planters. To supply them with labor, an increasing number of slaves were shifted west through the channels of the legal but not highly respected slave trade. Combined, these elements made the speediest conquest of a large area which United States history exhibits. They soon established a sectional civilization, which became highly self-conscious and distinctive.[1]

Other mountaineers left the Alleghanies by northern passes, and followed the National Road, branching out

[1] Mrs. Susan Dabney Smedes, *Memorials of a Southern Planter* (Balt., 1887), chaps. v, vi-viii.

to the north and south of it. They were strongest in Ohio, comparatively few stopped in Indiana, but before long great numbers were seeking Chicago. Adapting themselves to whatever type of civilization they found, these migrants retained both here and in the South their fundamental characteristics, and many rose to active leadership, contributing to the one side or the other their tenacity of purpose and strong sense of moral conviction.

Scattering before these purposeful settlers went the earlier type of frontiersman, whose chief impulse was adventure, discovery and untrammeled liberty. Never before had this element been more numerous or more varied in guise. The fur hunters were organized under the American Fur Company, the first great American "trust," but the opportunities for freedom that their life offered were immense. Their range was from near the Mississippi to the mountains. Scientists, and cranks disguised as scientists, roved with them. A new missionary impulse in the churches soon carried preachers into Oregon; already they had gone with our whale fishers to Hawaii. Teachers of new religious practices, such as the Mormons, sought virgin land for new Utopias. There were many, also, who dreamed not of farms and plantations but of being masters or fathers of new states, in most cases ultimately to come to rest under the United States flag. They were already operating beyond the borders of the United States, as in Texas.

Land seemed to nearly all Americans the key to happiness. With the vast majority the desire was for enough land to cultivate. With a very great number, however, the desire was to skim the cream of increasing land values. By 1830 most of the good land held by the states, companies and individuals under grants of the colonial period had been disposed of. Available land belonged to the public domain of the United States. A small portion of this was granted, for definite purposes, to each new state when it was admitted: one section out of thirty-six in each township for local education, a township or two in each state for a university, and varying amounts for roads or canals. These grants were at the disposal of the state governments. By far the greater portion of the public domain was, however, retained for sale by the United States government.

The United States land system was in 1830 familiar to the people by long usage, but was not entirely satisfactory to them.[1] The national government first acquired title by purchase from the Indians, made at public treaty. In 1830 it was felt that the government was not sufficiently vigorous in pushing for such grants, and that to the east of the Mississippi the Indians occupied more land than was proper. In fact the accepted feeling was that the Indians should be displaced from all this region and congregated into an Indian territory west of the Arkansas and Missouri boundaries, whither it was generally supposed white men would not care to go.

The land, once purchased, was divided by surveyors into townships six miles square, sections a mile square, and quarter sections, containing one hundred and sixty acres, which were again halved and quartered. Certain portions were set aside for town sites and divided into smaller lots. All subdivisions were carefully numbered. A district was then offered at auction at land offices which were situated conveniently near. To these sales the newly arrived migrants rushed and bid amid an excitement and bustle which has left its memory in the phrase "a land office business." No land could be bought at less than a dollar and a quarter an acre, and prices were often forced up beyond real value. They

[1] G. M. Stephenson, *The Political History of the Public Lands from 1840 to 1862, from Preëmption to Homestead* (Boston, 1917), chaps. i, iv, vii, xi-xii; R. G. Wellington, *The Political and Sectional Influence of the Public Lands, 1828 to 1842* (Cambridge, Mass., 1914), chaps. i-ii.

had to be paid in cash, or in land scrip which soldiers had received from services in various wars, but which was often presented by speculators who had secured it for but a fraction of its face value. Not less than eighty acres could be purchased. Land not sold at auction was put on sale at the minimum price of a dollar and a quarter an acre, and such land was often purchased by the new settler before leaving home through the medium of a land speculator, with the result that many found their lots in swamps or lakes.

It is evident that to start a new Western farm in 1830 required a cash investment of one hundred dollars for land alone. Many of those going West lacked this amount and settled down on land as yet unsurveyed, from which they might be driven by United States authorities, and which they were almost sure to lose when the land was surveyed and their land put up at general auction. Two ideas were frequent in their thought and conversation. One was that all public land should be turned over to the state in which it lay. The other was that land be given free to actual settlers. This latter idea came to be known as the homestead policy.[1] Both views were opposed by the older states, which feared that their populations would be depleted if emigration were made too easy. The second was particularly objectionable to the South, for public sentiment with regard to slavery had reached the point that, should land be given away, no special consideration would be given, as it had been in colonial Virginia, to settlers carrying slaves with them, but the same unit would be given to all heads of families.

Nevertheless, these frontier wishes were important, for never was so large a proportion of the population

[1] The best presentation of the case for homesteads is in the speech of Andrew Johnson delivered in the Senate of the United States, May 20, 1858. Andrew Johnson, *Life and Speeches* (Frank Moore, ed., Boston, 1865), 12-76.

migrating as between 1830 and 1850, or dominant in so large an area as measured by congressional votes. This was already true in 1830, and the impulses to migration continued to grow stronger and the obstacles less difficult to overcome as the facilities for transportation improved. While Ohio, Kentucky, Georgia and some other regions ceased by 1850 to be frontier, the pioneer had advanced by that date into regions unoccupied in 1830, and the frontier was as strong, though probably less proportionately strong, at the end as at the beginning of the period.

The first demand to be met was that for the elimination of the Indians. Two presidents owed their selection to this frontier element, Andrew Jackson and William Henry Harrison. Both had won its support in large measure by destroying the military and diplomatic power, the one of the Indians of the South, the other of those of the Northwest. One of Jackson's firmest determinations on entering office in 1829 was the removal of the Indian population to the Great Plains beyond Missouri, Arkansas and what was to become Iowa. Legal obligations seemed of small weight to a man whose customary associates had an interest involved and interpreted them from one point of view. That the Supreme Court held another view did not cause Jackson to condemn its chief justice, John Marshall, but to conclude that the president, the executive head of the government, need not be bound in action by the judiciary branch. He protected the states, particularly Georgia, in measures rendering the position of the Indians untenable, and pressed the sale of Indian land to the United States and the acceptance of the government's proposals for migration.[1]

Throughout the period, the process of removal was

[1] J. S. Bassett. *The Life of Andrew Jackson* (Garden City, 1911), II, 684-692.

being carried out. Tribal migrations shepherded by United States troops were a feature of the Western picture. Some Indians resisted. In 1831 and 1832 there was the brief episode of the Black Hawk War in Wisconsin. In Florida there was a ten-year struggle with the Seminoles moated about by their swamps. By the end of the period, except for a number of fixed reservations, the Indians were pretty well cleared out to beyond the first tier of trans-Mississippi states. With true Jacksonian spirit, the Indians of the Plains were left alone except for insufficient lines of forts along the trails of trade or migration to Santa Fé, to Salt Lake and to Oregon. This arrangement was by most regarded as final. Jackson himself opposed the rounding out of Missouri by the addition to that state of what is now its northwestern jog extending to the Missouri, for which Congress nevertheless provided in 1837.

The settlers demanded that the land so secured be speedily surveyed. By 1850 the survey had practically been completed in Michigan and in the southern and eastern third of Wisconsin and half of Iowa, was almost complete in Arkansas, and about half finished in Florida. During this period perhaps more than any other the United States government owned the land most desired and sold directly to the settler. The sale price, therefore, became a matter of high concern. Although this question was always at the forefront of politics and forced every party and leader to offer some solution in framing a general political platform, the migrants were not able to have their way. They wished the distribution of land to actual settlers at cost, but the older landless states regarded the public domain as a property to bring in income. The result was, politically, a deadlock in spite of a continual struggle for free homesteads, and the system of offering surveyed land first at auction, and then for sale at $1.25 per acre, was continued.

The land, however, was in the West and practice modified the law. Most settlers occupied their land before it was put on sale. When the auctions occurred the land office was surrounded by a crowd of respectable but determined men, sometimes organized to secure what they considered fair play, before whose set faces few were bold enough to bid for any section occupied by another or to force the price above the minimum.[1] This habit of anticipating the putting of the land on the market was recognized in 1830 by a law which practically granted indemnity to those who had already thus violated the federal statute. This charitable action but increased the habit and such laws were passed by each Congress. Finally in 1841 a general law recognized the fact. Henry Clay was responsible for a permanent "preëmption law" which gave the actual squatter a right to buy in at the minimum price in advance of the auction.

While most settlers purchased this land directly from the government, much was secured by speculation, particularly in the case of those portions set aside as town sites. Few of the leading men of the day, regardless of their place of residence, were without such property. Webster was a large landholder in Wisconsin, and a number of Southern politicians were interested in the development of Superior in that state. Some such speculators as Ezra Cornell of Ithaca held their land and made fortunes. For the most part, however, they were forced to sell before the competition of government land had ceased and prices had become much enhanced.

Government land must be paid for in cash. What this meant varied from time to time. Up to 1836 any paper money was accepted. From that date the United States government would receive only specie or its own

[1] Such a scene is described in A. W. Kellogg, "Recollections of Life in Early Wisconsin," *Wis. Mag. of Hist.*, VII, 489.

land scrip issued for various services. The policies of the states with regard to their land varied. In general they charged more than the national government. They also frequently accepted scrip, usually issued for services rendered in canal and road work. Such scrip was seldom presented by those to whom it was issued, but passed freely from hand to hand, serving the purposes of currency. The greatest period of land sales was while the United States government still accepted bank notes. This had, however, small relation to the use of land, as more was bought for purposes of speculation, particularly in 1835 and 1836, than for farms.[1] When specie was demanded, speculation decreased, and the annual land sales came to correspond to the area actually occupied each year. A dollar and a quarter an acre seems now a low price for land, but it is doubtful whether, except in cases of unusually favorable locations, frontier land has any value. At any rate opportunity to secure land for less caused pioneers to seek cheaper tracts where they existed. One of these was in eastern Mississippi, where the Chickasaw Indians, instead of selling to the government, commissioned the government to sell for them, while other such districts were Texas and Oregon.

The United States government was not only landlord but governor of these regions. Its system of government had been developed as part of the great constitutional work of the preceding generation. In its main purpose this system worked even more satisfactorily than previously in that it gave a government which actually preceded the settler. The spirit of the time, however, was opposed to the use of the military for such purposes and civil officers were always too few. New settlers had often at first to band together, and by the rough justice of lynch law deal with the desperadoes who accompa-

[1] D. R. Dewey, *Financial History of the United States* (A. B. Hart, ed., *American Citizen Series*, N. Y., 1902), 217, 224-227.

nied them. Still, courts and legal redress existed, and in a time incredibly short, representative institutions were functioning and territorial delegates were pressing the special demands of the new communities upon Congress. Necessity and desire rather than political philosophy inspired these demands, and no consistency runs through them. One tendency, however, was widespread. The frontier had more confidence in itself than in the national government. While it demanded favors of every kind and sort that the most paternalistic government might grant, it wished illogically for independence of action.

In framing new territorial acts, this sentiment was recognized, while upon their request these territories were made states. There developed, however, divergencies of view which were left over as one of the deeprunning problems of the next generation. One point of division, raised by William Pinkney, the Maryland senator and Webster's predecessor as leader of the bar, was as to the powers of Congress to impose permanent conditions upon a state, as had been provided for by the Ordinance of 1787. From this constitutional point arose a far less legally defensible point of view, which became, nevertheless, popular in the new regions, to the effect that even in the territories the actual sovereignty rested with the people, and that Congress could not limit their institutions, as, to cite the matter of chief discussion, by prohibiting slavery.

The land being occupied under such conditions was one of the easiest regions in the world to develop. Many of the new settlers were spared even the long task of clearing by occupying the prairie regions which earlier settlers had avoided because of the absence of wood, or still better, the "oak openings" of southern Michigan and Wisconsin. The development of transportation, however inadequate, produced results superior to that which any inland settlers had previously enjoyed. They were able to bring more with them. Mrs. John H. Kinsie, for example, coming to the wilderness of Wisconsin in 1830, found room for her piano. Those who brought money succeeded in securing carpenters to build homes which were soon adequately furnished. Those without it were able to market their crops with some profit, and few lived long in the one-room log cabins with which they started. Log extensions and porches were gradually added, and by the end of the period, brick making and the development of lumbering enabled a good number to move into real houses and relegate the original cabin to some farm use.[1] By 1850 public buildings, capitols, county court houses, schools, churches and colleges were rising not much inferior to those with which the generation had started in the East. Never had a civilization been established so quickly.

Between 1830 and 1850 the occupied frontier running north and west advanced to cover the remaining corner of Ohio, the northern third of Indiana, and the northern half of Illinois. It solidly occupied somewhat more than the southern half of the lower peninsula of Michigan. It found Wisconsin a wilderness and left it settled south of a diagonal from Green Bay to the mouth of the Wisconsin River. Iowa also began as a waste, and in twenty years a good third to the east and south was settled territory. Missouri, Arkansas and Louisiana began with lines of settlement along the Mississippi, the Missouri and the Red rivers, and ended the period with civilization pressing against their western boundaries.

More and more arose a further demand from the frontier upon the national government, or rather, two demands. From lower Iowa to the mouth of the Sabine

---

[1] Edwin Bottomley, *An English Settler in Pioneer Wisconsin* (M. M. Quaife, ed., Wis., Hist. Soc., *Colls.*, XXV), *passim*.

the edge of the frontier was a long artificial line, not the natural sawlike cutting edge of the frontier at other times and other places. In the upper part this line separated the territory which the United States designed for settlement from that which it planned to reserve for the Indians. The frontier was beginning to demand a revision of this Indian policy. From the lower boundary of Arkansas to the Gulf, the line separated the territory of the United States from that of the Republic of Mexico, and divided Americans of like stock and institutions from each other. Louder and louder grew the demand that the national government realize its "Manifest Destiny" by securing Texas.

Nor did the frontier stand alone in recognizing that destiny, and that it pointed not only to Texas but to a transcontinental republic, with California, Oregon and all that lay between them and the East. The difference between the frontier and the Eastern leaders, such as Calhoun, was that he regarded delay as advantageous to a nation growing daily stronger, while the frontier, especially when advanced groups of settlers ventured to anticipate our "destiny," regarded action as an immediate necessity. In order to understand the obstacles which the powerful frontier encountered in this its great adventure, it is necessary to consider how certain inhibitions were at the same time arising, a matter which is discussed elsewhere.[1]

The population which came together in the West was a mixed one. At its base was the family ambition for a good farm, which, after hard work, would bring comfort in late middle age and provide for the upbringing of the children. To most communities, however, came families with some wealth and background, who sought to establish themselves in prominence and rise to wealth. Everywhere were young men who sought freer oppor-

[1] Chapter xii.

tunities for distinction in law and politics, for this was a wholesome period when able young men consciously aimed at growing up with a community which would ultimately intrust them with its political destinies. Everywhere were those who had been discredited at home, and sought either opportunity to reform, or to resume under freer conditions careers of varying degrees of dishonesty.

In the speculations over town plats, in the struggles over county towns and state capitals, in the intrigues with the agents of prospective railroads, it was difficult to distinguish men of the latter type from the merely optimistic whose confident belief in the future caused irregularities in its attainment to seem trivial. At least a sophisticated generation such as our own would find it difficult to make such a distinction. A raw Western community rated its men by character, separated from their acts, and knew its successful scoundrels on whose side it was often worth while to be, from its well-meaning dreamers, to whom it was kind but whose undertakings it came to shun.

Some sought the West to escape the oppression of uncongenial families or communities, or to secure a greater moral latitude for themselves, or the power of imposing some particular system upon others. As compared with earlier times, however, there was less need to migrate for such purposes, and, with regard to moral and social aims, the frontier was often rather conservative than radical. Always hovering about each new community were numbers of the merely shiftless, endlessly seeking that turn of the wheel which would never come, while some were frankly criminal, who came to prey upon the less protected flocks of a new land.

Before this more solid mass of home seekers and their parasites continued to scurry the fringe of the still more adventurous and fantastic, and of those bent on finding new Utopias.   Thus in 1848 the Mormons made their great move out of the United States territory into the heart of the Rockies, and every year thereafter saw their thousands crossing the Great Plains to the Salt Lake region, where their new experiment was painfully striking its roots.   The American missionaries in Hawaii established themselves firmly and looked back to the United States for protection.   The fishermen, and the traders they attracted, were especially interested in the harbors of California, and, though few in numbers, they were in the early forties making their presence disturbing to the cabinets of Mexico and Great Britain.   Likewise, as we shall see, the Texan movement ripened into statehood.   Finally, in 1848, the last touch was given to this varied migratory movement by the discovery of gold in California.[1]

In general, as contrasted with earlier migration, there were fewer community movements.   As contrasted with later periods, the family, or at least the incipient family, played a larger part.   Families with young children were common, newly married couples frequent, groups of brothers with the purpose of sending back for parents and sisters were found in every district.   Young men with the plan of sending back for acknowledged sweethearts seem to have been as numerous as those who left home free-hearted.   Even the latter, once established, often returned to find a wife, or at least married the daughter of a neighbor from home.   During this generation it was much more common for the migrating husband and wife, whether of native or foreign birth, to come from the same home environment and thus to preserve the tradition of their strain than to marry into another provincial culture.

[1] See *post,* 308-311.

CHAPTER VII

Manners and Morals

THESE changes in transportation, in conditions of life and in the composition of the American people naturally produced changes not less important in their habits. Seldom have transformations so great been made anywhere in the lifetime of one generation. To create conditions so new and to make the necessary adjustments of life at the same time is something which is seldom satisfactorily accomplished. The United States of this period was not an exception, and it is doubtful if the surface of life was ever so fantastic and, except to an almost incredibly optimistic eye, so disagreeable. How deep these surface changes penetrated into the character of the people is a question more important but much more difficult, whether for the contemporary or for the historian.

Never before was the surface of life so exposed to the gaze of the public and the future. Never before in America were people so much out of their houses and on the move. Never before were there so many travelers to observe them, with so easy a market for their observations when put into print. Never had the busy reporters of the newspapers been so numerous and so alert to catch the mass or the individual in some unusual pose, some amusing gesture. The generation was exposed to a continual "close-up" without having learned how to appear before the camera. Whether this multitude of snapshots affords a better understanding of its real life than the materials existing for earlier generations is a question.   Certainly at the time there seemed to be less sense of direction, a greater variety of tendencies, than usual.   Whether this was a fact or was due to variety of report the cautious will be slow to declare.[1]

The travelers represented almost every variety of experience, prepossession and purpose.   De Tocqueville came in the thirties to study the working of our institutions from the point of view of political philosophy. Somewhat the same purpose animated Harriet Martineau, who, in spite of her deafness, had probably the best advantages of all for meeting the ablest minds and entering the finest homes of America.   Dickens had a popular reception and best saw America as the dominant democracy wished it to be seen.   He came primarily to make a book, and he probably was too little sensitive to understand that the Americans who had been laughing at an Englishman making fun of Englishmen would not laugh at an Englishman making fun of his foreign hosts. In America as in England, he saw rather the unusual and the comic than the ordinary.   Others came with special purposes.   George Combe lectured on phrenology in which he believed and to which he wished to make converts; George Lewis, to investigate our churches, Charles Lyell, our geology, and many others to report on opportunities for immigrants.   All these reports were read as attentively in the United States as elsewhere, and each new volume became at once the battle ground on both sides of the Atlantic for reviews which often equaled in importance, and almost in length, the works they dealt with.[2]

About some of the more constructive products of this generation, which are to be taken up later, such as the

---

[1] Compare J. B. McMaster, *History of the People of the United States* (N. Y., 1883-1927), with J. R. Green, *History of the English People* (London, 1877-1878).   The former seems generally throughout this period a much more confusing picture than any part of the latter.

[2] For a list of other important accounts of travel, see *post*, 347.

institutions for the blind and the insane, all were enthusiastic. On the great novelty of universal male suffrage perhaps none changed their preconceived ideas. As to the character of our public life, they were divided, but the intimate experiences of Miss Martineau at Washington are of more value than all the others taken together and are more favorable. Practically all disapproved of slavery; few traveled in the South to observe it.

One thing upon which the travelers were competent to report was the public manners of the Americans. On this point they were almost at one: the manners were bad. Foremost was the almost universal male habit of chewing tobacco and then spitting. Cigarettes had not come in, cigars were limited by social custom to certain times and places, but the "plug" was everywhere, and the bystander was fortunate when it was accompanied by its attendant spittoon. It is not necessary to suppose that there were no homes devoid of these articles, nor American men who were immune from the habit. It was, however, pervasive, and did not cause social ostracism or mark a social class. Equally distasteful was the manner of eating. The prevalent impression derived from hotel and boarding house was that the knife was too much in evidence, particularly in the consumption of peas; one noted merchant used his for ice cream also. Here again this habit was not universal, but the circles from which it excluded a person were small, and to most travelers inaccessible.

More general still was the practice of eating rapidly, without conversation. What they ate was again unsatisfactory to the observer, and if one may judge from the medical advertisements of the newspapers, to the digestion also. This impression would perhaps have been varied if more travelers had frequented the South. It was also true that in a country where most cooking was done or closely supervised by the housewife and where time was not considered a factor, there were more dishes of special excellence than there are today. In the church "socials" rivalry was keen in the production of cakes of elaboration and succulence, and if sauces were few, as Talleyrand had earlier remarked, relishes were many and recipes for them highly prized. The defect seems to have been the lack of balance in the ration. Meat was overabundant and fresh vegetables were too few. This generation did indeed learn to eat tomatoes, but not to make salads. The three meals of the day were practically identical.

Still again travelers were unfavorably impressed by the appearance of Americans. The women of the cities they reported as being of pleasing manner and costume but overdressed. New conditions meant that incredible numbers of Americans came to have, at least from time to time, unusual sums of money; the *nouveaux riches* came to swamp the aristocracy. The spirit of democracy was that all should rise to the top, and the first and easiest method was by overcoming the differences in outward guise. The increasing ease of ocean transportation meant a more and more rapid influx of fashion, in setting which the needle turned steadily away from London and toward Paris. More and more, therefore, the streets were crowded with women dressed in the extreme of fashion, and the shops displayed a greater and greater wealth of foreign goods. Less and less could foreigners distinguish the social position of these women, and, on the whole, social position came to be less and less significant.[1]

Such display was distinctly feminine. There was coming into existence that division of functions, which was to characterize the United States for several gener-

[1] C. W. Brewster, *National Standard of Costume* (Portsmouth, 1837); see particularly *Godey's Lady's Book and Magazine* (Phila., 1830, and throughout the period).

ations, by which culture was feminine, and masculinity was expected to distinguish itself by a lack of exterior polish. To a considerable degree the men could be more easily classed socially by their attention to their toilet, though such a criterion would have done an injustice to the birth and station of many a Southern planter. While the older men of the generation, such as Webster and Benton, still "dressed," it was becoming less and less desirable to do so. Equality expressed itself in the general vogue of the long-tailed frock coat, accompanied in the South by a broad-brimmed soft hat, in the North by the tall hat, less expensive than formerly now that silk had become its material instead of fur. Individual taste found its expression in the waistcoat, which rivaled the carpetbag in splendor. Still, men whose wives appeared in silks and satins slouched beside them in unfitted suits and dirty linen. For both, the bath was a weekly event, not always observed. Webster, when his second marriage brought him into the aristocracy, began daily to wash his chest; but this had more to do with his nasal troubles than with cleanliness.[1]

One of the first impressions that the traveler received on reaching New York in the later days of the period was of the newsboys. During the forties they were almost as characteristic of the city as were the dogs of Constantinople. They were new in America; they were almost unique in the world. It was one of the first occupations in which boys, who had always labored hard enough at home, began to receive money for their work. They were ragamuffins from the growing slums; they were sons of widows helping keep the family together; they were shrewd products of the business instinct who would save their earnings and rise to be

[1] G. W. Docine, *Manners Maketh Man* (Phila., 1852) ; Eliza W. R. Farrar, *The Young Lady's Friend* (Boston, 1836) ; *The Laws of Etiquette* (Phila., 1839) ; *The Young Man's Own Book* (Boston, 1832).

financial magnates. They fought, they divided their "beats," they had their regular days at the theater, they were among the most picturesque elements of the city.

The reason for their existence was the new development of the press which was one of the marked features of the period. The newspaper was, of course, not new. It had always enjoyed unusual advantages in America. Since the Zenger case in 1735 it had enjoyed a freedom of expression which the Federalists in the Adams administration had tried in vain to limit. It was free also from such imposts as the British "paper" duties, which laid so heavy a hand on the press of that country until Gladstone withdrew them. Nevertheless, American papers had but scantily rewarded their owners, because of their slight circulation. Many were maintained only by subsidies, direct or indirect, received from political leaders who needed them. Nearly all had been adjuncts, sometimes unimportant, of printing establishments. The most significant had been those of Washington, which relied on the profits of the national printing or on hopes of securing it.

The first new step was the establishment of the *Sun* in New York City by Benjamin H. Day, who, seeing the possibility of maintaining a low-priced paper by advertising based on large circulation, issued it in 1833 at one cent a copy. The *Sun* made also a second innovation in seeking to attract readers by the startling character of its news. Its famous moon hoax, detailing astonishing discoveries made by the astronomer Herschel which were proved by the arrival of the next packet from England to be without foundation, hit the funny bone of the public with a tingling sensation that was remembered and enjoyed. So successful was Day's experiment that in 1835 he began to turn the Napier press, upon which it was printed, by steam, and the need was created which stimulated inventive minds and brought about Hoe's rotary press in 1846.[1] Day's example was quickly emulated by the Scotchman, James Gordon Bennett, whose *Herald* by its collection of news and its brief and snappy editorials gave an impression of sophistication and cosmopolitanism. In 1841, a Vermont printer's boy, Horace Greeley, founded the *Tribune*, to which he gave distinction by its ardent advocacy of, or opposition to, the movements of the day, outside of politics as well as in that field.[2]

These papers soon began to compete with each other, their chief means of contention being the "scoop," or prior publication of some important or startling "story."[3] Such scoops were easier to secure than they are now when so much news is handled by press associations, and immense sums, considering the resources of the day, were spent in obtaining them. By the end of the period such papers were making large incomes. Their editors were free from political patronage though most papers were attached to some political party. Their influence had extended far beyond New York, and had changed the character of the whole press of the country and made the Americans a nation of newspaper readers.

The world as presented by such papers was a peculiar one. It is important to discount both the pictures of American life and the effect produced on the American mind. Political editorials were of the most exaggerated bitterness, and did not stop with the condemnation of men's opinions or the actual defects in their character. Their news was selected with reference to the unusual

[1] Robert Hoe, *A Short History of the Printing Press* (N. Y., 1902), 31-32, and *passim*.

[2] Horace Greeley, *Recollections of a Busy Life* (N. Y., 1868), 136-143, 167, 261.

[3] J. M. Lee, *History of American Journalism* (Boston, 1917), chaps. x-xiii; C. H. Levermore, "Rise of Metropolitan Journalism, 1800-1840," *Am. Hist. Rev.*, VI, 446-465; Allan Nevins, *The [New York] Evening Post* (N. Y., 1922), chaps. v-viii; G. E. Payne, *History of Journalism in the United States* (N. Y., 1820), chaps. xv-xvii, xxi, and 393-394.

and the sensational rather than with the desire of creating a photograph of life. One may almost conclude that things mentioned in the papers were exceptional, and look elsewhere, or at least read between the lines, for the real life of Americans. Facts were generally presented from the point of view of optimism; the conception of some public improvement was presented as if it were completed. On the other hand there was little, if any, of the later practice of selecting news with reference to the editorial policy.

Special value must be given to the advertisements which were paid for; one can safely conclude from these that the consumption of patent medicines was immense, and their patentees among the new members of the money aristocracy. The press, too, was so flexible, it cost so little to establish a new paper, and the habit of doing it was so strong, that in time most new ideas and points of view found somewhere an expression, and a survey of the whole press gives at least the elements of which American life was composed, although their proportionate importance must be fixed by other means.

At the time, most Americans read a paper with which they fundamentally agreed, and whose suggestions on small matters they were apt to follow. The respect for the printed word was still strong, and the influence of newspapers was probably somewhat more powerful than it is today. On the other hand, the population was keen, and there was ever present a standard of comparison between the knowledge each one had of local happenings and the newspaper reports. The new press began not only to give the Americans news but to develop their critical faculties. On the whole, the people obtained a better impression of what was taking place outside their personal experience than had their fathers, but it was still strangely and somewhat maliciously distorted.

The theater made no such sensational change as did the newspapers.[1] Actors were still mainly of English birth and training and of theatrical families like the Kembles. As the cities grew, however, they played to a larger proportion of the people and their position became more a matter of debate. On the whole the theater gained in standing, and Americans began to enter the profession without losing caste. In the forties some fifty stock companies were supported in moderation. Stars traveled individually and played in each city with the company established there. The demand for these stars became so great that, at the end of the period, their salaries threatened to reduce managers and regular staff to a very low compensation. Throughout the period Edwin Forrest was the chief hero of the stage. In 1849 Edwin Booth appeared at the Museum in Boston, and already Americans were becoming proud of Charlotte Cushman. Just after this period, the dramatization of *Uncle Tom's Cabin* brought to the theater tens of thousands who up to this time had regarded it as the chief weapon of the devil.

Theaters were of all types, and the ancestry of the Great White Way was in full swing in the Bowery. Plays were chiefly, however, of the classic type, all such authors from Shakespeare to Bulwer Lytton contributing. Melodrama often held the boards. Comedies were often of native authorship and supplemented by impromptu dialogue. The humor tended to be broad and for that reason they were all the more discredited. The outstanding vogue of Shakespeare must be attrib-

[1] Lawrence Barrett, *Edwin Forrest* (Laurence Hutton, ed., *Am. Actor Series*, Boston, 1881), chaps. iv-vi; N. M. Ludlow, *Dramatic Life as I Found It* (St. Louis, 1880), chaps. xxxviii, xli, xlv-xlvii, l-lxv; Anna C. R. Mowatt [Mrs. A. C. Ritchie], *Autobiography of an Actress, or Eight Years on the Stage* (Boston, 1853), chaps. ii, xii-xxi, xxv-xxvii; A. H. Quinn, *A History of the American Drama to the Civil War* (N. Y., 1923), chaps. vii-xi; *Charlotte Cushman, Her Letters and Memories of Her Life* (Emma Stebbins, ed., Boston, 1878), chaps. ii-vi, viii-x.

uted largely to the emphasis given to the action, and to the wondrous mouthing of his verse which hypnotized by its music this oratorical generation. As always, there was the appeal to sensuality made not without response. The chief expression of this was in New York in the forties, in the form of living pictures taken from the Bible and from classical mythology. The exact degree of nudity which they involved was the subject of newspaper discussion and court testimony.[1] Except perhaps on the Bowery, however, it was not absolute disclosure, but the human form revealed by tights.

A more significant development, and one dependent on the other accomplishments of the time, was the coming to America of actors, not unsuccessful at home but of the first rank, to extend their reputations and fill their purses. Americans were beginning to be willing to pay prices before unknown in order to see with their own eyes what the world was talking of. The first of these distinguished visitors was the Viennese dancer, Fanny Elssler, who arrived in 1840 and remained nearly three years with mutual satisfaction. Edwin Forrest attempted to reverse the process, but his second professional visit to England, in 1845, was not an entire success. National pride was aroused, and when William C. Macready returned the visit in 1849, the public feeling of New York resulted in the Astor Place riot, during which the militia were called out and fired at the mob, one of the earliest occasions when force was used to preserve order in an American city.[2]

In 1847 New York society sought to consolidate its position as the metropolitan aristocracy of a democratic

[1] *N. Y. Tribune*, Dec. 1, 1847; *N. Y. Herald*, Feb. 23, Mar. 1, 20, 23, 1848.
[2] Meade Minnigerode, *The Fabulous Forties* (N. Y., 1924), 185-209. George Ticknor wrote: "The people here about twelve years ago first began to feel that a mob impaired the popular sovereignty. . . . But this at New York was the most decisive of all." George Ticknor, *Life and Letters* (G. S. Hilliard and others, eds., Boston, 1876), II, 240.

country by organizing opera, which had already been introduced, as an aristocratic function. A company headed by the father of Adelina Patti, who then a mere child began her first acquaintance with America, sang a season of Italian works, which failed financially and socially. In 1850 Jenny Lind, brought over by P. T. Barnum for the people and not for a class, sang herself into the hearts of the masses, and really established an artistic *entente* between the two continents.[1]

More far reaching than the theater, which required a permanent roof, was the circus, which indeed needed shelter but now set up its tent in the wilderness and drew in the lonesome farmers from a widespread countryside.[2] It has been said that the modern circus is but a reproduction of the Roman and that the revival took place in Europe and not in America. There are, however, marked distinctions. For one thing the new circus was more humane, not only than that of Rome, but than the traveling shows and street amusements of the preceding generation, with their baiting of bears and bulls, and cock-fighting. An indigenous feature, moreover, was the presentation of hoaxes, which delighted this generation, no matter how barefaced they were, perhaps because they gave so many a sense of superiority in fathoming them. The supreme artist in such matters was P. T. Barnum, whose nurse of George Washington, mermaid, mechanical chess player and similar genial frauds never lost their charm. In fact he brought them to such a point of popularity that he established a permanent museum in New York, as successful and infinitely more amusing than the correct museum of Madame

[1] The arrangement Jenny Lind made, 1849-1850, was for $1,000 each for 150 concerts, and all traveling expenses. The total receipts for 95 concerts were $712,161.34. *The Life of P. T. Barnum, Written by Himself* (N. Y., 1855), 300, 343.

[2] I. J. Greenwood, *The Circus: Its Origin and Growth Prior to 1835* (N. Y., 1898).

Tussaud in London.[1] More important, however, was the traveling circus, which penetrated almost to the frontier, and brought cheer to laborious millions.

Of sports the most general was horse racing, which was universally American, though it did not become national in the sense that horses and owners competed from all parts of the country.[2] During this period the trotting race began to press hard on the running race, and in both sulkies were occasionally used. Crowds became larger, and in the North more democratic. Hiram Woodruff acquired fame as a driver, but not so great as that of the horses, the famous blinded Lexington, Flora Temple and Lady Suffolk, who between 1838 and 1853 ran between four and five hundred heats and won $35,000.

American men were not devoid of the innate desire to develop and test their strength, but this was rather rural than fashionable and private rather than public. Abraham Lincoln became the chief wrestler of his community, but was not challenged by the champion of the adjoining district, and no one paid admission to see him. Shooting, trapping and fishing were, except in the Southeast, an occupation rather than a sport. The volunteer fire companies, founded in the preceding period, had an enormous vogue; in the forties three thousand members paraded in New York; but their connection with athletics was slight. In fact, few American men had sufficient leisure for much participation in or attendance at games. Rowing was organized on the coast, and there is mention of baseball clubs, although it was not the game as now known. Cricket matches were held

---

[1] M. R. Werner, *Barnum* (N. Y., 1923), 118-119, 153-157.
[2] For baseball see Thurlow Weed, *Autobiography* (Harriet A. Weed, ed., Boston, 1884), 202. Agricultural fairs and horse racing need scientific treatment. Consult *History of Delaware County* [Ohio] (Chicago, 1880), 259-276, and Robert Peter, *History of Fayette County* [Kentucky] (Chicago, 1882), 106-179.

between New York, Philadelphia, Montreal and Toronto. The wealthy did some racing of yachts, "Corinthian" yachting, as they called it, and while some of the generation still lingered, in 1856, the *America* off the Isle of Wight won the cup, the most famous of modern international trophies that still remains with us.

More time was found for the swapping of yarns than for sport. In inns, in country stores, on trains, and in the ubiquitous saloon, there was developing a folklore of humor which had in it something distinctively American and racy of the soil. Practical joking extended to remarkable proportions. It remains a mystery who made and buried the "Cardiff Giant," which on being excavated near Syracuse in 1869 set the scientists agog with stories of a petrified man.[1]

In the East a further public diversion was the growing publicity given to "society." As the close and established circles of the colonial period began to give way before the inroads of the newly rich and the imitations of those not even wealthy but merely ambitious, society, more perilously poised than in the past, resorted increasingly to display. A considerable portion of America talked of the ball Mrs. Brevoort gave in New York in the forties. Still more spectacular was the increasing seasonal migration to resorts, with their colossal hotels whose genial hosts, such as Mr. Paren Stevens, performed to some degree the functions of Beau Nash. This new development was confined chiefly to the North, the less changing South following for the most part the older, more civilized custom of moving to the small family cottages of the various Virginia springs. The great fashion show was at Saratoga, but many were attracted by the seashore and began tentatively, heavily clothed and isolated, to indulge in sea bathing. By 1850

[1] Andrew Dickson White, *Autobiography* (N. Y., 1905), II, 468-485.

such vacation resorts were frequented by no inconsiderable a portion of the population, and the summer flitting, with trunks of increasing number and size, had become a feature of travel.[1]

In the middle of the forties, at such resorts, on steamboats and in the more fashionable homes, the insidious polka began to make its appearance and to displace the dignity of the square dances.   Its advent was proclaimed as a first step toward a degradation to the social standards of effete Europe.   Still, the majority of Americans had always danced.   French dancing masters found employment even beyond the mountains, and new steps spread with considerable rapidity, though the country boy coming to the city had to wait for the Virginia reel before he could join in.[2]   Cards, tabooed in many districts and by certain sects, nevertheless were common enough to call for the arbitrariness of Hoyle's rules.[3]

Conditions on the frontier were such as necessity required rather than what people chose to make them. Social life was mainly what could be fitted in with the requirements of labor, and was largely connected with neighborly assistance on such occasions as harvesting, house raising, corn huskings and the like.   Such events were infrequent, and Margaret Fuller, who was sent West by Horace Greeley to report on conditions, gave a sympathetic picture of the drabness of the women's lives and the tragedy of sensitive souls wrenched from the closer knit civilization of the East.[4]   Still, in the

[1] G. M. Davison, *The Fashionable Tour* (Saratoga Springs, 1830) ; Philip Hone, *Diary, 1828-1851* (Bayard Tuckerman, ed., N. Y., 1889), I, 20, 366-368, 372-376; II, 36, 188.

[2] Count Alfred d'Orsay, *Etiquette, a Guide to the Usages of Society, with a Glance at Bad Habits;* to Which is added the *Theory of the Rhenish or Spanish Waltz, and of the German Waltz, à Deux Temps* (Phila., 1843).

[3] Edmond Hoyle, *Improved Edition of the Rules for Playing of Fashionable Games* (4th edn., Phila., 1838).

[4] Margaret Fuller Ossoli, *Woman in the Nineteenth Century* (A. B. Fuller, ed., Boston, 1855), 217-227.

Cartoon—"The Studio of Henry Clay." The typical Kentuckian attempts to explain away his pet vices in defer-ence to the Eastern standards of Frelinghuysen, his partner on the Whig ticket of 1844.

seasons when farm life was less exacting, parties did occur, and were attended by those within the distance that a farm nag could reach.

In most homes the new lamps aided in creating increased hours for reading. The magazine was in its experimental stage and not a general feature, but nearly everywhere the newspaper arrived daily or weekly and was read from first page to last. Equally important was the religious press. Nearly every denomination published periodicals, which discussed some religious matters, much more the affairs of the churches, with picturesque glimpses of the outside world through the reports of missionaries, and gave a varying degree of attention to secular politics. The effort was to make such periodicals cheap, and some were distributed free; they reached an astonishing proportion of the population.

The increased facility of the printing press was taken advantage of also to turn out literature of the gutter, which was surreptitiously hawked about, and was available for those who wished it in cities and on routes of travel.[1] This seems to have been less sought, however, than the simpering *Souvenirs, Galaxies* and *Keepsakes,* full of death, attenuated love and moral sentiments, which were the appropriate gift of a young gentleman to the lady of his affections. Among the magazines *Godey's Lady's Book* guided the feminine aspirations of most well-to-do homes, and at the end of the period its popularity began to be shared by Nathaniel P. Willis's *Home Journal.*

The market for good literature was much larger, more varied and active, than previously, although not sufficient to support many authors in more than moderate comfort. Whereas the preceding generation had for the most part ordered such books from England and France, American publishers such as Harper and Brothers,

[1] Anthony Comstock, *Frauds Exposed* (N. Y., 1880), 388.

D. Appleton, Lea Brothers, J. B. Lippincott, Little, Brown & Company, and Ticknor & Fields were now publishing not only American but foreign works. Books such as Longfellow's *Evangeline* were known to be forthcoming and sought hot from the press. Among comparatively wide circles the fate of Dickens's characters, as they developed week by week, was a standard topic of conversation. French was less read than previously but translations brought Dumas into many homes. This was a period everywhere in which the chief authorities on such subjects as history, economics, science and political theory wrote to be read, and to a very large extent they were read. From the evidence at hand one gets an impression that public men were rather better read than they are today, but their reading was that of the time; ideas were more emphasized than facts, and sentiment considered more important than subtlety.

The presentation of "morals" is not today a delicate subject in America; in the thirties and forties it was tabooed. Its treatment remains difficult. Immorality in most countries conceals itself and is but a small portion of the record. It is generally treated as relatively unimportant, and plays a small part in serious studies. By way of reaction, other writers, discovering evidences of what has been concealed, rush to the conclusion that the whole picture has been distorted, and inflate the scraps they find with the hot air of suspicion until they produce a new distortion which, in our own generation, has destroyed the tradition of a Golden Age and clothed races and individuals of the past with habits quite inconsistent with their visible accomplishments.

On the matter of sexual relationships the code of the thirties and forties was exceptionally strict. Violation of this code was almost the sole meaning attached to the word immorality. Marriage was somewhat more optional than in the colonial period when economic necessity rendered a widowerhood of more than one year both inconvenient and unpopular.   Once entered into, it was for life.   Divorce was legally permitted for causes varying in the different states, but socially was little tolerated.   The rural condoning of anticipated marriage, which had been common in some districts during the colonial period,[1] had for the most part passed away, although marriage was still a sovereign balm to wash away past sins.   A double code existed in the difference in the punishment meted out to the offending man and woman.   In the South there was little reprobation for the incontinent male.   Still, everywhere the ideal was complete purity for man as well as for woman.[2]

This code was accompanied by a prudery which was almost universal.   The living pictures of the early forties yielded to the public clamor enforced by the police.   It was a period in which legs did not exist at all.   While Powers's "Greek Slave" was admired by the daring, Edward Everett in Boston draped his copy of the Apollo Belvidere.[3]   Probably at no period was an ankle so exciting.   With its own peculiar inconsistency, which was actually a little greater than that of most ages, the most conspicuous advertisements of the newspapers related to sex functions with a directness and completeness which would disgust if not shock even the present generation.   The presumption must have been that women were protected by their own modesty and ignorance.   Yet from the modern point of view the

[1] T. J. Wertenbaker, *The First Americans* (*A History of American Life*, II), chap. vii; J. T. Adams, *Provincial Society* (same series, III), chap. vi.

[2] Rupert Hughes, *The Golden Ladder* (N. Y., 1924); Frances Anne Kemble, *Journal of a Residence on a Georgian Plantation in 1838-1839* (N. Y., 1863), 14-15, 23 and *passim;* Meade Minnigerode, *Fabulous Forties*, chaps. iv, ix; Herbert Quick, *Vandemark's Folly* (Indianapolis, 1922), a novel which gives an admirable picture of frontier opinion; George Ticknor, *Life, Letters, and Journals*, II, 240.

[3] Allan Nevins, ed., *American Social History as Recorded by British Travellers* (N. Y., 1923), 245.

most interesting are of drugs to prevent conception.   In spite, however, of this glaring exhibition of the facts of life, it remains true that most girls and an amazing number of women did pass through life in an ignorance touching if not appalling.

The facilities for the incontinent were almost universal and subject to little disguise.   In the leading theater of New York, one of the galleries was a regular place for the making of assignations, and in most towns the house of ill fame was known to boys and men of all characters, sometimes mobbed, but more often jeered at.   It was an accepted aspect of life, disapproved but recognized. On the other hand, vice was strictly segregated.   Irregular relationships in normal society, of course, existed, but were extremely rare and received neither charity nor tolerance.   One can only do the very American feat of guessing, but by that process one comes to feel that the proportion of male incontinence was large, particularly among the planter class of the South where slavery afforded so great opportunities, and that the proportion of social irregularities among those considered social equals was strikingly small.

On the positive side the picture is more pleasing.   The attitude of the American man towards woman was exceptionally good.   Women not avowedly for sale were not expected to protect themselves nor to be protected by their male relatives.   Any and every man was supposed to protect them at any time and place.   Passion was no excuse for a failure of this trust.   The charm of social relationships which came from justifiable confidence was something that gave grace even to this awkward age, and was the secret of that charm which American girls undeniably possessed.   Even in the case of "fallen women," without place in the social order as they were and with little opportunity even for the gilding which in foreign capitals concealed the fundamental dross of their position, their treatment by the public was not physically brutal. It may be said that an American woman was practically safe in doing whatever she would. According to her character, for which by the men her word was generally accepted, she was placed upon the right hand or the left. Of the attitude of the respectable women towards their fallen sisters little is to be said—they were not supposed to know of their existence, and many, miraculously, did not. Their literature told them little; heroine and hero were spotless, and the unfortunate girl who enters most novels dies, or is made "honest" by marriage. However Magdalene societies did exist, and the recognized and unrecognized worlds had here and there their contacts.

Of the men it is obvious that large numbers were not pure. On the other hand, there was among them no gospel of "wild oats." While youth was accountable for much of the degradation that existed, it was in general much more true that the men like the women were divided into two classes, the pure and the impure. In small communities they were almost as well known. The difference lay in the fact that the sinning man was not excluded from society. With fewer drawbacks to deter, the impure class of men was much larger than that of women. On the other hand, the number of men who responded to the idealism of the time, and kept themselves pure for marriage and devoted to their wives afterwards was very large. It is probable that it was larger proportionately in America than elsewhere, and larger in America than in previous generations.

As difficult to estimate as sexual morality is honesty. Yet some distinctions of the time may be marked out. However much they might copy it in the writing books, this generation was little impressed by Benjamin Franklin's dictum that "honesty is the best policy." Honesty was a virtue, a simple virtue existing or absent, not an art requiring knowledge and practice for its successful attainment.   It was not a practical device for success.   In fact it was believed, and to a greater degree than in some other times and places was true, that the wicked flourished mightily.

Honesty was in the Northeast confused to a great extent with legality, and the American distaste for equity in law gave to many individuals a fictitious reputation for the virtue who were zealously weaving webs to catch less legally minded flies.   Particularly the novel developments of coöperative business gave a great advantage to the shrewd.   The law had not been developed to meet such complexities and yet served to salve the consciences of those who took advantage of its inadequacies.[1]

In the South and those portions of the West subject to Southern influences, honor was to a large extent confused with honesty.   This led to many tragedies from its misuse by the careless and by the unscrupulous.   A real Southern gentleman could rarely refuse to endorse a note if asked by another seeming gentleman.   The number of families driven to penury by such careless assumptions of the risks of others is beyond belief, and in many cases the original signer of the note had nothing to risk, or protected himself by assignment to his wife or others. This latter practice made partnership, which was the most usual form of business combination, in many cases most unfair, for when calamity came one partner would frequently be ruined, while the other retired to live on the profits of the business which he had carefully concealed.   The standards and the methods of simpler times, when each individual had been able to watch over his interests, when credit rested on individual reputation

---

[1] See for example, Bouck White, *The Book of Daniel Drew* (N. Y., 1911); Daniel Webster, "Speech on a Uniform System of Bankruptcy, June 5, 1840," *Writings and Speeches* (Nat'l edn., Boston, 1903), IX, 26-39.

protected by the knowledge of the vicinage, when a man must perforce be honest or be known to be the opposite, were breaking down now that business became a matter of combination, and when a lost reputation could be transplanted to a new environment.

The general optimism of the times also affected the practice of honesty. Where men believed, in innocence and simplicity, that fortunes were to be picked up from every new invention, or by each new section of land opened up for settlement, there was but a weak inhibition against taking the funds of others to start the flow. The number of thieves was not greater than at other times, but the number who used any money that came into their hands for the purpose of their own speculation, was never so great.

A striking illustration of the working of these tendencies was to be found in the condition of the civil service, already referred to, when the Panic of 1837 dimmed the first glow of these bright hopes. In 1840 Clay stated that of the sixty-seven officials of the land office, sixty-four were defaulters. This statement by the leader of the opposing party was more or less confirmed by the agents of the government who investigated conditions. Hardly an officer had refrained from using the public funds in his possession to buy the land which was rising in value each day; they would sell out, repay the government, and retain fortunes for themselves. Quite as significant was the finding that scarcely an officer could keep books; why worry over dollars when thousands were flowing by?

The ablest of the government investigators was V. M. Garesche. One of his characteristic reports is on an Ohio officer: "The man seems really penitent; and I am inclined to think, in common with his friends, that he is honest and has been led away from his duty by the example of his predecessor, and a certain looseness in the code of morality which here does not move in so limited a circle as it does with us at home.   Another receiver would probably follow in the footsteps of the two.   You will not, therefore, be surprised if I recommend his being retained in preference to another appointment, for he has his hands full now, and will not be disposed to speculate any more. . . . He has, moreover, pledged his word that, if retained, he will strictly obey the law. . . . Lenity towards him . . . might stimulate him to exertions which severity might perhaps paralyze." [1]   The reader will not suppose, as did the historian Von Holst, that the collector had "his hands full" of ill-gotten gains.[2]   The point, of course, was that he was so involved by his obligations that he might be supposed to have learned a lesson, and so be apt to observe more caution in the future.   In the customs service were defalcations of a different kind.   Numbers of mere crooks simply stole the money of the government, and the Panic so overwhelmed them that they were no longer able to cover up their tracks, and fled. The intentionally dishonest always exist.   At this period they were a little more apt to secure public office than at present, and inspection was not sufficient to restrain their activity.   The involuntary dishonesty, resulting from lack of public standards of conduct, is what was characteristic of the time.

It must be kept in mind that in the West, at least, the conditions of private business were not very different from those of the public.   Appointments of clerks and agents were as carelessly made, and even partners were as carelessly chosen.   Among them were the same standards and upon them fell the same consequences, consequences in some cases borne with poise and leading to

---

[1] *House Documents,* 25 Cong., 2 sess., IX, no. 297, 241-258.
[2] Hermann von Holst, *The Constitutional and Political History of the United States* (8 vols., Chicago, 1889-1892), II, 355 *n.*

restitution, in other cases escaped by decamping to newer communities, or, if enough profits had accrued, to Canada or some other foreign country.   In New England there was no such atmospheric excuse for loose dealing, and losses were due to sheer dishonest intention or to dishonesty cloaked by law.   In New York also it was less easy to be an innocent thief, but the gathering there of representatives from all sections of the country, and the knotting of schemes covering all sections, made it to some degree a microcosm of the whole country; and sound finance, loose finance and fraud mixed without distinguishing insignia to the confusion of those who made use of that mart.   In the South there was less change of conditions, except at New Orleans, which was confidently in the thirties, and not despairingly in the forties, rivaling New York, whose conditions it somewhat reproduced.

Not only was there the complexity of sectional differences, but that resulting from the inconsistency of a problem not thought through.   While laxity in the use of others' funds was regarded with so much lenity, the sane relief of bankruptcy, as we have seen, was generally disapproved.   In 1841 a bankruptcy law was passed.   When congressmen went home, however, they found that they had misinterpreted public sentiment and on their return to Washington they promptly repealed it.[1]   While it was in operation, four hundred and forty millions of liabilities were wiped out for forty-four millions of assets—a picture of the business methods of the time.

One need not conclude that the moral virtue of honesty was less prevalent among the people than at other times.   Its practice, however, upset by the incoming of new conditions, was at a very low point.   The public funds were less unsafe than in the next generation, but

[1] McMaster, *History of the People of the United States*, VII, 48-49.

probably private investment was never such a gamble. Protective measures had not developed, and one had to rely chiefly upon one's ability to read character. Men, such as the great Chinese capitalist, Houqua, who could read character, could always find agents of the most sensitive reliability as he found J. Murray Forbes, but few possessed the discriminating power.[1] Nor was the code of honesty developed to meet the new temptations. The generation handed the problem over to their children unsolved.

Rather different was the reaction to the somewhat kindred question of gambling. Gambling was in the blood of the time. When such a proportion of the population was taking its future into its hands by venturing forth to seek new homes, when those with little capital were risking it in such precarious new enterprises as railroads and gas companies, it is not surprising that men bet on horse races, and that lotteries were a feature of the day. The very prevalence of this custom, however, began to breed a moral feeling against it, which with some ran to the point of condemning the use of chance, even in cases where all history and convenience authorize it. By the end of the period probably more Americans played cards without stakes than the people of other countries, and the number who condemned cards because some did play them for stakes began to be formidable.

Another phase of the moral attitude was that lotteries were seldom indulged in purely for the sake of chance. They were usually undertaken for the purpose of building a church or school, for sweetening a public loan or with some other such idea of having the end justify the pleasure of the means. If one combines speculation in business with the more ornamental forms of gambling,

[1] H. C. Pearson, *An American Railroad Builder, John Murray Forbes* (Boston, 1911), 5, 8, 9, 107; J. M. Forbes, *Letters and Recollections* (Sarah Forbes Hughes, ed., Boston, 1899), I, 62, 63, 72, 77-80, 98-101.

one may say that most Americans of the period were generally slightly unbalanced by the chance that they might win or lose something.[1] They were much more conscious of the dangers of the less essential forms than of the risks of unstable business.

Somewhat different again was the moral position of dueling. This product of chivalry had in the preceding generation prevailed in all sections except New England and Pennsylvania, but had been made illegal. The law, however, had little effect upon the practice. It is popularly supposed to have received its death blow when Burr so killed Hamilton. It is possible that this was so, but in that case the blow must be considered as having very lingering effects. Twenty years later one of the most advertised of American duels took place between Clay and John Randolph of Roanoke—the West against the South. Nor did the duel die out during the lifetime of this generation. Some changes, however, gradually came about. Sentiment on the subject became sectional. In the North condemnation was complete, and public sentiment was practically prohibitive. In this respect, too, Northern sentiment came gradually to extend to most portions of the Northwest. In the South and the Southwest, while some shared this feeling, the condemnation of public sentiment was chiefly from the mouth and the man who took an insult without demanding satisfaction, unless the episode were very trivial or there were circumstances of age or position which extenuated the refusal, was ruled from public favor. Here was an

---

[1] *Lottery Argus, Commercial and Exchange Telegraph, or National Miscellany* (Palmer Canfield, ed., Balt., from 1827); *Cohen's Gazette and Lottery Register* (Balt., from 1826); Palmer Canfield, *Petition on the Subject of Lotteries to the Legislature of the State of New York, April 13, 1833* (Albany, 1833); A. R. Spofford, "Lotteries in American History," Am. Hist. Assoc., *Report for 1892*, 173-195; J. H. Stiness, *A Century of Lotteries in Rhode Island, 1744-1844* (Providence, 1896); J. R. Tyson, *A Brief Survey of the Great Extent and Evil Tendencies of the Lottery System as It Exists in the United States* (Phila., 1833).

illustration of sectional moralities which were as serious obstacles to the growth of nationality, and as dangerous to the maintenance of national unity, as rifts over material interests.

Most significant of all is perhaps the fact that morals were among the most serious interests of the time, and the subject of hot controversy and debate.   In this chapter have been treated those features of the question which it is essential to know in dealing with the everyday life of the people.   Those problems which by the clamor they aroused called for group or community action will be treated in connection with the reform movements.[1]

[1] Chapter xi.

CHAPTER VIII

THE POLITICIANS

ASIDE from the making of a living or the accumulation of a fortune, the main preoccupation of most American men was politics. Politics was a male function not merely because the vote was confined to them, but because it was supposed to be unsuited to the female mind and inconsistent with that "delicacy" which was the current ideal. It was, however, a time when man proposed and woman disposed. In the South, the social mingling of the sexes made the women of the governing class almost as politically minded as those of the English aristocracy, though without their influence. The glimpses one gets of feminine opinion in the South lead one to suppose that their influence might well have been extended. In the other parts of the country it was only the exceptional woman who was informed and interested, but when so inclined she made her opportunity.

The call of politics as a career was not so general as in the preceding generation, and became less compelling as the years went on and opportunity came to be more varied by new inventions and business opportunities. Conditions remained less changed in the South, where the man whose plantation was in running order took to politics as naturally as did the English country gentleman. Some few of the poorer also entered the arena to fight the aristocracy or to make a place in it for themselves.

In the West, too, politics was the premier profession. The irregularities of frontier farming left able young men plenty of leisure intervals to build up a connection, and office once attained afforded a living wage. More particularly was this true of the lawyers whose circuits gave an exceptional chance for making acquaintances and for whose profession politics was the best advertisement. In the West, therefore, a large proportion of ability went into political leadership.

In the Northeast was the greatest change. Here the revolt against aristocracy was keenest. The public tended to reject the candidate of wealth and social position, while the character of the contests rendered politics unfashionable. It was not until the next generation that George William Curtis gave his call for the educated to come back into public life. This attitude not only kept the supercilious out of politics, but meant that politics was not a road to social recognition for the untutored. It had much less to offer financially or in distinction than the new forms of industrial activity. It attracted on the whole the less favorably placed and the less able. Of the great numbers necessary for the conduct of politics but few could expect the very moderate rewards of office. It was a condition which encouraged petty corruption.

Though between 1830 and 1850 the population somewhat less than doubled, between 1828 and 1848 the vote increased about three times.[1] This increase was partly due to the extension of manhood suffrage and partly to silent organization and noisy advertisement. The increase from eleven hundred thousand to sixteen hundred thousand between 1828 and 1836 was, apart from natural circumstances, quite apparently the result of organization, especially the development of the Jacksonian organization in New England and Ohio. Speeches were made and published, newspapers clashed in their scurrilous attacks, broadsides were distributed,

[1] Edward Stanwood, *A History of the Presidency* (Boston, 1898), 163, 185, 203, 223, 243.

"Major Jack Downing" introduced the humorous reaction of the supposedly rustic commentator; [1] but probably more important was the quiet work of the local organizer with his hand on the pulse of every voter in his district.

The increase of eight hundred thousand in the next election was in large part due to the counter attack of the Whigs. Never as successful as their opponents in organization, some genius or geniuses among them evolved the idea of blatant penetrating publicity, pitched in a moral key, but affording a degree of amusement. It was founded on a hoax little more subtle than the articles on the moon in the *Sun* a few years before. Their candidate, quiet old General William Henry Harrison, of one of the first families of Virginia, well-to-do and living as a gentleman, a scholar stored in a rather schoolboyish fashion with historic parallels for modern conditions, was represented as sitting in a log cabin, in a coonskin cap, drinking hard cider. With less untruth, but with exaggeration, the Democratic candidate, Martin Van Buren, was pictured as an aristocrat, eating with gold spoons and maintaining the White House on the scale of a king's palace. A description of its furniture, appalling in very truth to the frontiersman, was the leading campaign document. [2]

The Whigs thus appealed to the democratic sentiment of the time, and in a measure even to class hatred. The judicious must have marveled at this spectacle of a party that had boasted its support by gentlemen of both North and South sounding all these phrases of Fraternity. Whatever the Whigs may have lacked in logic

[1] [Seba Smith], *The Life and Writings of Major Jack Downing, of Downingville, away down East in the State of Maine. Written by Himself* (Boston, 1833); same author, *Letters of J. Downing, Major, Downingville Militia* (N. Y., 1834).

[2] Charles Ogle, *Speech on the Regal Splendor of the President's Palace* (Boston, 1840); same author, *Rede über die Königliche Pracht und die Verschwendung im Präsidenten-Palast* (Phila., 1840).

they had psychology on their side; they shouted that a great crusade was on, and called on all to participate in the assault. The parades, which had for many years been held, elongated and decorated themselves with floats and banners to an extent previously unknown. Songs were sung by these great gatherings, some of which caught the popular ear. Gigantic balls, representing the growing Harrison majority, were rolled from city to city. In the West crowds, sometimes amounting, according to popular report, to a hundred thousand, were drawn in from miles around by the prospect of what amounted to a circus with a serious aim—a thing which this generation could not resist; in which they did not stand alone but only a little more on tiptoe than their forefathers and descendants.

The Whigs in this election had a perfectly good case. The significance of the campaign is that their leaders recognized that the people ruled but did not trust the people's judgment. Men of aristocratic tendency and of great ability, they hit upon the susceptibilities of the time and played on them with unusual skill. They won the election but not complete control of the government. Their insight, however, into the weaker sides of the American character was correct, and the political methods they introduced lived for over fifty years. This election for the first time brought out the full voting strength of the American people; in the succeeding election, the vote increased but normally.

During the forties practically all Americans were either Whigs or Democrats. Some were sufficiently dissatisfied with both parties to organize on the outside. Some changed their votes from the one side to the other. More than nine tenths of the electorate, however, were tagged and proud of their tag. The two-party system never stood higher in the public regard. The Whig party really existed only about fifteen years, from 1839

The Whigs in 1840 thought it good American politics to represent their candidate as living in a log cabin,

Whereas his home was really that of a typical Ohio country gentleman.

to 1854, and yet for twenty years after men were spoken of as Whigs and their political fortunes were affected by their early record.

Perhaps this sentiment for party was a result of the fact that this generation found an unusual degree of difficulty in forming its two great parties. The element that in 1828 supported Adams for the presidency, called by its opponents "Adams men," and claiming as its title National Republican, represented the Federalist point of view, with the added result of a generation's schooling. Holding to a considerable degree the belief in government by the "Best," it ceased to believe that democracy would ride to a catastrophe, and on the contrary accepted it as a fact which must be dealt with. It retained to the full the belief in community guidance and would have directed the new developments of the period from halls of Congress. This policy may be epitomized in Clay's "American System" of protective tariff, internal improvements by the national government and the distribution of public-land revenues among the states. It was perhaps the strongest single political group in the country, and particularly powerful in the leadership of such men as John Quincy Adams, Webster and Clay, the political skill of such men as Thurlow Weed, and the commanding genius in publicity of Horace Greeley. It never, however, constituted a majority of the electorate.

The winners of the election of 1828, on the other hand, were not a party. Their element of cohesion was their leader, and they were properly known as "Jackson men." They were united about him, moreover, not because he stood for a program but because he might stand for anything. In office Jackson did stand for definite things. The political history of his administration is that of the successive breaks he made with factions which had supported him but which became alienated by his actions. By 1836 the process was complete, and the consolidated Democratic party had been organized, the oldest of our present party organizations.

A student of political statistics would have been at a loss to understand how Jackson could have driven out South Carolina, the Virginian element throughout the South, the supporters of internal improvements in the West, and those rural elements in the East that were attracted by the Anti-Masonic attack on secret societies, and still remain in power. The figures of 1828, subjected to such an analysis, would have spelled defeat. The persistent success of Jackson himself and the continued control maintained by his followers were due to the increase in the electorate, for he and his program appealed particularly to those elements which had not previously taken part in politics and whose inclusion was his outstanding aim. Even in 1840 a remarkable proportion of the new voters drummed out of their holes voted for the Democratic party.

The most important of the decisions of Jackson, which caused the loss first of one element and then another, were three. His veto of the Maysville Road bill detached those who wished an active policy of federal control of internal improvements. Its practical result was to split the frontier element, and by 1836 the frontier, which had been solidly for him, was not unequally divided. The second was his highly nationalistic proclamation in answer to South Carolina's nullification, which alienated those in the South who felt their chief danger to be in the establishment of national sovereignty. The third was his war on "Nick" Biddle and the United States Bank, which alarmed those interested in the stability of finance.

To coalesce these dissentient elements with the National Republicans was a problem rather of politics than of high statesmanship. In 1839 such a combination was actually effected largely by the political skill of

Thurlow Weed. It was at this time that the Whig party was really born, although the name had been used for some years before. While the Democratic party had achieved unity by following the biblical injunction of cutting off the hand that offended, the Whigs had acquired substance by the articulation of the dissevered members. Its constituents were divided on policies, but united in their growing hatred of the Democratic party—a bond most powerful when they were in opposition—in their belief that they could better administer the government, and in a certain social cohesion. They included in both North and South those who were less inclined to accept the voice of the people as the voice of God and who were disposed to retard the modification of representative government by democratic control.

To have evolved two national parties, even though one was but precariously united, was no small achievement for this generation. While more stable organizations have since been attained, never since have both parties been national in the sense of including North and South. While the two parties represented in mass two opposing attitudes toward government they embodied also many subtler but equally permanent divisions. A study of successive elections in Ohio, for instance, shows that from the period of Federalists and Republicans, through that of Whigs and Democrats, to that of Republicans and Democrats, there has been a continuity of sectional majorities quite amazing. Causes dependent upon original stock, geographical location, religion, migration, immigration and mere tradition have at all times modified the natural division based on political theory or economic interest.[1]

While the struggles between the parties were carried on with more noise than at any other period and polit-

[1] Consult C. B. Going, *David Wilmot, Free-Soiler* (N. Y., 1924), 80-84, for an example of the currents in Pennsylvania.

ical attacks were made by the new undisciplined press with unseemly vulgarity, it would appear that there was less real bitterness affecting daily relationships than before or immediately after. Men changed parties frequently and without permanent breaks in the circle of intimates. While individuals enjoyed this freedom of action, the question of the party allegiance of elected officers was being fought out. One aspect of it was whether a senator was a representative expected to use his own discretion, or an agent of his state to vote as the local legislature instructed him. State after state issued its instructions; some senators obeyed, some refused to listen. No conclusion was reached, but the senators with their terms of six years were in the stronger position, and the practice of instruction gradually fell into disuse.[1]

The two most important cases involved vice-presidents. In 1840 John Tyler was elected vice-president on the ticket with Harrison. His strict-constructionist views were well known, and he owed his selection to the desire of the Whig political leaders to hold that element by giving it recognition without power. The unexpected happened: Harrison died one month after his inauguration, and Tyler was destined to be president for nearly a full term. The moral question of whether he was to act as agent of the party which had elected him, or to be true to his own views and the faction whose votes his nomination allied with that party, was one for the casuist. This situation was made peculiarly delicate by the vanity and the sensitive integrity of Tyler, and still worse by the tactless dictatorialness of Clay, who assumed the position of party head. The result was that after disagreeable bickering, in which the more charitable view is that there were misunderstandings

[1] F. W. Whitridge, "Instruction," *Cyclopedia of Political Science* (J. J. Lalor, ed., Chicago, 1881), I, 357-364.

rather than misrepresentations, Tyler vetoed the bank bill which was the essential feature of the Whig program. The closing of Tyler's career with his presidency, and his rejection by the Democrats with whom he became anxious to affiliate himself, seem to show that in popular opinion the acceptance of office from a party involved loyalty to its program.

This seems to have been the lesson learned by George Mifflin Dallas of Pennsylvania, elected vice-president in 1844 by the Democrats. His president, Polk, did not die, but he was placed, by the political maneuverings of his enemies in a position not unlike that of Tyler. The Democratic tariff bill of 1846, the first avowed step in the direction of free trade, was in the Senate brought to a tie, and it was necessary for Dallas to give the casting vote. As a protectionist from a protectionist state, should he stand by his convictions and his local supporters, or by the party which had elected him? Dallas cast his vote for his party's bill. From the people Dallas received no further recognition, but from his party he received in 1856 the position of minister to Great Britain.

In spite of tricks, deceits and organizations growing less and less flexible, the important elections of this period seem to have expressed the dominant desires of the electorate.[1] When the electorate wanted two or three inconsistent things, it could not get them all, and it is with these secondary considerations that politicians chiefly play. It was their task to satisfy as many group enthusiasms as possible without sacrificing the great principle of cohesion.

When one turns to the accomplishment of politics in constructive legislation, the first impression is that this

---

[1] Stanwood, *A History of the Presidency*, 151-243. For the election of 1844 see C. R. Fish, *Development of American Nationality, 1783 to the Present Time* (N. Y., 1913), 305-306.

is the most barren period of our history and that the effect on everyday life failed completely to justify the effort put into political debate. This is not true, but is the consequence of the character of the leading legislative achievement aimed at and secured. The object of the majority was consistently the freedom of the individual and the reduction of the functions of government. This predominant purpose was none the less attained because it was negative. From the time this generation got into the saddle until they passed over the reins to their successors this object dominated national politics in spite of the apparent fluctuations of parties. One cannot say that politics failed to affect life because they left it loose instead of controlling it.

The chief accomplishments of politics may be considered the removal of questions of currency and banking from the control of the national government, the adoption of the spoils system, of party organization, manhood suffrage, and the wrenching of public office and financial control from the aristocracy. With the exception of party organization and manhood suffrage, these proved to be, in the main, temporary results. Nevertheless it must be kept in mind that during the period they prevailed there developed from these conditions indirect results which have proved lasting: the laying out of a system of transportation by private initiative under the control of corporations, the working out by state initiative of the elements of a new system of currency and banking which later was made national, and the development of a new aristocracy of wealth.

It must not be supposed, however, that the opposition, the Whigs, though never really controlling the national government, were powerless. Led by such men as Webster and Clay, often with the support of Calhoun, that party generally possessed the greater weight in debate, and it frequently possessed a veto by having a majority in the Senate. Combining these advantages with favoring breaks of circumstance, they were able to exert a strongly modifying influence on legislation.[1] One important victory was the compromise on the land question; another was to modify somewhat the detachment of the national government from the development of transportation by the evolution, at the close of the period, of the policy of land grants made, indirectly, to transportation corporations.

The most remarkable deviation from the predominant policy of the generation, however, was with regard to the tariff.[2] It would certainly have been in harmony with the philosophy of the time to have levied such taxes as were to be derived from imports purely with regard to revenue, and to make no attempt to use them as a means of directing industry. Toward this logical position the Democratic party slowly moved, but for the greater portion of the time protection existed. The law of 1828 was properly known as "the tariff of abominations." Jackson wished its repeal, but he favored at least such protection as would develop industries necessary to give the country military independence in war time. In 1832 a well-drawn protective bill was worked out by the committee on ways and means headed by John Quincy Adams, and was signed by Jackson. It was this bill, aggravating from the very fact that its reasonableness threatened to make it permanent, that was the signal for separate action by South Carolina representing the cotton-growing interest, to which alone no plausible advantage could be offered by any manipulation of rates. Faced by nullification, Jackson volleyed

[1] A. C. Cole, *The Whig Party in the South* (Wash., 1913), 64, 74 77, 134, 219, 223 n.
[2] Edward Stanwood, *American Tariff Controversies in the Nineteenth Century* (Boston, 1903), I, chaps. vii-viii, x; II, chaps. xi-xii; F. W. Taussig, *The Tariff History of the United States* (N. Y., 1892), 68-154.

and thundered, and at the same time, as was his custom, counseled compromise. Brought together by young Senator Tyler, Calhoun, leader of South Carolina, and Clay, the political leader of the protectionists, found common ground. In 1833 they agreed to the tariff of 1832, with slight changes, on condition that it should be gradually reduced by percentages until in 1842 all rates would become equal at twenty per cent, approximating thus the ideal of the antiprotectionists: a tariff without discrimination and for revenue only.

This gave ten years of comparatively good protection, and Clay argued that in this way he had saved the system which would have otherwise been sooner overthrown. By the close of the period the Whigs were in control of Congress. The Southern Whigs, however, were not enthusiastic for the protectionist principle, and a satisfactory bill was passed only by a combination of the National-Republican Whigs with the protectionist Pennsylvania Democrats, the latter being won over by the offer of exceptionally favorable terms for the iron of their state. Protection met its final defeat with the election of Polk and the appointment of Robert J. Walker as secretary of the treasury. Walker's recommendation was to look toward a tariff for revenue, and indeed "free trade" on the economic principles of Cobden, but that steps should be taken discreetly, particularly in the case of the iron of Democratic Pennsylvania. His bill of 1846 brought the tariff into harmony with the legislative program of the generation. The people, however, were not strictly logical, and one remains uncertain whether, in spite of theory, the majority did not really believe in protecting American manufactures.

The influence of the Whigs, however, cannot be estimated by looking at the national government alone. In some states, such as Massachusetts and Kentucky, they **were** almost continuously in power; in many others they divided control; in none were they powerless. Every function that the national government threw off might, and in some cases must, be assumed by the states. There were no limits, except their constitutions, to the functions they could assume. This situation produces a chaotic impression when one turns from studies of the legislation of Congress to states like Massachusetts which began to control the labor of children, to plan a transportation system and to appoint commissioners to control its new corporations, and then to states, such as Wisconsin and Iowa, which proposed to exclude banks not only from politics but from very existence. To some degree, however, it was the chaos of evolution. The federal system was doing its distinctive work. States were experimenting with different systems and ideas.

The most striking illustration of this legislative experimentation was in the case of banking and currency, after the struggle between Clay and Tyler made return to a United States Bank practically impossible.[1] Men of affairs set to work to build up state systems. By 1850 the freeing of banks from politics by general incorporation laws had become an accepted idea. The fact that bank notes should be protected by safety funds was equally approved, though one more panic, that of 1857, was to be necessary before it was discovered how large these should be and another half century before it was realized of what they should be composed. By 1850 the more advanced thinkers realized the advantages of the Massachusetts "Suffolk system" for frequently test-

[1] D. R. Dewey, *Financial History of the United States* (A. B. Hart, ed., *American Citizen Series*, N. Y., 1903), 153-161, 259-262; W. M. Gouge, *An Inquiry into the Expediency of Dispensing with Bank Agency and Bank Paper in the Fiscal Concerns of the United States* (Phila., 1837); same author, *Short History of Paper-money and Banking in the United States* (N. Y., 1835); same author, *The Fiscal History of Texas* (Phila., 1852); A. B. Hepburn, *History of Coinage and Currency in the United States* (N. Y., 1903), 122-133.

ing solvency, and shortly after 1850 clearing houses were to be legalized institutions. There was much that remained to do, but this was a very reasonable contribution of new and tested ideas, to constitute the legacy of the generation on a subject which they refused to discuss collectively or to act upon nationally.

Politics can never be confined to one objective; there are always questions of internal policy and of foreign relationship which combat each other, and in the first century of United States history the equally compelling problems of community relationships within the country. During this period nearly every citizen discussed the relations of the states and the Union. These discussions, based as they were upon interpretations of the Constitution, were carried on in an atmosphere of rarefied subtlety. The amount of reality behind them may be easily exaggerated; and it may be easily underestimated. Georgia, profiting by Jackson's removal of the Indians, supported him against South Carolina's nullification, although the interests of the two states on the point in question were practically identical. States had personalities and insisted upon them; state pride was evidenced by the infliction of their names upon countless children. General Sam Houston had the cruelty to name a daughter Patience Elizabeth Texas Louisiana. Nevertheless the states can hardly be regarded as the units, political, historical, economic and social, which disturbed Washington and his associates. Eager to escape the Union as South Carolina was in 1850, the majority of her citizens would not try it alone. Secession always carried the *arrière pensée* of a new union with at least some of the sister states.[1]

On the other hand sectionalism was growing daily, but by the men of this period its growth was feared,

[1] M. J. White, *The Secession Movement in the United States, 1847-1852* (New Orleans, 1916).

not relished. Clay and Webster became steadily more national; their last great work was the Compromise of 1850.[1] It must be remembered, moreover, that when Calhoun in 1850 opposed the compromise, it was not with the glowing enthusiasm of an apostle but with the awe of a prophet of disaster. The impending separation that he saw was not a new heaven, as it seemed to his younger *confrères*, but the failure of a life work.

Politicians on a less elevated stage played in the main the same part. To no point did Jackson more unequivocally commit the Democratic party than to this: "The federal Union, it must be preserved." When in 1837 Texas, a true child of the Union, was knocking at the door, Van Buren turned a deaf ear for fear of disturbing the peace of the household. The sage Blair, the wily Weed, the astute Van Buren, all agreed that the question should be kept out of the national politics. It was before the election of 1844 that Van Buren, who expected the Democratic nomination, visited Clay at his home, Ashland, and the two agreed to continue the same policy. Party organizations were national; their managers dreaded the demoralizing effects of sectional conflicts; their conventions afforded a preliminary cleansing room to wash them out before they reached the halls of Congress. It was a period of intense patriotism. Politicians had learned to use foreign controversies to win votes at home.[2] The same patriotism led them to be cautious in arousing sectional hatred. It was necessary for each to stand for the basic facts of his section's interests, but the politically minded more and more feared these very facts. Webster's attitude in his debate with Hayne did not change but his language did. The forces that throughout the period were strengthening

---

[1] See *post*, 319-323.
[2] For example, see M. E. Curti, " 'Young America,' " *Am. Hist. Rev.*, XXXII, 34-55.

sectionalism were not political. The influence of the parties, politicians and statesmen was increasingly in the direction of counteracting it. They kept the Union through their own day.[1]

[1] An interesting picture of the confused situation in the Democratic party in 1850 is to be found in R. F. Nichols, *The Democratic Machine, 1850-1854* (Columbia Univ., *Studies*, CXI), chap. i.

CHAPTER IX

THE RELIGIOUS SCENE

WHILE politics was the predominant preoccupation of the men, religion was that of the women. This is by no means to say that religion did not interest the men, but merely that, taking them as a whole, it came after politics. This was distinctly and increasingly a religious period. It was not merely that the interest in religion itself was stronger than in the preceding generation, but that the union between religion and morality was so strong that they became practically indistinguishable, and that almost every subject was invested with the religious qualities of certainty and enthusiasm. Every orator had to prove that his position was endorsed by the Constitution and the Bible.

This religion was Christianity. Deism may have been held by as many as in the preceding generation, but at least not so many distinguished men professed it, and the rationalistic attitude of the eighteenth century melted under warmer rays. Atheism was unimportant. The distinction between the two generations was in spirit rather than in form. The outward evidences of religion continued to be for the most part the same. Travelers, except from Great Britain, were impressed by Sunday observance, and this impression was generally favorable even in the case of Catholics. It was a genuine power in the land, and was nowhere more in evidence than in the schedules of the new railroads.[1] For over fifty years after the period only mail trains ran through Connecticut

[1] Emerson Davis, *The Half Century* (Boston, 1851), 183-188.

179

on that day. In the second place, church attendance was general. It was both respectable and fashionable. It included far greater numbers than the rolls of church membership carried. It pressed hard on the facilities provided, and on the frontier was checked only by the lack of churches.[1] Another evidence was the fact that while religious taxes were withdrawn, religion was, on a basis purely voluntary, better supported than ever before.

The call of the ministry was stronger than in the preceding generation. Sainthood for its own sake attracted few, but Christian service was more than usually attractive. More than in the Revolutionary period it afforded a means of distinction as well as of usefulness. Preachers such as William Ellery Channing, Theodore Parker and Henry Ward Beecher became national figures. At the same time the development of missions added the call of adventure to that of religion itself. Peter Cartwright, the frontier itinerant, and Adoniram Judson, the first great foreign missionary, continued to illustrate how a life of varied experience might be combined with religious service. The number of able boys attracted increased, but the total number of ministers was never sufficient. The opportunity for women who wished to lead a life devoted to religion, which had previously been restricted to sects such as the Quakers and Shakers, was increased by the introduction of Roman Catholic sisterhoods, the semiofficial recognition given by the Protestant bodies to missionaries' wives, and by the open forum which existed for those few women who felt called upon to preach without denominational sanction.

[1] The *Census of 1850*, however, reported accommodations for 14,-234,825 in a population of 23,191,876; the value of church property was $89,983,028. J. D. De Bow, comp., *Statistical View of the United States . . . Compendium . . . Seventh Census* (Wash., 1854), 39, 138.

In spite of this revival of interest in religion, the idea remained unchanged that the basis of its relation to the state should be separation. During this period the last taxes for church support were abolished, in Massachusetts in 1833, and nearly the last religious disqualifications for office.[1] In this separation education was the contested field and remained so throughout. This was, however, mainly a contest of competition between public and religious schools, not for elimination. There was some struggle for state support for religious schools but the principle of separation was strong enough to prevent serious controversy. In the free field, opinion, perhaps for practical reasons of expense, swung toward the public rather than the religious schools, although in the realm of higher education denominational colleges continued to be more important than those of the states.

It was, of course, impossible for two such forces entirely to escape contact. In general, the attitude of the state was benevolent, exempting religious property from taxation. Religious questions of great delicacy came before the courts. The most interesting concerned conflicts between the Roman Catholic episcopacy and separate congregations over the ownership of property, in which the courts followed the canon law.[2]

Public policy again was sometimes involved. There was every reason that the United States should be represented at the Vatican as the Pope was temporal ruler of a considerable area in Italy. Protestant sentiment, however, prevented this until 1848, when the liberal pronouncements of Pius IX gave him a general popu-

---

[1] *Constitution of the Commonwealth of Massachusetts* (Boston, 1873), art. xi, 35-36, 44; S. H. Cobb, *Rise of Religious Liberty* (N. Y., 1902), 514 ff.

[2] Thomas O'Gorman, *A History of the Roman Catholic Church in the United States* (Philip Schaff and others, eds., *The American Church History Series*, N. Y., 1893-1897, IX), chaps. xxii-xxiii.

larity which allowed the sending of a representative to his court.[1]   More important was the involving of the government in the activities of missionaries.   To those among the Indians it afforded not only protection but actual financial assistance under the guise of employing missionaries for educational work.   In this way an annual governmental appropriation was made and considerable sums set aside from the trust funds of the Indians.[2]   In the case of foreign missions, the government was bound to protect the lives and properties of missionaries, and actually it did what it could to gain them opportunity for work in foreign lands.[3]

It was undoubtedly true that, in spite of the principle of separation, very large numbers, overlooking minor differences, regarded the United States, some as a Protestant country, more as a Christian country.   This latter idea, in fact, infused the speeches and proclamations of nearly every president and governor.   It had, however, no tangible result, and Jews were not treated differently from Christians.

Religion was, indeed, too vital a thing to escape connection with politics.   The churches paid little heed to the ordinary conflicts of parties, except in New England, although such sermons as that of Robert Little, the Unitarian at Washington, when Jackson was about to be inaugurated, from the text: "When Christ drew near the city he wept over it," were not uncommon.   So many matters, however, began to come before the public which were regarded as fundamentally moral and yet called for legislative action, such as the care of the insane, temperance and particularly slavery, that public men found it

[1] C. R. Fish, *American Diplomacy* (N. Y., 1924), 280.

[2] M. L. Edwards, *Government and Indian Missions* (unpublished thesis, Univ. of Wis., 1916).

[3] Rufus Anderson, *History of the Sandwich Islands Mission* (Boston, 1870), 196-208 and *passim*.

impossible to ignore them. In fact during these years the connection of religion with life was more and more emphasized, and preaching took on more and more a humanitarian and social cast.

The mingling of these semipolitical questions with religion was deeply resented by many and caused not a few ministers to lose their places and not a few congregations to divide. This hostility was, however, chiefly due to the political instinct to avoid dangerous discussion rather than to a real desire to restrict religion to its especial field. With opposition the practice grew. More and more ministers took a stand on this question and that, and in the forties the meetings of the governing bodies of the various denominations came to be rent between those wishing their church as a whole to declare itself, one way or the other, and those who wished it to keep silent. This practice was strongest in New England and in New York. It extended gradually West. In the South there was more feeling that ministers should keep out of politics; yet even there on one conspicuous subject, advocacy of slavery, they were encouraged to declare themselves.[1]

This was hardly an atmosphere in which one would expect tolerance, and yet, except in the Eastern cities where religious differences were emphasized by those of race and riots occurred between a rather rowdy type of Protestants and Catholics, intolerance did not often run to violence. There was, indeed, some development of a broad-minded charity but not enough to account for the lack of strife. Rather, it seems to have risen from the fact that all the sects had come really to stand equal before the law, and that it was so easy for divergent elements to separate and form new sects. This was in-

---

[1] For example, see Rev. Richard Fuller, *Domestic Slavery Considered as a Scriptural Institution* (N. Y., 1847), and S. B. Howe, *Slaveholding Not Sinful* (N. Y., 1855).

deed a period particularly marked by the formation of such new groups.

The geographical and social pattern of denomination-alism was inherited.   In New England the Congrega-tionalists, just disestablished, barely maintained the posi-tion they had inherited.   Rich and energetic, they were forced to divide social and intellectual Boston with the Unitarians; Providence had always been Baptist, and Newport, Episcopalian.   More important was the fact that, by an unfortunate bargain with the Presbyterians, the Congregationalists had, in the preceding generation, given the latter control of mission work in the West. Migrating Congregationalists entered Presbyterian con-gregations, and it was hard to recall them later.   For these and other causes the Congregationalists never dom-inated expanded New England as they did the home districts.[1]

In New York the Dutch Reformed and the Epis-copalian bodies, each at one time established, divided the social and financial classes but in competition with prac-tically every other known variety of Christian organiza-tion.   In New Jersey the Episcopalians and Quakers were in the most conspicuous position.   In Pennsylvania the Quakers found their capital.   Never did their ideas pervade so much of the community nor were their works more effective; but their numbers did not grow.   Here, too, were numerous German sects, as that of the Mennonites, for the most part settled as communi-ties.   In Baltimore, as in New Orleans and to some extent St. Louis, long settled Catholic families gave the tone to society, and played the leading rôle in the religious and social life.   They shared the field with the Episcopalians who, from the Potomac to beyond the Savannah, occupied much the position which the Congregationalists held in New England, though

[1] Davis, *The Half Century*, 373.

slowly giving way before the Presbyterians in many sections.

None of these groups had as yet struck root in the West. At home, moreover, they were, each in its own locality, weakened by the inroads of certain denominations of a less local character. Numerically the strongest Protestant denominations were the Baptists, with a tradition of revolt going back to the early days of the Reformation, and the Methodists who in the eighteenth century had separated from the officialdom and ritual of the Church of England. Divided on minor points of theology, they were alike in their appeal to emotion, insistence on the necessity of personal conversion and a strict code of moral taboos. Both were democratic in government, but the Methodists were more strongly knit by the employment of bishops and a well-developed representative government. Both were especially strong among just the element that was most moved to migration, and so spread rapidly into the West, the Methodists more particularly into the Northwest, the Baptists into the Southwest. Dozens of sects, less important numerically but each with a devoted membership, were scattered throughout the country. Among them the lenient theology of the Universalists attracted perhaps the most attention.

With comparatively few representatives in New England, the Presbyterians were numerous, and more powerful in all other regions than their numbers gave evidence. Theologically they stood very close to the Congregationalists of the period, the distinction between them being in their systems of church government, which are indicated by their respective names. The real control among the Congregationalists rested with each separate church, although they came together in associations for conference. In the case of the Presbyterians it was based upon the presbyteries, or local associations of churches, and the synods which represented larger units. There had always been in America, in spite of the struggles of Cromwell's day, a close association of the two denominations and even interchange of ministers.   Thus Jonathan Edwards' first charge had been a Presbyterian congregation in New York.   Early in the nineteenth century, the agreement mentioned was made, that Presbyterian churches receive migrating New Englanders, though in time many of these latter extricated themselves and organized such churches as they had been accustomed to.   In the thirties and forties the Presbyterian organization included the great majority of the Scotch and Scotch-Irish element, and such migrant New Englanders as were not Baptists or Methodists.   The Presbyterian influence was powerful wherever these two racial elements were to be found.   They controlled the mountain area, radiated influence from their citadel, Princeton, and became nationally important with the rise of the migrating mountaineers to power.   Particularly in South Carolina they divided influence and position with the Episcopalians and the still surviving Huguenot congregations, and in Tennessee contributed the more powerful political leaders, including Presidents Jackson and Polk, who made the First Presbyterian Church at Washington the church of the presidents.[1]

To these inherited alignments this generation added several new elements.   From the point of view of numbers the most important resulted from the teachings and preaching of Alexander Campbell, who came to this country in 1809 from Ireland.   His chief purpose was Christian unity, and his method a rereading of the Bible. In practice he united something of the logic of Presbyterian theology with emotional preaching and conversion.   Beginning in Western Pennsylvania, he succeeded

[1] Martha L. Edwards, "Religious Forces in the United States, 1815-1830," *Miss. Valley Hist. Rev.*, V, 436-449.

in bringing together large numbers of Presbyterians and Baptists. He organized the Church of the Disciples in 1827, but his followers were popularly known, first as Campbellites and later as Christians.[1] Their numbers grew with great rapidity and they soon became formidable because of their concentration in the regions near and west of the mountains from Georgia to Indiana.

A movement whose influence rested rather on the ability of those taking part in it than on numbers was that of the Unitarians. In so far as their movement was a denial of the principles of Calvin, upon which in some form most of the Protestant denominations of the United States rested their theology, it began in the preceding generation and had now grown into a strong denomination of itself. By 1832 its ideas were sufficiently formulated to cause Ralph Waldo Emerson to resign his ministry in Boston, and there had come to be a new orthodoxy among the unorthodox.[2] The new body was numerous only along the New England seaboard. Scattered congregations, however, were organized wherever the New England element was to be found, and the Unitarian pulpit, with its exceptional independence and the wide range of subjects which it treated, was no mean power. There were only a few Southern congregations like that in St. Louis and that founded by the New Englanders in Charleston; and the South, in spite of the sympathy of Calhoun for its views, denounced and distrusted the movement with as much fervor as that which had moved the Connecticut pulpit to thunder at the supposed atheism of Jefferson.

Another Protestant movement was of more import-

---

[1] W. W. Jennings, *Origin and Early History of the Disciples of Christ . . . 1809-1835* (Chicago, 1919), chaps. v-vii; T. W. Grafton, *Alexander Campbell* (St. Louis, 1897), chaps. viii-ix. See also William Phillips, *Campbellism Exposed* (Cincinnati, 1860).

[2] J. E. Cabot, *A Memoir of Ralph Waldo Emerson* (Cambridge, Mass., 1887), I, 154 and *passim*.

ance symbolically than in its actual effects.   About 1833 William Miller, of the village of Low Hampton, New York, began to preach the second coming of Christ.   The greatest interest centered in his literal reading of the biblical prophecies and his statistical calculations from them, a form of thought which was very popular at the time on both sides of the Atlantic.   In particular he predicted the new dispensation for a certain date in 1843, and so convinced his followers that they disposed of their worldly goods and in some places assembled in white robes to meet their Lord.   Failure did not discourage him, though predictions as to other dates brought out decreasing numbers.   His personality, however, was so strong that in spite of repeated disappointments, he established in 1845 a lasting sect of followers, the Adventists.[1]   One of their special tenets was the observance of the seventh day, Saturday, in place of Sunday.   This practice, not indeed a new one, made it inconvenient for them to live scattered among a population differing on so practical a point, and so they tended to congregate in communities stretching from Maine to Wisconsin.

More fundamental was the question they raised as to whether, at any date, the millennium would be realized in the world, or whether it was to be reached only by death and in a heaven located beyond the ken of man. In maintaining the first position, as indeed in their belief that such a millennium was close at hand, they struck a note strictly in accord with the optimism of the period. These views were endorsed by tens of thousands who rejected their chronology and their organization.   Or, perhaps, the whole movement was but an extreme expression of a widespread attitude of mind.

It is not surprising that in a period so individualistic

[1] The fullest account is Clara E. Sears, *Days of Delusion* (Boston, 1924).

there developed one important movement that was less a modification of Protestant Christianity than a brand-new religion. This was Mormonism, which was founded by Joseph Smith, a member of a family of New England migrants that had drifted into central New York.[1] He provided for his followers a new Bible, the Book of Mormon, with a history of the adventures of the Lost Tribes of Israel and with a continual revelation of the divine will through the perpetual presence of a prophet, he being the first of this new line. In 1830 he founded his church. He soon associated himself with Sidney Rigdon, who brought to the church a new element of popularity and strength.

This was a period when there was a strong movement in the direction of communism. It did not go to the extreme form of sexual communism, and it did not seek immediately to communize the state. It rather fitted in with the dominant individualism by stimulating the formation of experimental units. It had its immediate roots in religious communities emigrating from Germany in the eighteenth century, reënforced in the preceding generation by such American sects as the Shakers. In the thirties and forties it was based on the desire to return to the simplicities of early Christianity, and on philosophic concepts, such as those of Charles Fourier, and on economic doctrines, such as those of Robert Owen, who founded New Harmony in Indiana in 1824. Between 1840 and 1850 more than forty communistic projects were attempted.[2] Most of them were short lived; but some of these experiments, like that of Brook Farm, as we shall see, commanded the attention of ex-

---

[1] E. H. Anderson, *A Brief History of the Church of Jesus Christ of Latter Day Saints* (Salt Lake City, 1902), pts. ii-iv; William Berriam, *Catalogue of Books, Early Newspapers and Pamphlets on Mormonism* (N. Y., 1898) ; William Clayton, *Journal* (Salt Lake City, 1921).

[2] Morris Hillquit, *History of Socialism in the United States* (5th rev. edn., N. Y., 1910), pt. i.

ceptionally able minds.   Of all these movements perhaps the most successful was that organized by Rigdon, supported by the fervor which Joseph Smith inspired, and carried out after 1846 by Brigham Young.

Although the Mormons were not anti-Christians, and although the revelations commending polygamy were not given until 1844, the fact that they represented a new religion in a country, which, however tolerant, was Christian, combined with a great variety of other causes to render them unpopular with their neighbors. Their community moved from New York to Ohio, thence to Missouri, next to Illinois, always growing and always hopeful.   In 1844 Joseph Smith was killed by a mob.   They thereupon determined to move beyond the borders of settlement and finally in 1848, under the leadership of Brigham Young, succeeded in occupying the Valley of Great Salt Lake, which they hoped to keep a distinctive land for themselves.   To this new home they had brought by 1850 not merely the bulk of their adherents, but also the beginnings of a stream of European immigrants which their missionaries persuaded to cross the Atlantic.[1]

Another great change was the enormous increase in the number of Roman Catholics as the result of immigration.   Practically all of the Irish immigrants and perhaps a half of the Germans, with the French Canadians, belonged to that faith.   Distributed over most parts of the country except the South, they brought a new factor into all populous communities and many of the smaller towns.   The Church of Rome was not unaware of this great extension of its influence and responsibilities, and its shifting followers were not left entirely to their own resources for the development of their complex life.   Missionary organizations and the orders sup-

[1] H. H. Bancroft, *History of Utah, 1540-1886* (*Works*, San Fran., 1883-1890, XXVI), chaps. iv-xiii.

plied funds for beginnings, and priests were often designated to the American field. By the end of the period the church was fully established, with archbishops, bishops, monasteries and convents, and the opportunities for the development of its own priesthood. Although still organized under the missionary department, the Propaganda, its bishops holding commissions as *in partibus infidelarium,* the church was fully cognizant of its position of equality before the law, and felt at home in the United States.[1]

The innovations in religious methods during this period consisted chiefly of those brought with them by the Roman Catholics: ritual, contemplation and the religious life. These were nearly exclusively confined to the members of that church. The Episcopal Church was about to introduce them, but rather as a result of the Puseyite movement in England than of copying their neighbors at home. A change more general was the increase in the use of music in the churches. Many Protestant bodies, and particularly the Quakers, held out against instrumental music and set forms. Nevertheless, hymns, supported by organs or melodeons, rapidly supplanted the versified psalms and the tuning fork.

Much greater use than before was now made of the forms of worship and religious expression developed in the preceding generation. Revivals were constant and took place frequently at the camp meeting which became general and better organized. Few countrysides were without a grove devoted to such uses, and they came to be equipped with open-air auditoriums which were surrounded by the frail cottages of habitués. The Methodists extended their system of itinerant preachers, and *colporteurs* carried the Bible and local news to thousands

[1] J. R. G. Hassard, *Life of the Most Reverend John Hughes* (N. Y., 1866), chaps. vii-xx; O'Gorman, *A History of the Roman Catholic Church in the United States,* chaps. xxii-xxv.

of isolated farmsteads on the frontier. Religious manners varied with the locality, and, where necessary, religion sought the soul by acquiescence in exterior crudities.   It was probably by the wide extension of these essentially democratic methods that the migrating folks were held, and that the gradual intensification of the religious impulse was carried forward.

One striking manifestation of the religious spirit was the development of missionary work.   Christianity has always been a proselyting faith, but the insistence of the call for extension has varied from time to time.   One significant movement began in the last years of the preceding generation, signalized by Bishop Heber's great hymn, in 1819, *From Greenland's Icy Mountains.* Bishop Heber found that though in Ceylon "Every prospect pleases and only man is vile," the fault was rather with the Christians than the heathen:

> Can we whose souls are lighted,
> With wisdom from on High,
> Can we to men benighted
> The Lamp of Life deny?

In 1848 Bishop Doane of Albany expressed the spirit of his time.   It was only necessary to let the light be shown.

> Fling out the banner!   Heathen lands
> Shall see from far the glorious sight,
> And nations crowding to be born,
> Baptize their spirits in its light.

More particularly this call was to the distant and the unusual.   Perhaps religion shared the spirit of the Jacksonian democracy and felt that those at home, being freed from ignorance, were responsible for themselves and that the first duty was to carry the gospel where it was not known.   Something, too, must be attributed to the combination in individuals of the spirit of adventure with the religious impulse. At least during this period there was a wide extension of the range of missionary activity.[1]

Missionaries were active in India, China and the Mediterranean. In Hawaii (the Sandwich Islands) the missionaries arrived at a strategic moment and, within limits, civilized and christianized the kingdom. In 1842 Webster recognized their accomplishments by declaring that Hawaii lay within the American sphere of influence; just at the close of the period annexation was discussed. Maintaining themselves in the island, their families became the nucleus of the American element which finally gained financial and economic control.[2] Another popular field was among the American Indians, particularly of the South. Here the missionaries performed what came to be their customary feat—the putting of the spoken language into writing—established schools, and acquired a strong hold which led them to oppose Jackson's policy of Indian removal. After the blow of that defeat they never quite regained their position.

The Methodist Episcopal Missionary Society, organized in 1819, had from the first been particularly active among the Indians, although it also carried on systematic work among the Germans and the Swedes.[3] In 1833 four Flat Heads from beyond the Rockies made their way to St. Louis where they interviewed General William Clark, of the Lewis and Clark expedition, who was at the time superintendent of Indian affairs with

[1] Hiram Bingham, *A Residence of Twenty-one Years in the Sandwich Islands* (Hartford, 1849); H. H. Jessup, *Fifty-three Years in Syria* (N. Y., 1910), *passim;* Francis Wayland, *Memoir of the Life and Labors of the Reverend Adoniram Judson* (Boston, 1853), I, chaps. xii-xiii; II, chaps. i, iii-v, vii.

[2] Rev. and Mrs. O. H. Gulick, *The Pilgrims of Hawaii* (N. Y., 1918), chaps. xiv-xxi.

[3] Davis, *Half Century,* 312-313.

headquarters in that city. Their object was to secure missionaries to be sent among them. To this call the Methodists enthusiastically responded. In June, 1833, Jason Lee departed for the mission, accompanied among others by one young man who devoted all his property to the undertaking. By this time the rivalry of the different denominations for attractive fields was keen, and in 1836 Marcus Whitman was sent out by the Presbyterians as a medical missionary to Oregon. There soon arose a different kind of rivalry. Not only did the Protestant denominations compete with each other, but when occasions arose, as in this instance, with the long organized but newly revived missionary activity of the Roman Catholics. The latter in this Oregon field were French, supporting the claims of the British government which in Canada had given their church so many advantages. The echoes of this contest in a region jointly held and severally claimed by the United States and Great Britain were not long in reaching the two capitals, and in exciting interest, international and political as well as religious.

Other denominations soon felt the movement. When one includes the Mormon missionaries actively at work in Western Europe, there was by the end of this period practically no section of the world in which Americans were not calling men to Christ and diffusing some elements of American civilization. The influence of these contacts upon the nations in which they worked is one of the most important subjects for study in modern history; the effect at home was far from negligible. The amounts contributed were not large. The Methodists between 1820 and 1833 spent but $101,947.24; the American Board a little later had worked up steadily to an annual budget of something over eighty thousand.[1] These sums were at first secured with difficulty and in spite of

[1] For other figures, see Davis, *Half Century*, 305, 311, 313, 315.

Marcus Whitman's mission at Waiilatpu, Oregon, in 1843.

In Salt Lake City, 1847, then the capital of a little Mormon republic. President Young's house (right), theater (left), mint (in background).

opposition.   In Alabama the Methodist Conference split
into two bodies on the issue.   Arguments against foreign
missions varied from insistence on home needs to the
fear that the heathen unenlightened might be saved after
death, but if preached to unsuccessfully, would go to
hell.   Contributions, however, grew, and grew steadily.
The very fact of making them at all, the information
about foreign lands and habits gained from the sermons
and reports required to secure them, the examples of
heroism and devotion which the work afforded, gave
this generation an almost new impulse to altruism, and
was an important element in the development of American philanthropy, which so much needs study and
analysis.

Theologically this period was important, but it is an
unsatisfactory one for study.   New ideas originated and
became potent without affecting the structure of theology.   Among the Catholics there was little doctrinal
disputation, and little contribution unless one reckons
as such the voluminous polemical writings of Orestes
A. Brownson begun in the early forties.   Protestant
creeds remained practically unaltered.   Like the national
Constitution they were accepted as fundamental while
controversy raged about their interpretation, often
breaking up bodies of the same creed, such as the
Methodists and Baptists, into many independent organizations, sometimes bitterly opposed.   Preaching was
often extremely narrow, and it was probably as a reaction from the bitter denunciations and bigoted exposi-
tions of the frontier enthusiasts that the young Abraham
Lincoln wrote his uncharacteristic attack upon religion.[1]

This instance of Lincoln is an illustration of a situation far more important than most people then realized.
Among a people imbued with optimism, self-confidence

[1] W. H. Lamon, *The Life of Abraham Lincoln* (Boston, 1872), 157-
158, 486-504.

and a sense of equality, it could hardly be expected that the dolorous version of Calvinism which had animated so much of the preaching of America could continue to make an appeal.   To keep the population religious, it was necessary that some adjustment take place.   The direction of this change was indicated by views expressed by a number of the leading minds of the time.   From 1833 to 1859 Horace Bushnell preached at Hartford to a congregation of exceptional influence and culture. The characteristic theme of his sermons was the search for truth through multifarious channels.   He differentiated intention from attainment, and gave credit to all who earnestly sought.   Nor did he claim to see the whole but only one facet of the jewel.   He taught that all who asked would be given some glimpse, that the only error was to claim to have the whole.   In all religions and sects he could find something, or at least admitted there was something, special and choice.   This "comprehensivism," setting sympathetic understanding in the place of either dogmatism or tolerance, developed an intellectual following, but still more was it in harmony with the spirit of equality, and so influenced the tone of preaching of many denominations.[1]

A second development, which was not so much a change of theology as a change of emphasis, is illustrated by the preaching of the Unitarian, William Ellery Channing, first at Newport and later at Boston.   A man of extreme dignity and reasonableness, with an ability to write as well as to preach, he influenced not only his congregation and denomination but a conservative class far beyond these confines.   In its earlier stages Unitarianism had insisted most strongly on its denials, not only of the divinity of Christ but of salvation by grace.   Channing spiritualized the positive aspects of its teaching, the in-

[1] Horace Bushnell, *Life and Letters* (Mrs. Mary B. Cheney, ed., N. Y., 1880), chaps. iv-xii.

sistence on the merits of good works.   Practically all the
reforms of this period found support from his pulpit,
and he almost forced those who believed in grace to
urge that the works of the righteous must exceed those
of unbelievers who relied on works alone.[1]   He was
probably more influential than any one person in uniting the forces of religion with humanitarian reforms,
and in developing the idea of social service by the
churches which has become so characteristic of American
Christianity.

More important than either was Ralph Waldo Emerson.   Theologically Emerson walked by himself.   Absolutely individual, he was yet the most representative
of all the aspirations of the people.   Whatever their
creed, Americans were restive under the constant insistence that they were born in sin.   No theology denied
the possibilities of men, but American Calvinism had
never emphasized it as did the Catholic Church in which
men and women might rise to recognized sainthood.
This longing for spiritual joy while still on earth had
never been absent.   Anne Hutchinson had felt it when
she proclaimed that the Lord had personally revealed
the truth to her.   The same possibility of direct sancti-
fication had been one of the compelling graces of Quaker-
ism.   Among the Methodists some sects believed such
an attainment possible.   This feeling Emerson voiced,
not in effusive oratory, but in a clear calm voice that
penetrated far.

Just what Emerson believed cannot be exactly defined, for its merit was its mysticism.[2]   In raising human
possibilities to the elevation of divine stature, he cer-

---

[1] J. W. Chadwick, *William Ellery Channing* (Boston, 1903), chaps.
viii, x-xi.
[2] Woodbridge Riley, *American Thought* (N. Y., 1913), chap. vi; see
also R. W. Emerson, *Complete Works* (Boston, 1903-1912), *passim;*
same author, *Journals* (E. W. Emerson and W. E. Forbes, eds., Boston,
1909-1914), *passim.*

tainly did not look to unification with God in a Nirvana;
he was too keen an individualist. Perhaps he looked to
a divine democracy in which, as all were gods, there
would be no strife, and all decisions would be unanimous
because all would see alike in seeing all. Historically,
at least, this is unimportant, for few were really interested in an Emersonian system. The important point
was that he exalted man to the highest point of conceivable attainment, emphasizing that he was born with
a spark of the divine instead of in sin, and at the
same time he incited to effort, in a way that Jackson's
philosophy never did in politics, by raising the goal of
human achievement to the skies. While Emerson's influence was much greater in the succeeding generation,
even in the forties he influenced the tone of preaching
of ministers of all kinds of creeds, and, where they
caught his note, they held their self-confident congregations without cheapening religion.

In presenting Emerson as a product of American conditions and as a religious force, it is not overlooked that
his views were influenced by German thought and that
he is chiefly regarded as a philosopher. Among the
Americans who at this time were influenced by the
philosophy of Kant, developed by Fichte and interpreted to the English by Coleridge and Carlyle, Emerson was neither the first nor at this time the most
prominent. George Ticknor and a few others brought
their interest fresh from their studies in Germany, and
they regarded Henry Hedge of Boston as their leader.[1]

Few in numbers, they were very able, and concentrated chiefly in or about Boston. An informal club
united such of the interested as George Ripley, Margaret
Fuller, James Freeman Clarke, Emerson, George Ban-

---

[1] Cabot, *A Memoir of Ralph Waldo Emerson*, I, chap. vii; H. C.
Stoddard, "Transcendentalism," (W. P. Trent and others, eds., *Cambridge History of American Literature*, N. Y., 1917-1921), I, 333-334.

croft and others. This club was known among its members as the Symposium or Hedge's Club, but soon acquired popularly the name of Transcendentalist. In 1838 it brought out fourteen volumes of *Specimens of Foreign Standard Literature,* and few groups of so small size have attracted so much attention. This association, based on a study of philosophy, was in intent religious only in its purpose to batter down the traditional Calvinism of New·England. Quite as interesting is the evident fact that the religious atmosphere of New England enveloped the group, and that Transcendentalism came to be with them for the moment a religion, or at least was held with all the spirit of religion.[1]

The influence which these Transcendentalists exerted must not be even largely attributed to the power of their ideas or their skill in propaganda. As in the case of Emerson's religious views, this philosophy fitted in with the state of the American mind, and Kant was received, as Locke had been earlier, because he gave expression to what Americans thought. The particular phase of his system as developed by his followers and turned into a flame of action by the American Transcendentalists was that problems of reality could best be studied by the subjective consciousness. As a consequence their philosophy appealed strongly to this self-educated generation who loved the abstract and disliked detailed study. It was, too, emphatically the philosophy of the reformers.

[1] O. B. Frothingham, *Transcendentalism in New England* (N. Y., 1876), chaps. vi-ix, xi-xiii.

CHAPTER X

EDUCATION FOR THE PEOPLE

THE ideals and the resources of one generation determine the education of the next. There are wide differences between the education which the generation reaching its maturity in 1830 had received, that which it devised for its children, and the education which its chaotic maladministration actually gave them. Its own schooling, moreover, was not the embodiment of the ideas of its fathers, for they had been too devotedly concentrated on problems of political construction to revolutionize the schools. Rather it was an inheritance from grandfathers and still earlier ancestors, touched here and there by revolutionary "Liberty" and by more or less unconscious gains or losses from the mere change of conditions. It is not surprising, therefore, to find that educational practices differed widely from section to section, that they were not based upon the sense of equality, and that they were better at the top than at the bottom.

In no field has the use of terms been more careless than in relation to education, and endless disputes have proceeded therefrom. Thus "public" schools in England and "public" schools in the United States have meant quite different institutions; thus "compulsory" education is free, and the term "free" schools is applied to those representing three quite distinct stages of development. To avoid confusion of terms, the essential points in the development of modern education may be looked upon as two. First came the acceptance by the community of its responsibility to educate its children

200

by taxation, a position which it reached by stages, rising from acceptance of the responsibility for those whose parents could not afford it, and finally attaining the view that it was desirable to extend tax-supported education to all. Secondly, the principle of compulsion was applied to education, which involved two quite separate conceptions; the one, that every community should offer such opportunities, the other, that every child must be made to take advantage of them, so as to conserve the public safety. To these two points different communities have progressed by every conceivable variety of route and combination, and wise men will continue to differ as to the extent of the education to which public support should be extended and compulsion applied.

There was, when this generation was growing up, a general expectation that all Americans should receive a primary education in the "three R's," reading, writing and arithmetic. In Massachusetts and New York school maintenance was by law compulsory. In all New England opportunity was provided in various ways, by the assistance of taxation, if necessary. In the little white frame schoolhouses scattered over the countryside instruction was carried on with all degrees of efficiency. Teachers' salaries were small, but, eked out by free board and lodging with first one and then another of the patrons of the school, were sufficient to tempt ambitious boys seeking the little actual cash needed to give themselves a higher education. There was no such thing as "grading," but the system had in New England been so long in operation that most of the scholars were of proper school age. Noah Webster's spelling books and "spelling bees" helped fetter one fine freedom which the earlier generations had enjoyed.[1]

In New York the idea of universal education went

[1] E. P. Cubberley, *Public Education in the United States* (Boston, 1919), 174, 216-217.

back to the Dutch. There was in 1830 no general provision for it by taxation, but a School Society spent perhaps a hundred thousand a year in New York City; the Lancastrian system was an economical method of using some pupils to instruct the others, and on the whole there was little excuse for not learning the fundamentals of social intercourse. In Pennsylvania conditions varied. Nowhere were better schools than those maintained by such religious bodies as the Quakers and the Moravians. On the other hand, absolutely free education was seldom available and some communities were without educational opportunity. In the South was still more diversity in 1830. Here it was a matter of class more than of locality. People of means educated their children regardless of local institutions. On the other hand, there was very little provision for the really poor whites and many grew up in self-respecting and excusable ignorance. According to the will and energy of the mistress, Negro house servants were taught to read and write, or left in ignorance. Such an ambitious boy as Andrew Johnson left Raleigh at the age of ten unable to write and he seems not to have acquired the art until after his marriage in Greenville, Tennessee. Indeed, desire to learn seems to have been one incentive to his marriage.

The mountain area was practically illiterate. West of the mountains this generation suffered not only from the poverty of their parents but from an economic fallacy of their parents' generation. It was supposed that in all the area where ownership of the land passed through the hands of the United States government, that is north of the Ohio, west of the Mississippi, together with Alabama and Mississippi, education had been provided for by land endowment from the famous "sixteenth section." It escaped notice that unoccupied land does not sprout schools. Probably in no part of America before or since, except in the Alleghany region, was it so difficult to start an education as in this area before 1840.   The story of Lincoln shows the difficulties, but it must be remembered that not everyone was a Lincoln to overcome them.

The opportunities for education beyond the primary schools were most numerous in New England in 1830, and its institutions were of more than local importance. Nowhere was the impulse behind education so general and so strong.   Unusual numbers consecrated themselves to the carrying of education to others.   New England became for a time the seed farm for education throughout the United States, except for New York and Pennsylvania with their self-sufficient cultures.

The oldest establishments for what we call secondary education were the "Grammar" or "Latin Schools," of which the Boston Latin School with its sound drill in the basic branches of languages and mathematics was justly the most famous.[1]   In the twenties a few high schools had been established in Massachusetts and at Portland, Maine; and the Massachusetts statute of 1827, requiring a tax-supported high school in every town of five hundred families or more, set a pattern that was soon copied by Maine, Vermont and New Hampshire.[2] We will see that this development spread rapidly between 1830 and 1850; much more numerous throughout this period, however, and certainly in the beginning, were the academies which had been rapidly increasing in numbers since the Revolution.[3]   These were generally founded by endowment, were frequently assisted by the towns in which they were located, but also charged tuition.   One striking thing about them was that with their

[1] A. V. G. Allen, *Life and Letters of Phillips Brooks* (N. Y., 1900). I, 53-67, 100-143.
[2] Cubberley, *Public Education in the United States*, 190-194.
[3] E. E. Brown, *The Making of Our Middle Schools* (N. Y., 1903), chaps. ix-xii.

independence of each other and the absence of such a governing tradition as bound the colleges, they differed more among themselves, and expressed more readily the new ideas of the time.   The most famous, Phillips Exeter and Phillips Andover, by this time considered venerable, resembled the English public schools such as Rugby.   Others, with little remark, became coeducational.

For most of their students these academies were finishing schools, and their commencements and exhibitions were the rallying points of educational interest for all the surrounding communities.   In New England they were usually held in the Congregational Church, which, of course, had been built originally as a town "meeting house" for all public purposes.   Their character reveals in part survival of a Puritanism that has been somewhat misunderstood and in part the new impulses of the rising generation.   The pulpit end of the church was boarded over to make a stage, and curtains and sometimes scenery were provided.   Here oftentimes exercises were offered all day long to an audience of relatives, friends and patrons, whose chaises were tethered about as thickly as Fords are now parked round a county fair, and who refreshed themselves during the intervals not only with the lunches that they brought but from stands where lemonade and confectionery were sold.[1]

The program opened with prayer.   This was followed by the Salutatory Oration in Latin.   Then came the Dialogue, probably descended from the medieval defense of the thesis, and English orations.   Then were presented—before this audience which did not know but disapproved the theater—dramas, tragedies and comedies, classic and original.   John A. Dix describes with zest the performance of the *Taming of the Shrew*, with a realis-

---

[1] A. C. Tilton, "Literary and Debating Societies in New Hampshire Towns and Academies," *Granite Monthly*, LI, 306-318.

tic interpretation of the drunken tinker.[1]   He himself
followed, with high success, in Miss More's poetical version of the contest between David and Goliath.   By
their performances on such occasions, men like "Long
John" Wentworth and Henry Wilson attracted the attention of the neighborhood as lads of promise whose
cause it was worth furthering.

More somber were the Quaker or Friends' schools
which represented a different type and from which at
this time instrumental music was excluded, but where
high educational standards attracted many students from
outside the membership of the "Meeting."   The earlier
academies in the South were generally founded by Scotch
teachers with little outside assistance and were conducted
with less display than those of New England.   Nor in
general did they become educational centers for the communities, for the youth of the best families continued
to be prepared for college by private tutors.   In time,
however, New England teachers took the place of the
Scotch, and the academy life was modified in the direction of New England habits.   Here, however, none were
coeducational.   Educationally, this was important, for
the "female academies" offered a curriculum designed
to meet chiefly the ornamental requirements of the
Southern lady, whose practical education was given by
her mother and her "Mammy."   Wax work and hair
flowers played a prominent part in her formal schooling.   Socially, the difference was not so great as it might
seem; for where there was a "female" academy there
usually was a male academy also.[2]

The pride and joy of any fortunate community,
however, was the college.[3]   The college constituency

[1] John A. Dix, *Memoirs* (Morgan Dix, ed., N. Y., 1883), I, 27-29.
[2] W. M. Meigs, *The Life of John Caldwell Calhoun* (N. Y., 1917),
49-66.
[3] Transylvania is a good example of the local interest in colleges.
Robert and Johanna Peter, "Transylvania University, Its Origin, Rise,

was not purely local. Except for the University of Pennsylvania, the University of Virginia and state-aided colleges in a few other Southern states, colleges were the creation of religious denominations with the original object of training their clergy. It is from this point of view that their restricted curricula should be viewed. When in the middle of the eighteenth century the interest of the most ambitious youth began to turn from the ministry to law, the change was reflected not so much by the introduction of new subjects, as by gradual curtailment of the requirements in theology and logic. Some opportunity was here and there afforded for natural science and public law. In 1806 John Quincy Adams became professor of rhetoric and oratory at Harvard, and in 1810 he published his lectures, which had wide effect in introducing this popular subject into college teaching.[1] In the main, however, courses remained grounded on Latin, Greek and mathematics. Nor can it be denied that the teaching was generally of an uninspiring character, and that the instructional staffs were in many cases inferior in intellectual caliber to the average of their students, and not far above them in training.

Here and there were great teachers, and in the twenties there began to be a few scholars, such as Jared Sparks, among the college faculties. What saved the colleges from dry-rot, however, and what caused them still to appeal to the ambitious and train them for the work they had to do, was the development of extra-curricular activities by the students themselves, assisted by the more alert of the professors and tutors. These

Decline, and Fall" (Filson Club, *Publs.*, no. 11, Louisville, 1896), *passim*; Robert Peter, "The History of the Medical Department of Transylvania University" (Johanna Peter, ed., Filson Club, *Publs.*, no. 20, Louisville, 1905), *passim*.

[1] Josiah Quincy, *The History of Harvard University* (Boston, 1860), II, 290-291.

activities did not take the form of athletics. Students did, indeed, play, but there was nothing resembling the organized sports of later times. As in the preceding period, surplus energy showed itself chiefly in the life of the literary societies. A new development was the growth of the Greek-letter fraternity system in the colleges. Although Phi Beta Kappa had been founded as a secret society at William and Mary in 1776, it had had no imitators until the mid-twenties when three new fraternities, Kappa Alpha, Sigma Phi and Delta Phi, were founded at Union College in New York.[1] The Greek names reflect the strong classical tone of the higher education of the times. The example once set, chapters of these fraternities spread to other colleges, and what was more important, new fraternities were set up here and there. As early as 1839 students in the Western colleges caught the fever, and Beta Theta Pi was started at Miami University in Ohio.

Despite the Greek-letter designation, the activities of the fraternities did not, in this period, differ essentially from those of the preëxisting literary societies. In both cases, their substance was of debates and orations on the current problems of the day, the declaiming of literary selections, and the production of plays, classic or original. It was, however, in the older literary societies that the men of this generation were trained. One of the chief rivalries of these societies was the creation of libraries.[2] In 1817 the college library of Dartmouth consisted of about four thousand volumes, chiefly antiquarian. A fee was collected for each book borrowed and the library was open one hour a week. In 1825 the libraries of the Dartmouth societies numbered about six thousand volumes, they were open daily, and books

[1] R. C. Alexander, "History of the College," *Union College Centennial Anniversary, 1795-1895* (N. Y., 1897), 65-66.
[2] A. C. Tilton, "The Dartmouth Literary or Debating Societies," *Granite Monthly,* LII, 157-169, 202-213, 249-263.

were loaned freely, even for vacation use. One would dislike to say that this was a measure of the relative enlightenment of the faculty and the students, but it is to some extent an indication that the rising generation was taking its education into its own hands.

Such self-education conducted under the classical traditions of the time had its effect upon the mentality of those who were the leaders of the American people between 1830 and 1850. They naturally were not lacking in self-confidence. They had a wide general knowledge of public law, of political theory, of world conditions in so far as they were crystallized into books, which means, in general, conditions of twenty or thirty years previous. They indulged freely all their lives in the habit of unchecked generalization. Conditions did not favor the development of scholarship, or of specialization, or of the habit of laborious accumulation of details. Men so trained would be more apt to attack their problems by intellectual conception than by measurement. For public debate they were well prepared, which was fortunate in an age when an orator had to prove that each of his proposals was constitutional as well as expedient, and that those of his opponents were not only unwise but immoral. For drastic mental training the interpretation of the Constitution was to some extent a substitute for the theology of the colonial period.

The opportunities for securing such an education were best in New England, with Harvard, Yale, Dartmouth, Brown and other colleges. The Middle states were fairly well supplied, with Columbia, Union, Princeton, Pennsylvania and many good though smaller schools. Virginia with William and Mary and the new University of Virginia educated most of her own sons who went to college and some of those from the South and West. The states to the south were not without colleges in 1830 and even west of the mountains was Transylvania with its hundred-thousand-dollar library. The edge of distinction was taken off the institutions of these regions, however, by the fact that the genteel thing was to send sons away. Where before the Revolution they went to England or France, they now went North, particularly to Yale. For women there were no institutions that were distinguishable from "female academies."

Training for a livelihood, whether in trade or profession, was still chiefly a matter of apprenticeship at the opening of the period, though the organization of professional education had begun. The senior profession was the ministry. Probably a larger proportion of the ministers were college-trained than of any other professional group. For them, too, the college training was most nearly adequate, while divinity schools like those at Harvard and Andover had now come to a flourishing condition.

Greatest in the eyes of the rising generation, as of their sires, was law. The law school at Harvard had been opened in 1817, and that at the University of Virginia in 1826.[1] More common was office training; almost every prominent lawyer had one or two clerks who were studying and who hoped for partnership. A certain standard of legal learning was maintained by the examinations for entrance to the bar, but these did not keep out young men who relied solely on their assiduous reading of Blackstone, the Constitution and the statutes of their own state.

Medical schools existed in 1830, as at Pennsylvania and Harvard, and their graduates and those of foreign training were held in much higher esteem than the much

[a] Josiah Quincy, *History of Harvard University*, II, 374-380, 404, 586; Thomas Jefferson and J. C. Cabell, *Early History of the University of Virginia* ([J. W. Randolph, ed.], Richmond, 1856), 387-390, 424, 520-522.

larger number who had picked up their knowledge in the office of some old practitioner. On the whole, however, the medical profession had less standing than that of law. The public credited the quack as readily as the honest apprentice-trained doctor; the conservative trusted much to the age-old lore passed down in families from mother to daughter; the speculative indulged first in one "Universal Specific" and then in another. All Americans, stirred thereto eventually by their hastiness of diet, took a deep interest in their own interiors and bought generously and read persistently the many medical books arranged alphabetically by symptoms and drugs, which keen producers furnished to a ready market.

For the learning of trades apprenticeship was the only reliance.[1] An institution affecting the whole structure of society and the lives and happiness of so many of its members could not but undergo constant change and modification. These changes, however, in the period when the generation of the thirties and forties was being educated, had not attracted serious attention and were the result of more or less unconscious yielding to the pressure of circumstances. One was that the authority of the master over the apprentice, except in seamanship, was lessened in law and much more in fact. Another was that the trades had less attraction than in the eighteenth century, when Benjamin Franklin was their typical product. There seemed clearly a greater future in marketing great numbers of articles, such as Connecticut-made clocks, than in laboriously producing a few articles of extraordinary merit, which after all would but come into competition with similar articles more cheaply made in Europe. Moreover, the lure of tending one's own flocks under one's own

---

[1] P. H. Douglas, *American Apprenticeship and Industrial Education* (Columbia Univ., *Studies*, XCI), chap. iii.

vine and fig tree, as Webster with an imagination rather poetic than exact described the life of the American farmer, was over all the land.   Craftsmanship, therefore, on the whole, decayed and little of the work of this generation is cherished as is some of that of the preceding.   In speed and ingenuity, however, the American skilled laborer had few if any equals.

The whole economy of the farm and of the household was taught in the home, and passed on, the first in the male, the second in the female line.   In both fields there was some progress.   Some planters sent their chefs to be trained in France, and recipes went by favor from family to family.   Dress, furniture, fancywork and table etiquette by slow degrees responded to European influences, chiefly those of London.   The farm was subject to the influence of agricultural societies to which belonged many of the leading men of the time, and whose publications were of some influence in sowing new ideas in the minds of farmers' sons.[1]

It is difficult to assess the differences which formal education placed between those who enjoyed it, and those subject only to the casual educational opportunities about them.   In the rural districts there was a difference in speech, but there were also marked differences among the educated from different localities.   Education meant a livelihood, but all could secure a livelihood.   The influence of training upon such minds as those of Webster and Calhoun, as distinguished from the slightly trained native intelligence of such men as Clay and Jackson, is plain to one who studies them.   It has seldom been more easy to enforce on the public the spurious brilliancy of an educational veneer, yet the prestige of education has seldom been higher.   It brought somewhat grudging respect for those who pos-

[1] See G. M. Tucker, *American Agricultural Periodicals* (Albany, 1909), 72-76.

sessed it; it was considered as the key to success and there was an overwhelming impulse to possess it. The spirit of the times was expressed in a report of working-men in Philadelphia in 1830. They unanimously resolved "that there can be no real liberty without a wide diffusion of real intelligence; that the members of a republic, should all be alike instructed in the nature and character of their equal rights and duties, as human beings, and as citizens; . . . that until means of equal instruction shall be equally secured to all, liberty is but an unmeaning word, and equality an empty shadow. . . ." [1]

The changes which the people so educated desired to make for the benefit of their children were more of extension than of content. It was part of the democratic movement of the time to provide for the education of the children of the common man, but the general satisfaction with things American and the absence of any effective critique of life prevented any systematic and general change in the character and aim of the education afforded. It was part of this condition that people were best satisfied with education at the top, and changes in the colleges were less important than those in the schools—nor did universities really develop in the period under review. [2]

To take up first the colleges with their less vital changes, one notes again the leadership of Harvard and Yale. Both fostered the development of science and of literature. By adding irregularly one new subject and then another, they widened the opportunities of their

[1] J. R. Commons, ed., *A Documentary History of American Industrial Society* (Cleveland, 1909-1911), V, 94-107, esp. 99-100.

[2] Educational statistics are very unsatisfactory, but it is significant that between 1840 and 1850, the number of colleges and universities was reported as increasing from one hundred and seventy-three to two hundred and thirty-nine, while academies and such schools increased from 3,242 to 6,085. *Seventh Census, 1850, . . . Compendium* (J. D. De Bow, comp., Wash., 1854), 141-143, 151.

students, but did not weld the whole into any new educational scheme.   Some of their professors, as Benjamin Silliman at Yale and Jared Sparks at Harvard, came to be nationally known, and smaller institutions began to take pride in having men of distinction on their faculties.   In 1827 Francis Wayland became president of Brown University, remaining until 1855.[1]   Stimulating successive generations of students, he thought also profoundly on educational methods and devised an approach to the elective system.   In 1826 Mark Hopkins became president of Williams, in which position he remained throughout the period.   Hopkins's remarkable influence over the students of Williams for half a century emphasized the value of strong men for such posts.[2]

The famous statement that an ideal college would consist of Mark Hopkins on one end of a log and a student on the other might have dangerously popularized the idea that equipment was not a necessity.   In fact, however, the stream of generosity had been clearly set toward the colleges and reasonably continued.[3]   Its chief sources were the loyalty of alumni of wealth and the mass contributions of the religious of various denominations.   The vast gifts of the very rich were a thing of the future.   The actual college equipment was generally more imposing to the eye than in reality. Practically always the site was commanding, the grounds large and well-shaded, and the buildings free from the

[1] W. C. Brown, *The History of Brown University, 1764-1914* (Providence, 1914), chap. vi; C. E. Hughes, "Historical Address," *The Sesquicentennial of Brown University, 1764-1914* (Boston, 1915), 179-186.

[2] L. W. Spring, *A History of Williams College* (Boston, 1917), 155, 214-226; Calvin Durfee, *A History of Williams College* (Boston, 1860), chap. xiii.

[3] In 1850 the two hundred and thirty-nine colleges and universities were reported as receiving annual incomes as follows: endowments, $466,614; taxes, $15,485; public funds, $194,249; and other sources, $1,288,080. *Seventh Census, 1850, . . . Compendium*, 141.

architectural fantasies of the time—all evidences of the rule of the classically trained. Most of the buildings were dormitories, the president was well-housed, the younger faculty accommodated about the college, while the professors lived more commodiously than their salaries would seem to have justified. The library was a separate building in few institutions, and its use had not yet been discovered. The equipment for the natural sciences varied from the fairly adequate down to a small cabinet of minerals.

The multiplication of such colleges was more remarkable than the growth of any one of them. Something like eighty were founded between 1830 and 1850.[1] This was due, in large measure, to denominational rivalry. Each aimed at being represented in each new state. Members everywhere would contribute to such a cause. Within the new states communities were keen to secure the institutions so planned, and people often gave beyond their means. Many colleges that have proved permanent were begun with less than ten thousand dollars in subscriptions; fifty thousand was a firm basis. It might have seemed that American youth were to receive their collegiate education in colleges not larger than those of an English university but separated from each other. All these colleges charged fees, which, like the cost of college living, were very low. It was becoming more and more customary for boys to earn their way. A chief purpose of most colleges was still the preservation of a learned clergy. Revivals were habitual, and the pledging for foreign missionary service was frequent.[2] It was, however, already true that most colleges drew more heavily from their community than

---

[1] Cubberley, *Public Education in the United States*, 203-204.
[2] For the influence of a revival on the mind of Salmon P. Chase, then (1826) a Dartmouth undergraduate, see A. M. Schlesinger, ed., *Salmon Portland Chase, Undergraduate and Pedagogue* (Columbus, 1919), 130-132.

from their denominations, and each student body was of many beliefs.

The most interesting of the new foundations was the coeducational, coracial Oberlin, which was founded in 1833 by a group of liberal Congregationalists who wished to experiment with new ideas in education and to foster new causes.[1] Another striking institution, not of college rank, was Girard College, founded at Philadelphia under the will of Stephen Girard, from which the clergy were rigorously excluded.[2] But more striking than the gradual improvement of the colleges and their multiplication was the lack of any vital change either to meet their defects existing at the beginning of the period or to tune them to the times. Barring a few scattered brilliant teachers instruction was poor and laborious. While science was slowly making its way in, there was no general change of importance in the curricula. The thing that boys longed for, and girls envied them the chance for, was the opening of doors of opportunity by language, mathematics and scientific method and the inspiration of some leader. The persistent few got them, chiefly by their own initiative. What made most persons glad that they had been at college continued to be the training obtained by constant clash and adjustment with their fellows in a society where, on the whole, the majority modeled themselves on the best.

Professional education made more substantial advances. While most doctors and lawyers still continued to receive their instruction by apprenticeship, supervised by the medical societies and the bar associations, an in-

---

[1] W. G. Ballantine, ed., *The Oberlin Jubilee, 1833-1883* (Oberlin, 1883), 141-146, 153-179, 322 and *passim;* C. G. Finney, *Memoirs* (N. Y., 1876), chap. xxiv.

[2] H. W. Arey, *The Girard College and its Founder* (Phila., 1853), 30-44; C. A. Herrick, *Stephen Girard* (Phila., 1923), 135-141, 155-158.

creasing number sought schools of medicine and law. These were generally attached to a college and through them some colleges were on the way to become universities.   A simple college course was no longer regarded as sufficient training for an educated clergy and theological seminaries increased in number and attendance. The medical school at Harvard was in high estimation, and the University of Pennsylvania drew many from the South, though those who could afford it still resorted to Edinburgh, Paris and Vienna in some numbers.   The great advance, however, was in scientific and in technical training.   The Rensselaer and Franklin Institutes, begun in the twenties, grew in influence, but probably the best school of engineering during the period was West Point.   Certainly appointments to it were highly prized, and while made by the personal favor of members of Congress and the president, were of high character.   As the army was too small to absorb the number who graduated, many went into general business, and its graduates played a large part in the development of the railroad system.

In 1846, by the influence of George Bancroft, at the time secretary of the navy, there was founded at Annapolis a school to provide trained officers for the navy as West Point did for the army.   The training given by these schools, however inadequate it may seem today, is approved by the marked difference between their graduates and the untrained volunteer officers when tested by war.   In 1846 what became the Sheffield Scientific School at Yale was founded, and in 1847 the Lawrence Scientific School at Harvard.

The vital and exciting problems of the period in education were not those of this higher training, but revolved about the questions of equality of educational opportunity, tax-supported education, the functions of church and state in elementary education, and the organization of a system of schools adapted to American conditions.[1]

Though in 1830 the principle that education should be provided for those who could not pay for it was accepted in New England and New York, it was not national; it was not yet decided how far such an education should be extended; and in particular, it was not recognized even in the Northeast that education should be free for the children of those who could pay as well as of those who could not.[2]   The key state in this controversy was Pennsylvania.[3]   Here labor, which was largely that of craftsmen, strongly urged the adoption of the free system.   In Philadelphia such a system was established, and in 1834 a state law was passed.   This produced a violent reaction.   Petitions with 32,000 signatures were delivered in protest, and a large majority of the legislature was believed to be in favor of repeal. The Senate passed a substitute bill "making provision for the education of the poor gratis."   This was opposed by the Democratic governor and by the brilliant young Anti-Masonic, later Whig, and still later Republican leader, Thaddeus Stevens.   In one of the great orations of American history he stood for a general free public system; he won the legislature, and the act stood.[4]   Some states had preceded and most followed, but this contest may be taken as the turning point toward a public school system free to all on equal terms. It must be kept in mind, however, that the Pennsylvania

[1] Cubberley, *Public Education in the United States*, chaps. v-viii.

[2] As late as 1840 only one half of the children of New England were given free education, one seventh of those of the Middle States and one sixth of those of the West. *Seventh Census, 1850, . . . Compendium*, 150-151.

[3] J. P. Wickersham, *A History of Education in Pennsylvania* (Lancaster, 1886), chaps. xv-xvi; J. A. Woodburn, *Life of Thaddeus Stevens* (Indianapolis, 1915), 41-54.

[4] Thaddeus Stevens, "Speech in Defense of the Pennsylvania Free School System," U. S. Commissioner of Educ., *Rep. for 1898-1899*, I, 516-524.

law involved compulsion neither on the community to maintain schools nor the individual to attend. In Massachusetts, which had always stood for compulsion upon the community, a law of 1842 made an additional point by forbidding manufacturers to employ minors of certain ages who had not received a minimum of education.

The adoption of these principles was the most notable educational accomplishment of the generation. The actual practice of tax-supported education made rapid but uneven progress. It was a matter of time and circumstance. It was undoubtedly delayed by the still flourishing hope that education might be supported by land endowments. The newly created Western states received government grants, and when the surplus revenue was distributed in 1837, the older states created permanent funds in hopes of assistance to an indefinite amount, hopes which were speedily dashed by the Panic and consequent change in policy. The actuating motive was the rising desire for better schools, and as plans and systems were made definite and attractive, they steadily won support.

A preliminary problem was the relation of education to religion. Undoubtedly the majority of citizens interested would have preferred some religious teaching in the schools. Most Protestants were able to agree upon the reading of the Bible, and they were the majority in an overwhelming proportion of United States territory. The Catholics, however, strongly objected, and, while localized, they represented a large vote which would be opposed to any tax-supported education involving such use of the Bible, particularly in the King James translation. This situation was so acute in New York that the state was divided for purposes of education into its component areas: "Up-state," where on such matters the New England ideas prevailed and school districts were provided, each supporting its schools; and the "City" where there was a "Public School Society," with a centralized Protestant control, entirely removed from the popular vote. When William H. Seward became governor in 1839, he declared strongly for extending the "Up-state" system to New York City, although this would give the control of portions of it, at least, to the Catholics. In this he was supported by the Reverend John Hughes, who in 1842 became Catholic bishop of New York and in 1850 archbishop. The two became fast and lifelong friends, and in spite of violent attacks upon Seward by ultra-Protestant elements, the next legislature adopted a uniform state system.[1] The ideal aimed at in this system was a school which all could attend regardless of faith, and supported and managed by the local majority; it was intended to separate religion and politics. Compulsion was absent. There was no prohibition against the maintenance of parochial schools by denominations that were willing to support them or against private schools in general. Where the matter was of importance, permission was generally given to conduct such nonpublic schools, even in a foreign language. The reading of the Bible in the public schools was not prohibited, but in practice was generally discontinued in case of protest.

The organization of a system of schools under these conditions was most largely the work of Horace Mann, although he stood by no means alone. Mann graduated from Brown in 1819, and taught school and studied education for many years. The general interest in education which was rising contemporaneously took two forms which gave him his opportunity. In the first place, there was an increasing feeling that the schools of each state needed a certain amount of correlation and

[1] J. G. R. Hassard, *Life of the Most Reverend John Hughes* (N. Y., 1866), chap. xiv; F. W. Seward, *W. H. Seward* (N. Y., 1891), chap. xxv.

supervision.   In 1826 Maryland created the office of state superintendent but two years later abolished it; between 1825 and 1835, the secretary of state was given oversight of the schools in Illinois, Vermont, Louisiana, Pennsylvania and Tennessee.   In 1837 Massachusetts set an example for other states by creating the first real state board of education, and to the responsible post of secretary Mann was appointed, a position which he held from 1837 to 1848.[1]   The second asset was the tendency of individuals to study the systems of Europe. Perhaps the first of such investigators was Henry Barnard of Connecticut, but other individuals, including Mann himself and agents appointed by groups and communities, were continually bringing before the public material showing the inferiority of most American schools as compared, for instance, with those of Prussia.[2]

Thus supported, Mann issued a series of annual reports which had an influence far beyond the confines of his state.   His first attempt was to improve, or rather create, the teaching profession.   American school children were, here and there, not badly off, for nearly all the distinguished men of the North and West taught school during some portion of their careers.   In general, however, teachers were pensioned incompetents.   Mann urged the necessity of special instruction in the art of teaching, and secured in 1839 the foundation of the first state-supported American normal school, at Lexington, Massachusetts.[3]   In the meantime a professional spirit was being aroused, and some training was being

[1] Mrs. Mary P. Mann, *Life of Horace Mann* (Boston, 1865), chaps. iii-iv; A. D. Mayo, "Horace Mann and the Great Revival of the American School, 1830-1850," U. S. Commissioner of Educ., *Rep. for 1896-1897*, I, 715-767.

[2] See Henry Barnard, *Normal Schools* (Hartford, 1851); C. E. and L. B. Stowe, *Harriet Beecher Stowe* (Boston, 1911), 98-99 and *passim;* E. D. Mansfield, *American Education, its Principles and Elements* (N. Y., 1850), chaps. iii, viii-xi.

[3] See A. O. Norton, ed., *The First State Normal School in America, The Journals of Cyrus Peirce and Mary Swift* (Cambridge, 1926).

The first state-supported normal school, Lexington, Mass., 1839.

*Oberlin College: **Ladies'** Hall,
First home of college girls.*

*Oberlin College: Tappan Hall,
Gift of an abolitionist.*

given by teachers' institutes. In 1845 Mann secured the formation of a state association of teachers in Massachusetts. Other states followed rapidly, and teachers emulated others in taking advantage of the improvements of transportation to meet frequently for the purpose of mutual acquaintance, self-training and influencing public opinion. How speedily such ideas spread is indicated by the fact that by 1849 fourteen states had appointed superintendents of education. Buffalo was the first, in 1837, to appoint a city superintendent, Providence followed in 1839, New York in 1841, New Orleans in 1843, and by 1850 it showed promise of becoming the custom.

As to the limits of the system one may say that outside of the South, public responsibility was fully acknowledged for elementary education, was strongly felt to extend to secondary schools, and was beginning to extend to collegiate education. The contest was a local one. In the older states it was between the idea of a private academy, supported chiefly by private generosity and fees, and a tax-supported, free high school.[1] The academy still received strong religious support. Protestants were most anxious to control education at this level, whereas Catholics generally devoted their efforts to the separate maintenance of lower schools. Nevertheless the high school gained steadily on the academy.[2] In New England financial stress led in many cases to combinations. Academies were taken over by the public and high schools were assisted by donations. In the West, as cities developed, the general equality of financial conditions caused the high school to outdistance the academy.

[1] Charles Hammond, *New England Academies and Classical Schools* (Boston, 1877); G. F. Mills, *The Academy System of the State of New York* (Albany, 1922); E. E. Brown, "History of Secondary Education in the United States" [bibliography], *School Rev.*, V, 84-94, 139-147.
[2] Brown, *The Making of Our Middle Schools*, chaps. xiii-xiv.

Standardization was far off. It was in secondary education a period of lively experimentation. One high school which was greatly admired was that at Providence. Here was a three-year course, including reading, writing, geography, history, American history, logic, philosophy, "evidences," arithmetic, bookkeeping, surveying, astronomy, Latin, Greek, natural philosophy and vocal music. Hartford received a donation and built a school the description of which shows that an extraordinary amount of thought was given to its construction. It was for the purpose of coeducation, and its well-equipped classrooms contained umbrella stands, for the girls places for their overshoes, and for the boys bootjacks to draw off their high boots in place of which they would don slippers. It contained an "apparatus room," a library, a few periodicals, outline maps, astronomical maps, a "magic lantern" and surveying instruments. It was observed with interest and pleasure how friendships among its scholars were formed across class lines. Such schools were of course exceptional, even in New England. In the West the desire for schools was stronger than the feeling for standards.

In the South the high school was scarcely to be found. There was, however, in certain other directions more state effort than in the North. The first real state university in the country was the University of Virginia, which was opened in 1825. Virginia and South Carolina founded military academies. In the meantime the Western states had been granted large tracts of land for university purposes. In 1842 Michigan opened its university, and it became the expected thing that new states would establish such institutions. By 1850 the foundations of fifteen state universities had been laid, most of them in the West and South.[1] These new in-

[1] C. F. Thwing, *A History of Higher Education in America* (N. Y., 1906), chaps. x-xv.

stitutions had neither free tuition nor coeducation, nor did they receive continuous appropriations from the state. They resembled in most respects the colleges of the East. The state university as it is known today was still a thing of the future; but its development was almost certain, when the responsibility of the state for providing higher education was thus established.

As in the case of most other developments of this period one is saved from an impression of chaos only by concentrating one's attention on constructive work actually accomplished, not on quantitative comparisons. Everything was existing at once, and the philosophic contemporary could see little drift one way or another. Fortunately few of the workers were philosophers, and most of them drove ahead, each confident that his own scheme of salvation was winning out. For instance, while the scheme of public education was developing, private education was also flourishing and advancing. Complete private systems from the elements through the professional schools still drew the majority of the well-to-do in the South and East. Nearly all colleges were still denominational and more were founded on that than on the public basis. Many regarded the public system as adding to, rather than substituting for, the other agencies.

Sectional differences were actually greater than laws would indicate. As between East and West disparity of resources was the most significant, and it carries its own explanation and description. In general the Alleghany Mountain region resisted education. There, a virile population, somewhat depleted by the migration of its most ambitious sons and daughters to the East and West, maintained one of the most inflexible civilizations of the continent and an oral tradition of song and speech. In the South the ruling class was satisfied with its opportunities, and the other classes were leaderless and too indifferent to demand that these be extended. Of the states which within this period adopted a state system with a superintendent at the head, the only Southern states were Maryland, Kentucky and Louisiana. New Orleans was one of the most alert cities of the country in recognizing educational ideas, and its high school was established in 1843; but such instances were spasmodic, and where a system was established, the immediate results were much less tangible and widespread than in the North.

While the lines were being laid down on which the school education of the mass of the American people has been developed, the forces that kept them alert and sharpened their faculties after school was over were being strengthened to a notable degree. Before 1830 organized religion, with its regular sermons, its facilities for the publication of books and its innumerable periodicals representing each form of activity of each denomination, was the most potent intellectual influence in the country. The next twenty years merely developed this activity. Political discussion, however, gained enormously in its power of presenting problems to the people. It copied many of the methods of the churches, and it outranked them in its employment of the newspaper press. Between 1830 and 1850 there was also an increase in the influence of the secular and nonpolitical magazine. Besides the "parlor magazines" like *Godey's Lady's Book* and *Peterson's Magazine*, the *New England Magazine* was founded in 1831, the *Knickerbocker Magazine* the next year, and the *Southern Literary Messenger*, of which Poe was for a time editor, in 1834—all of them periodicals of reassuring literary merit. Numerous others were started, especially in the South, but died untimely deaths, though near the close of the period, in 1846, *De Bow's Commercial Review*, a journal of a somewhat different type, began a successful career in New Orleans.

Despite these promising developments, however, the most important educational agency touching the lives of adult Americans was the one known as the Lyceum movement.[1] This was originated in Millbury, Massachusetts, in 1826 by Josiah Holbrook. Its main activity was the establishment of lecture courses. Soon it became nationally organized, and sent forth some of the ablest and some of the most specious men of the times, from New England to the far stretches of the frontier. Similar work was undertaken by mechanics' institutes and other bodies. Of single instances, the most important was the Lowell Institute of Boston, endowed in 1836 with a quarter of a million dollars by the will of John Lowell. The fees received for such lectures were an important element in the support of intellectual workers in the United States, who were thus enabled and, indeed, almost forced to carry their intellectual life to the people in a manner never before equaled.

A remarkable feature of the period was the part played by New England in the actual extension of education. Its belief in education, its opportunities, the thrill of its renaissance combined to make it a second Scotland, sending forth countless apostles of intellectual training. Schoolmasters, professors, college presidents, lecturers and state superintendents swarmed out, generally flying over the mountains and alighting beyond wherever there was a job, often trusting to the future to develop a salary. The influence of this New England element varied in the different sections.[2] In the Lake

[1] H. B. Adams, "Educational Extension in the United States," U. S. Commissioner of Educ., *Rep. for 1899-1900*, I, 284-299; *The American Lyceum (Old South Leaflets*, no. 139, Boston, n. d.).
[2] H. A. Bridgeman, *New England in the Life of the World* (Boston, 1920); L. K. Mathews, *The Expansion of New England* (Boston, 1909).

regions its members at once took the lead in educational affairs, and strongly influenced the region, through education and example, in its attitude toward life. In the Ohio Valley it reënforced the New England elements already there and built up a strong and self-conscious community centering largely at Cincinnati. This was, however, a community among strong rivals, the Southern and the German. Sometimes the three blended, sometimes they stood apart, sometimes they contended. In the South, New England educators were almost as numerous. They took the place of the Scotch tutors of earlier times, and they almost halved the leadership of higher institutions. Their influence, however, was very slight. Most left after a term of years, retaining some mutual relations of sentiment but few of agreement. Those who stayed for the most part, as Sergeant S. Prentiss of Maine and Mississippi, adopted the Southern point of view, although they retained much of their self-discipline and carried the earnestness of their moral conviction to the new views they adopted. Many came to be among the most ardent advocates of the Southern position.

In spite of these diversifications it should remain the last impression that this period saw the acceptance of the fundamental principles of the American public-school system by the nation and that it laid the actual foundations. In 1850 there were in the country at large some eighty thousand elementary schools, with more than ninety thousand teachers and three and a third million pupils, and something over six thousand secondary schools, with more than twelve thousand teachers and over a quarter of a million pupils. The income of the former was derived in most part from public sources; and a growing proportion of the secondary schools were on a similar basis.[1] Such an accomplishment is con-

[1] The income of the elementary schools, amounting in all to $9,529,542, was derived as follows: $182,594 from endowments,

vincing evidence of clear thinking, and forces one to conclude that the unfavorable picture of American life presented by the travelers and the newspapers is a hasty and ill-drawn picture of superficial traits.

$4,653,096 from taxes, $2,552,402 from public funds and $2,141,450 from other sources. The secondary schools were supported by $288,855 from endowments, $14,202 from taxes, $115,724 from public funds and $4,225,433 from other sources. *Seventh Census, 1850, . . . Compendium,* 142-143.

CHAPTER XI

ART, SCIENCE AND LITERATURE

BUT a small proportion of the energy of this generation was devoted to art and its accomplishments were small. In the beauty of skilled workmanship it cannot be compared with that which preceded it. In taste, again, it was far inferior to its ancestors and superior only to its immediate successors. In creative art it produced nothing that could compare with some of Stuart's portraits or with Jefferson's University of Virginia, and there was no such promise of the development of American schools of art as appeared in the seventies and eighties. Such genius as originated in America still sought its inspiration abroad and remained chiefly imitative.

The decay of taste was rather the result of the political revolution of Jackson and the economic revolution produced by invention than of intrinsic causes. It was, in other words, not necessarily true that there were fewer people in the country with an eye trained to reject the unsightly than there had been, but that their views made less impression on the public. Every man's opinion became equal, and in the absence of standards, the absurd, the crude, the ugly and the pretentious competed on even terms with the proven products of inherited appraisal. On the other hand, American taste had been confined within narrow limits, and had allowed but slight native deviations from imported models. It might be hoped that in this new freedom America would develop new forms of art, and that taste would rise to an ability to judge more independently and to react to a greater variety of influences.   It would, of course, be too much to ask that a new constructive and discriminating background for artistic effort be formed in the same generation that was breaking down the old; and no such miracle occurred.

In architecture America had admired the white, the pure line, more than color; first the Greek—the washed Greek that still remained rather than the colorful temples of the original builders; secondarily the Roman; and after that, the architecture of the earlier Georges preceding the regency.   New Englanders admired Chinese porcelains and china and lacquer work brought home by their traders.   During this period Americans continued to look to France for ideas in personal adornment; and at the very end a small but scattered group of the esoteric discovered the charm of Italy, and Florentine jewelry became almost a mark of caste.

A cult of nature arose, a strange conventionalized or sentimentalized nature remote from reality.   The gorgeous flora of carpets was perhaps its worst expression. Gardening did not improve beyond the accomplishments of George Washington and his friends; but it continued to be one of the leading avocations of the rich, and it joined itself a little to the science of botany through the pride taken in exotic specimens.   It is significant to find one of the leading manifestations of such taste in the horticultural society of so new a city as Cincinnati. It became customary to pay nature the compliment of enthusiasm over landscapes and people actually traveled to see the White Mountains.[1]   It was, of course, not new to admire scenery; the point is that such admiration now became a merit.   Its character is indicated by the

[1] *Scenery in the United States,* forty engravings (N. Y., 1855) ; Robert Sears, *New and Popular Pictorial Description of the United States* (N. Y., 1849) ; N. P. Willis, *American Scenery* (Phila., 1842).

special interest taken in the startling and the curious aspects of nature, and the fact that art was expected to enhance their fantasy or to invest them with some sentimental quality, most often gloom—the thick black gloom of a happy people.

These tastes found expression in the fancywork of the leisured women. The growth of wealth is indicated by the increased numbers who so employed themselves; the tradition of labor, by the monumental tasks of patience which they undertook. Among these women was preserved the eighteenth-century conception of fine workmanship and delicacy of manipulation, and the following of conventional standards was more admired than originality and uniqueness. Most impressive perhaps was the exquisite embroidery of microscopic minuteness in soft white thread wrought on the beautiful white Indian cottons, a material whose use greatly irritated American cotton growers and which the competition of the harder American fibers drove out of the country during the thirties. A craze for the exquisite enameled watches of Geneva was perhaps accountable for the delicate designs of the bead bags which young ladies wove, carried and presented to their friends. Perhaps the forties are not yet far enough behind us to allow a full appreciation of fairylike deftness of creation to overcome the distaste for the hair wreaths, highly personal materials out of which, during patient hours, the most skillful built up monuments of their families and intimate friends. Most pervasive of these female accomplishments was the work in wax. It is probably not true that a Kentucky college offered the degree of "Maid of Waxwork," but at least in every fashionable school the subject came to take place above the "use of globes" of Becky Sharp's day.

Beads and hair and wax were all wrought into the forms of nature, flowers and fruits; few aspired to rival

Madame Tussaud with the human figure.   It was indeed a teleological nature.   It was the generation in which Edward Everett spent much of his time at a Harvard banquet in picking over the fruit that he might find one specimen to illustrate the divine perfection of the handiwork of God.   In contrast with the earlier samplers with their words of wisdom writ in all the stitches of needledom, these new toys mark a turning point from Heaven above and Hell beneath to the earth between; the young ladies were finding that the works of nature were worthy of attention at the same time that the theologians were discovering that man was not all vile.

The chief encouragement to paint was in the desire for portraits,[1] though before the period was over, this demand was weakened by photographic devices.   Chester Harding, one of the leaders of the day, had won the wherewithal for his European training by painting in Paris, Kentucky, one hundred portraits at twenty-five dollars each during a space of six months.   None of the portrait painters quite equaled Copley or Stuart. Charles Loring Elliot preserved some of the Bostonese in perhaps the most striking portraits of the generation. Hardly of this generation, though living into it, was Washington Allston, who, after seventeen years in Europe, settled in Boston and Cambridge, and found time between portraits to paint scriptural subjects.   In Philadelphia, Thomas Sully, an Englishman of about the same age, gained some reputation for historical and contemporary portraits.   Paintings like Emanuel Leutze's "Columbus before the Council of Salamanca" (1841) were engraved and reproduced by thousands.   Such circulation was another source of the artist's income.[2]

[1] Samuel Isham, *The History of American Painting* (N. Y., 1905), chaps. vii-viii; S. W. Price, *The Old Masters of the Blue Grass* (Filson Club, *Publs.*, no. 17), *passim*.

[2] Frank Weitenkampf, *American Graphic Art* (N. Y., 1912), chaps. iv-vii, x-xii, xv.

More characteristic of the period were the group of painters who sought to put on canvas the beauties of the American landscape, now seen for the first time. The leaders of the "Hudson River School," as it has been called, were such men as Thomas Cole, A. B. Durand, J. F. Kensett and Thomas Doughty.[1] Though from the standpoint of today much of their work is deficient in technique and fundamental composition and their landscapes often seem abstract and sentimental, their efforts marked a distinct advance over those of their predecessors who were never interested in nature for its own sake but only as a background for an historic or religious event.

Most of the artists of the time were self-taught, but sooner or later they fell under European influences and the more fortunate among them traveled and studied abroad.   London ceased to be the artistic metropolis for America, as in the days of Benjamin West; towards the end of the period its place of primacy was taken by Düsseldorf.   Meantime, at home, New York succeeded in establishing itself as the principal art center of the nation.   The growing interest in painting was amply attested by the formation, in 1828, of the National Academy of Design in that city.

Newer to America was sculpture.   Here again the chief financial support came from orders for busts or statues of men with adoring families or admiring friends or of women with devoted husbands.   Such bids for future fame were naturally fewer than painted portraits, but orders for them from private individuals were supplemented by contracts from the nation, states and cities for public statues or for the sculptural decoration of the newly rising public edifices.[2]

[1] C. H. Caffin, *The Story of American Painting* (N. Y., 1907), 66-79.

[2] Importations of paintings and sculpture produced by American artists abroad were in 1849-1850, $27,123—$7,407 from the Hanse Towns,

Fame came first, perhaps because urged on by the ever active Boston claque, to Horatio Greenough, who designed the noble but slightly squat shaft on Bunker Hill, classified numbers of New England countenances, and erected some well-balanced but somewhat uncomfortable allegorical groups.   Born in 1805 as was Greenough, but at Cincinnati, was Hiram Powers.   His fame, which became considerable, rested on his uniqueness, though he possessed a decided delicacy of touch and fineness of finish.   His most famous work was his "Greek Slave." This the historian McMaster pronounced in the early eighties to be almost the only native work of art worth surviving, but in a modern auction room it would be barely worth its marble.   It was a nude female figure. In the generation of the forties nudity was a distinction, a scandal or a flag of freedom, and no other work of American art was so much discussed.   It brought Powers fame and patronage, but perhaps lost him the contract for sculptures on the capitol newly rising at Washington, which was won by a younger rival, Thomas Crawford of Pennsylvania.   Crawford gave far more evidence of strength and originality, but his work was less perfect, and he died at forty-three before he had fulfilled his promise.   Like the others he followed classical forms and set his American heads on the bodies of Italian models clothed in togas.[1]

American sculpture by the end of the period was far below the level of painting.   There was in it scarcely a trace of America in spirit or technique.   It had, however, secured wider popular attention and had done more to interest American youth in the possibilities of art as a career.   Still more, it had begun to develop an atmosphere of appreciation.   Artistic education had to be

and $11,357 from Italy.   Importations of foreign productions were listed at $16,313.

[1] Lorado Taft, *History of American Sculpture* (rev. edn., N. Y., 1924), 15-128 *passim*.

sought in Europe. Painters trained in Europe returned and most of them gradually deteriorated when deprived of the talk and criticism of the foreign art quarters. Sculptors could work less readily at home, and established themselves in Europe. Powers and Greenough settled in Florence; Crawford with his wife, the sister of Julia Ward Howe, at Rome, where they developed a love for Italy which found such notable expression through another art by their son, Francis Marion Crawford. Their studios brought together small but influential groups of Americans who began to travel for pleasure and improvement. Margaret Fuller at Rome took an active part in the Revolution of 1848 and married the Marquis of Ossoli. These migrants, however, never ceased to consider themselves, or to be considered, American. Their circles became distinctly American colonies whose purpose it was to exploit the artistic riches of Europe for the benefit of their fellow countrymen.[1]

By the end of the period some Americans had added to their desires that of artistic beauty. A cult of Italian art had begun, architectural motives, jewelry, some paintings and more statuary had been brought over, and the range of American appreciation had been extended. The founding of colonies at artistic centers was no mean achievement, and its results were to grow with the years. Out of them grew a coterie of Americans which has continued to furnish a nucleus and stimulus for creative art. With the breakdown of aristocracy, however, their dictums did not attain the sanction which culture had exercised in the days of Washington and Jefferson, and the vanishing of craftsmanship in the trades deprived native art of its true background.

America was not without the elements of music. Art had, however, here even less than in other lines devel-

[1] Julia Ward Howe, *Reminiscences* (Boston, 1900), 188-204.

oped the national resources.[1]   In New England the musical impulse had been almost extinguished by the Puritan discipline.   Folk song seems to have vanished even more than folk dancing, although some rather droning melodies, with words somewhat improper, either survived or grew.   Elsewhere the United States was fairly vocal.   Among the Dutch and Germans was some remembrance of old tunes.   In the Alleghany Mountains innumerable old songs of Scotland and England were kept alive, to be rediscovered to the world in our own generation, and occasionally frontier episodes reawakened the instinct for new creation.   On the northern lakes and western rivers Canadian boatmen sang at their work, and in the forests the Indians treasured melodies which have since then furnished themes for some of our best composers.[2]

Most important was the wealth of music among the Negro population, which lightened the monotony of travel in all the regions of the South and the Ohio. Whatever its origin, this music was quite distinctive and new themes and new words were continually coming from the cotton fields and lower decks of steamboats. In the forties this music began to receive recognition. White singers, with blackened faces, began to go about the country in troupes, singing Negro melodies.   That of E. P. Christy, organized in 1842, was at once successful.[3]   At the same time Stephen C. Foster was adapting this folk music to art songs, though his work

[1] L. C. Elson, *National Music in America and Its Sources* (Boston, 1890), *passim;* same author, *The History of American Music* (N. Y., 1925), 34-79; H. C. Lahee, *Annals of Music in America* (Boston, 1922), chaps. iii-iv; R. C. Winthrop, *Music in New England* [1857] (*Old South Leaflets,* no. 196, Boston, n.d.).
[2] Jennie T. Clarke, ed., *Songs of the South* (Phila., 1896); R. P. Gray, ed., *Songs and Ballads of the Maine Lumberjacks; with Other Songs from Maine* (Cambridge, Mass., 1924); Edith B. Sturgis, ed., *Songs from the Hills of Vermont* (N. Y., 1919).   Indian songs have been collected under the auspices of the Smithsonian Institution.
[3] Meade Minnigerode, *The Fabulous Forties* (N. Y., 1924), 230-244.

was rather suggested by it than an incorporation of melodies and words. His "Old Folks at Home," published in 1850, became immediately popular, and gave him for a time perhaps the largest income from art earned by any American.[1]

Perhaps the change which spread most widely during these years was that in church music. Here the leading figure was that of Lowell Mason of Massachusetts, whose native gift received its direction from the classic German composers. He was supported by the Academy of Music founded at Boston in 1832, and finally succeeded in securing instruction in music in the public schools. His greatest influence, however, was in the adaptation of selections from such composers as Haydn, Handel and Beethoven, with some of his own, to psalms and hymns, the preparation of such collections for churches and the encouragement of congregational singing.[2] By these means he gave great impetus to the use of music in public worship. Native piano manufacturers, such as Chickering of Boston, and German instrument makers, as the Wurlitzers of Cincinnati, were making music more possible than previously in the home. A Chickering piano became a mark of social and cultural distinction, while melodeons, invented by Jeremiah Cathcart in 1836, began to replace the tuning fork in the smaller churches and invade the home at the rate of twenty thousand a year.

Words meant more to most Americans than airs. The outstanding contribution was the writing of hymns, of which Amercan authors contributed a substantial number. Sentimental and humorous songs were

[1] H. V. Milligan, *Stephen Collins Foster* (N. Y., 1920), chaps. iii-v. Philip Hone notes negro songs as popular in New York in 1837. Philip Hone, *Diary, 1828-1851* (Bayard Tuckerman, ed., N. Y., 1889), I, 272.

[2] T. F. Seward, *The Educational Work of Dr. Lowell Mason* (Boston, 1885[?]); Elson, *History of American Music*, 40, 78-79; same author, *National Music of America*, 273-280, 286-287.

also produced in large numbers. The most highly considered was *Home Sweet Home,* written in 1823 by John Howard Payne, in London, as part of an operatic sentimental drama, and set by his English composer to a Sicilian air which Payne had picked up in Italy.[1] *America* was written in 1832 by an American, Samuel F. Smith, but to an air esteemed by many nations.

In the East, Italian music held the *pas.* Italian opera, with which the country had long been familiar, was in 1847 established in New York on a rather elaborate scale, and while this venture again failed, it proved to be an important step in naturalizing this expensive art. In New Orleans[2] French influences dominated. They inspired the young L. M. Gottschalk, perhaps the first American to exhibit the signs of musical genius, who soon after the close of the period went to study in Paris and quickly returned to play his dreamy compositions from one end of America to another. Most substantial of foreign influences was the German. Boston had had a Handel and Haydn Society since 1815, and German immigrants, bringing to America a musical literature at its zenith, were able to continue it, to interest those of their neighbors who possessed a real musical sense, and to lay the foundation for a musical taste in America which soon placed German compositions in the forefront and left native American sources undeveloped for many years.[3]

Much more American than the development of art was that of science. In certain respects this period cannot be considered so brilliant as that of the Revolution when Benjamin Franklin and Benjamin Thompson

---

[1] C. H. Brainard, *John Howard Payne* (Wash., 1885), 24-52.
[2] A. O. Hall, *The Manhattaner in New Orleans* (N. Y., 1850), 91-100; Eliza Ripley, *Social Life in Old New Orleans* (N. Y., 1912), chaps. viii-ix.
[3] Francis Lieber, *The Stranger in America* (London, 1834), I, 292-301.

were peers in the world group who were laying the groundwork for modern science.   On the other hand America was making a more distinctive contribution than at that time.[1]   The interest shifted from universal laws to descriptive study based on material at hand, and the United States played its part rather by contributing new data than new ideas.   Such a tendency ran somewhat counter to the general trend of the times, and in this respect American scientists had much in common with the inventors of the time.   In fact, the greater support given them indicates that their work was regarded hopefully by their contemporaries as of immediate practicality.

This feature is illustrated by the coast and geodetic survey.   Established in 1815, its first important work was done under a Swiss, Ferdinand R. Hassler.   In 1843 Alexander Dallas Bache, a grandson of Benjamin Franklin, succeeded him as superintendent, and held the post until his death in 1867.   Under his direction the work was pushed with vigor and precision, and it gave him perhaps the leading scientific reputation of any American of his time.   His work was also typical in that it was in the nature of a continuation of that of the discoverers and explorers, carrying the revelation of the continent to a further stage.[2]   The recognition of this function is shown by the government's use of the army and navy for the carrying on of such work. Between 1838 and 1842 Lieutenant (later Admiral) Charles Wilkes was engaged in making an exploration of the Pacific which combined surveys of what is now our northwestern coast and investigations of the Antarctic continent with a strange medley of adventure,

---

[1] E. W. Brown and H. A. Bumstead, *The Development of the Sciences* (New Haven, 1923), *passim;* E. S. Dana and others, *A Century of Science in America, . . . 1818-1918* (New Haven, 1918), *passim.*

[2] *Centennial Celebration of the United States Coast and Geodetic Survey* (Wash., 1916).

A fantastic prophecy of the fate of the Wilkes Expedition, 1838. To many Americans government patronage of science seemed grotesque.

political activity and scientific results.[1]   With a similar variety of purposes Captain (later General) John Charles Frémont explored the mountain regions of the Southwest, while a further step in study was marked by the appointment in 1834 of the first United States geologist.

To the resources of the government were, by a curious romance and a strange twist of psychology, added an important semipublic foundation.   An Englishman, James Smithson, who died in 1829, bequeathed the then immense sum of $515,169 to the United States for the foundation of an establishment "for the increase and diffusion of knowledge among men."   Congress, under the careful direction of John Quincy Adams, who made it one of his many interests, chartered in 1846 the Smithsonian Institution, which in the course of time has come to spend infinitely more of the government's money than that of the founder's.[2]   As first head there was appointed Joseph Henry, the physicist, who was largely responsible for its sound scientific development.   New York and Pennsylvania began systematic geological surveys of their resources in 1836, and within twenty years most of the other states had followed their example.[3]

Aside from such public aid the scientists, unlike the artists, were able to secure posts in the colleges and universities, which gave them a substantial footing from which to work or to interest men of wealth in their undertakings.   In 1824 Stephen Van Rensselaer founded at Troy a school of science and engineering which has

[1] Charles Wilkes, *Narrative of the United States Expedition, 1838-1842* (Phila., 1845).

[2] W. J. Rhees, *An Account of the Smithsonian Institution, Its Founder, Building, Operations, Etc.* (Wash., 1857), 5-10, 31-32.

[3] G. O. Smith, "A Century of Government Geological Surveys," E. S. Dana and others, *A Century of Science in America*, 195-199.

become the Rensselaer Polytechnic Institute.[1]　In the same year the Franklin Institute was founded at Philadelphia.　In 1843 Ormsby M. Mitchell secured the establishment of an observatory at Cincinnati from which he made observations which attracted wide attention.　In 1847 Maria Mitchell, having studied not in Harvard (which no woman could) but by personal favor with Benjamin Pierce, professor of mathematics at that college, discovered a comet.　At Harvard Asa Gray was at work along lines particularly American, and making contributions of world-wide importance in botany.　He noted and classified a vast number of American plants, and published many works and textbooks which were very generally used and which stimulated others to similar work.[2]　In 1837 Professor J. D. Dana of Yale published his *System of Mineralogy*, long a standard work in that field.

The two most picturesque figures in the field of science, however, were those of J. J. Audubon and Louis J. R. Agassiz.　Audubon was born, probably in Louisiana, of French-Spanish parentage, and by natural interest devoted himself to ornithology.　True frontier scientist and an artist trained by David, he wandered through the forests and swamps, studying the birds in their native habitats and painting them with an exactitude which has been exceeded only by the camera.　His means were small, and he passed many years without recognition.　It was finally in Europe that he secured a publisher and a public.[3]　Agassiz, a French Swiss, educated with the best resources of Europe, came to America in 1846 as a field for his researches in geology

[1] R. P. Baker, *A Chapter in American Education* (N. Y., 1924), 3-74.

[2] Asa Gray, *Letters* (Jane Loring Gray, ed., Boston, 1893), I. *passim;* II, chap. v.

[3] John Burroughs, *John James Audubon* (Boston, 1902), 43-136, and esp. xiv-xvii (chronology).

and zoology at the age of thirty-nine. He was appointed to a professorship at Harvard, and remaining in the country, identified himself with it. In 1850 he published his study of Lake Superior, an important contribution to the development of the glacial theory. He soon became the leader in interesting new students of nature and in securing for them popular support; he was the most influential immigrant since Hamilton and Gallatin.[1]

The most energetic workers in the field of science were the geologists. Benjamin Silliman at Yale was perhaps the most popular and widely known of all engaged in this branch, and by means of the *American Journal of Science,* which he had founded in 1818, he provided a channel of publication for students and investigators in all domains of science. He also spread the knowledge of the new discoveries to the lay public, lecturing from one end of the country to the other.[2] As early as 1819 the geologists saw the benefits of coöperation, and in 1840, through the instrumentality of Edward Hitchcock, the American Society of Geologists was formed. Within two years the association broadened its field of activity, and added "and Naturalists" to its title. Out of this there developed, in 1848, the American Association for the Advancement of Science, embracing all the scientific activities of the nation and marking the dawn of the era of associative effort in the sciences.[3]

With less amiable coöperation, in fact with some heartburning, medical science made some advances of world importance. The most important of these were in the direction of anaesthetics, the basis for the devel-

[1] Elizabeth Cary Agassiz, *Louis Agassiz* (Boston, 1885), I, chaps. iv-xii; II, chaps. xiii-xvi; Jules Marcou, *Life, Letters, and Works of Louis Agassiz* (N. Y., 1895), I, chap. iii, and *passim*; II, chap. xiii.

[2] G. P. Fisher, *Life of Benjamin Silliman* (N. Y., 1866), I, 319 and *passim*; II, 1-100.

[3] H. L. Fairchild, "The History of the American Association for the Advancement of Science," *Science,* new ser., LIX, 365-368; LX, 134-135.

opment of American surgery which was to become so notable in a later time.[1] In 1844 Dr. Horace Wells, a dentist of Hartford, Connecticut, showed that nitrous oxide gas might be used as an anaesthetic by allowing a tooth to be extracted while he was under its influence, but he was not successful in bringing his discovery to the favorable attention of the medical profession. The subject, however, was attracting the attention of many. In 1842 Dr. Crawford W. Long, a Georgia physician, had ascertained that ether might be used successfully to deaden pain during an operation, but he did not publish his results until 1849. Meantime a Boston dentist, Dr. W. T. G. Morton, succeeded, with the advice of C. T. Jackson, a distinguished chemist, in establishing the same fact in 1846, and a successful operation performed upon an etherized patient in the Massachusetts General Hospital convinced medical men of the great utility of the anaesthetic. Unfortunately the fame of the codiscoverers is marred by their attempts to control the sale of the anaesthetic agent and by the later claims of each to the exclusive credit of discovery. It is a commentary on the inevitability of the event that the use of still a third gas, chloroform, for anaesthetic purposes was demonstrated by Sir James Y. Simpson of Edinburgh, Scotland, the next year.

It will probably be an eternal controversy whether history is or is not a science; it is not necessary to argue this question here. History was certainly not a profession, and its adepts can but be divided according as their work was most largely the undoubted scientific task of collecting data or the production of literature. Only one really distinguished name defies such a division, George Bancroft, and he by career and by purpose

[1] F. R. Packard, *History of Medicine in the United States* (Phila., 1901), app.; two *Reports* of the United States House of Representatives in 1852, and *Senate Reports* in 1853 and 1863; *Proceedings in Behalf of the Morton Testimonial* (Boston, 1861), *passim*.

belongs to the school of publicists.   The greater number of those engaged in historical work were, like the geologists and botanists, at work in accumulating and classifying material.   Among such groups they were the first to organize, the Massachusetts Historical Society, founded in 1791, being the earliest of state organizations devoted to a scientific task.   The example of Massachusetts was speedily followed, and during this period the organization of such a society was as much a part of the insignia of a newly created state as was the establishment of a university, although both might long remain on paper.[1]   The instinct for the preservation of national traditions influenced Congress as well.   The Library of Congress, founded in 1800, continued to be supported, and special acts purchased notable collections of historical material, as the libraries and papers of Thomas Jefferson and James Madison.

Congress went a step further and appropriated money for the editing and publication of some of this material. John Quincy Adams as secretary of state devoted no small part of his time to such work, and showed no small degree of acumen in separating the true and false; and his ever meticulous care was evident in the conduct of the publication.   The great authority on such matters, however, was Jared Sparks, from 1831 to 1853 first professor and later president of Harvard.   With a systematic conception of his task he pursued with indefatigable energy material which eluded him.   Full of information, his writings are yet of little importance as compared with his editing of the writings of Washington and of other correspondence and of documents of the first significance.   That the material in which he dealt was of a character to arouse emotions, of which the

[1] A. P. C. Griffin, *Bibliography of American Historical Societies* (Am. Hist. Assoc., *Rep. for 1905*, II), gives thirty-five historical societies founded between 1830 and 1850.

chief was patriotic pride, perhaps accounts for the fact
that his work has a touch of error not found in that
of the natural scientists.   He probably was not inferior
in technical equipment to Gray, but his love of country
would not allow the Fathers of the nation to appear
except in full dress.   Thus it was that he corrected the
spelling and the sentences of Washington to accord with
the standards of his own time; his changes, however,
were of taste rather than for concealment.[1]

The interest of these collectors of historical data was
centered in one great event, the American Revolution.
They could see some things behind it—the true historian
must always have some antiquarian zest for the old—but
practically nothing existed between them and the Revolutionary heroes.   For the study of the Old World they
had few resources; for America beyond the Alleghany
Mountains, little interest.   This latter field, however,
keenly appealed to one of the youth, though he remained dazzled by the period of the Revolution.   This
was Lyman C. Draper, who, born in 1815, began to
search for history as Audubon did for his birds, by
traveling through the Western country—an explorer-
historian seeking his living sources in remote huts and
bringing away their letters and account books and their
narratives which he took down as they told them.   Just
after the close of the period he obtained support from
the young state of Wisconsin, an achievement which
shows that he was not a voice crying in the wilderness
but an illustration of a widespread patriotic interest in
the nation and the men who had made it.[2]

In a generation so chaotic as that of the thirties and
forties, the popular interest out of which sprang these

[1] J. S. Bassett, *The Middle Group of American Historians* (N. Y.,
1917), 57-137; H. B. Adams, *The Life and Writings of Jared Sparks*
(Boston, 1893), II, chaps. xxv-xxviii.

[2] L. P. Kellogg, "The Services and Collections of L. C. Draper," *Wis.
Mag. of Hist.*, V, 244-263.

varied efforts in art and science was naturally not disciplined, heedful of leadership, or content to make smooth the paths of the masters. Quackery of every sort was more materially profitable than true progress. Phrenology was more popular than geology, and mesmerism than anaesthetics. The note of the time in such matters was still a tolerant equality. An attitude had been achieved like that of the Athenians who would listen to every new thing. Unlike the Athenians of St. Paul's day, however, Americans were filled with earnestness, and few preached without securing a band of devoted, if ephemeral, disciples.

The impulses to writing were stronger, the education for it better and the field of contestants more numerous than in art and science. Literature was not without some public support. The different political parties sought the aid of writers and rewarded some with office, as Washington Irving with a diplomatic mission to Spain. No appointments were more popular than such as these which few connected with the eighteenth-century practice of government patronage. For the most part, however, authors were dependent upon the response of the public. This popular approval can hardly be said to have been critical. Still there existed here a somewhat stronger aristocracy of taste than in any other field. Here, too, was less insularity, and foreign criticism, particularly that of the great English and Scotch reviews, played no small part in creating American reputations. The steadying effects of such criticism were felt by most of the major writers, but buyers were not bound by it and the only real taboos were those not of style but of the presentation of subjects and points of view considered immoral.[1]

[1] W. P. Trent and others, *Cambridge History of American Literature* (N. Y., 1917-1921), I-II, gives the most extensive treatment of the varied literature of the period.

At the beginning of the period New York was distinctly the literary center, already established by fifteen years of activity. Here the initiative had been taken by a number of the aristocrats who were not dependent upon popular support. First in importance and recognized in the thirties and forties as the leading literary figure in America was Washington Irving. Possessing a strong and individual sense of humor, he had begun by laughing out Dutch customs in his *Knickerbocker History of New York*. His interest, however, was more in developing a style based upon the study of English models. He turned sharply from tales of American life to a sympathetic presentation of foreign lands, first England and then Spain. As he grew older the patriotic impulse of the men of his age turned him again to American themes and he wrote a series of books on pioneer life. Toward the end of the period he started his researches on a life of Washington, which began to appear in 1855, a five-volume biography, excellent but rather admired than read.

In his desire to write on American subjects but to find such as were heroic and detached from contemporaneous life, Irving may be associated with the prevalent romantic school of the time, and was typical of an impulse very strong among American writers. The American Scott was another aristocratic New Yorker, James Fenimore Cooper. In choosing themes from the conflicts with the Indians, and pioneering, he was dealing with subjects which were actually contemporaneous in American life. They were not, however, contemporaneous in the life of New York, and he wrote from a point of view which never existed on the frontier. His novels, *The Last of the Mohicans* (1826), *The Pathfinder* (1840), and the others, presented material practically before untouched by literature and introduced American scenes to practically the entire youth of Western Europe.[1] His few essays to comment upon the life about him are forgotten except by students.

The literary strength of William Cullen Bryant, a New England boy who came early to New York, was in poetry, which was admired but was not sufficiently profitable to its author. Throughout this period he was editor of the *New York Evening Post*. Highly independent, he gave voice to views held largely by the more intellectual elements of the Democratic party. To his paper he gave a literary tone and to some degree he unified the literary work of New York. More and more New York became a publishing city. The firms of Harper and Appleton were in operation throughout the period, and at the end were in close rivalry with that of Putnam. There existed, therefore, the full equipment of a literary center.

No one city, however, could aspire to be the center. Competition was strong both between cities and between sections. Philadelphia won N. P. Willis, the popular poet of mediocrity, away from New York, and in 1848 he began to edit the *Home Journal*, which represented the tastes and intellectual capacity of the middle class. The firm of Lippincott offered the best of publishing facilities, and that of Lea Brothers, an already established reputation.[2] In Baltimore the very unliterary *Niles' Register* was the best recording agency of political affairs in the country. In Richmond the *Southern Literary Messenger* attempted to develop the talent of the South.[3] In Charleston William Gilmore Simms wrote historical

[1] P. A. Barba, "Cooper in Germany," *German-Am. Annals*, new ser., XII, 3-60.

[2] Lea Brothers and Company, *One Hundred Years of Publishing, 1785-1885* (Phila., 1885), passim.; A. H. Smyth, *The Philadelphia Magazine and Periodical Contributors, 1741-1850* (Phila., 1892), 204-244.

[3] B. B. Minor, *The Southern Literary Messenger, 1834-1864* (N. Y., 1905); M. J. Moses, *The Literature of the South* (N. Y., 1910), chaps. vii-xii.

novels of the Revolution and border wars and encouraged and influenced many younger writers.[1]

Connected with no section or center, the leading poetic figure of these years was Edgar Allan Poe, who was but twenty-one in 1830 and died in 1849.   His poetry was the finest expression of the weirdly romantic, and struck one of the most responsive chords of the time.   Full of music and mastery of form, his themes were treated with an imagery so far from any reality that ever was in America that they seem artificial.   More original was his prose.   Here, too, he toyed with the weird and the fantastic, yet in form and subject made the first distinctive American contribution to the scope of literature. Not the first to write short stories or detective stories, he was the first to master the essentials of both arts. Such contributions, being rather personal than the result of national stress, received recognition more promptly abroad than at home.   Particularly among the French were his works admired, and from Paris his reputation was reflected back to his home.   The inadequate support that brought on his premature death, however, was not entirely the result of nonrecognition. The United States in this generation did not support pure literature.   When Poe, as was to have been expected, failed as a magazine editor, the general public felt relieved of further responsibility for his maintenance.

This failure to remunerate American authors properly was perhaps in part due to the fact that much of the reading of the public was supplied to them without any compensation to the authors.   The "best sellers" were English, Scott and Dickens.   There was no provision for international copyright; in fact the situation had never before created a serious injustice as no such market as the United States had ever before been open since the

[1] G. A. Wanchope, *The Writers of South Carolina* (Columbia, S. C., 1910), 7-84, and *passim*.

days of printing, ready to take the untranslated products of another nation. English works were pirated when the first copy reached America. Numbers of American publishers, such as Harper of New York and Ticknor and Fields of Boston, voluntarily paid large sums to authors like Dickens; but they could not give adequate payment, for the foreign author could give them nothing except priority and a good word to advantage them over other publishers. This situation made it cheaper for publishers to produce foreign than American works, and particularly in magazines and reviews, with the notable exception of the *North American Review,* the American author who must live by his writing was hard driven by foreign competition. The increased guaranty of the United States copyright law of 1831, which extended the period of protection from fourteen to twenty-eight years with the former renewal right of fourteen years, was no protection against this competition.[1] Although Pennsylvania iron and New England textiles were able to secure national aid, the public preferred a cheap market to domestic production when it came to literature. Actually the failure of an international agreement, so strongly urged by Dickens on his first visit to the United States, was a greater blow to American than to foreign authors.

The outstanding development of the period was the rise of the New England literary movement, and the organization of Boston, though on the extreme eastern edge of the country, as its most productive literary center. Here Harvard was the nucleus both in training and in maintaining by its professorships the first literary leaders. The earliest to obtain distinction were, as in New York, members of the aristocracy, Alexander and Edward

---

[1] United States Supreme Court, *Rep. on Wheaton v. Peters* (N. Y., 1834); R. R. Bowker, *Copyright, Its History and Its Law* (Boston, 1912), 35-36; Francis Lieber, *On International Copyright* (N. Y., 1840); P. H. Nicklin, *Remarks on Literary Property* (Phila., 1838).

Everett, George Bancroft and William H. Prescott. Among them they illustrated the tendencies already noted. The Everetts combined politics with scholarship. Alexander was an essayist on many subjects and served as minister to Spain from 1825 to 1829. Edward, after being ordained as a minister, accepted a professorship of Greek at Harvard, and in 1820 became editor of the *North American Review*. In 1836 he became governor of Massachusetts, in 1841 minister to Great Britain, and in 1845 president of Harvard. His chief form of literary expression was the oration, carefully prepared and polished on the most exacting classical models.

Like Everett, Bancroft alternated between politics and literature, but his literary purpose was more persistent.[1] He was the precursor of a new type of American scholar who sought German training. He became active in politics, being that *rara avis*, an educated Northern Democrat, and served as collector of customs at Boston, as secretary of the navy, and as minister to London and, after the Civil War, to Berlin. In the meantime he was preparing for his life work a history of the United States, which should be a justification of the conflict with Great Britain and an exposition of American principles. His first volume appeared in 1834, and through fifty years the appearance of each of its successors was a literary event of the first importance. More detached was the historian Prescott, who sought also an American subject but, like Cooper, wished it to savor of romance. He found his field in the early relations of Spain and America, and while he sank himself in the sources he lost none of the romance his subject afforded.[2] His first work, *Ferdinand and Isabella*, appeared in 1838, and

[1] M. A. DeW. Howe, *Life and Letters of George Bancroft* (N. Y., 1908), I, chap. xx and *passim*; II, chaps. vi-vii.

[2] George Ticknor, *Life of William Hickling Prescott* (Boston, 1864), chap. vii and *passim*.

his most famous, *The Conquest of Peru,* in 1847.   In the forties his greater successor, the young Francis Parkman, was preparing for his pathfinding work on the other side of our colonial relations, those with the French and the Indians of our own territories.

Somewhat older than Bancroft was George Ticknor, whose interest was more purely literary.   From 1815 to 1819 he studied in Europe, and in 1819 was appointed professor of modern languages and literature at Harvard. His *History of Spanish Literature,* published in 1849, was well received and promptly translated into Spanish, French and German.   His letters show him to have been a man of culture, whose judgments on current events were always sound.   His cousin William D. Ticknor was founder of the publishing house of Ticknor, Reed & Fields in 1839 (later Ticknor & Fields), which promptly became a vital factor in the literary life of New England and the nation.   Seldom has any city possessed publishers so gracefully fitted to develop its literary resources as did Boston in Ticknor and his junior associate, James T. Fields.

Perhaps the greatest product of this aristocratic culture was Henry Wadsworth Longfellow, who was born in Portland, Maine, in 1807.   In him were combined the scholarly interest, a sense of the romantic and a choice of American subjects having in them the possibility of embodying American ideals.   Becoming a professor of *belles-lettres* at Harvard in 1836, he published his *Psalm of Life* two years later and followed it presently with his *Voices of the Night* and *Evangeline.*   By instinct he avoided the realities of life around him, and painted in ready and charming verse a world and human nature in which men delighted to believe.   Already by 1850 he had equaled Irving in the popular estimation and exceeded him in the affection of the public.

Of about the same age as Longfellow, but different

in spirit, was another group of New England writers.
These men were more deeply affected by the impulses
of the time. Oliver Wendell Holmes, who was born
in 1809, has vividly described their attitude in his tale
of the "wonderful one-hoss shay." This remarkable
vehicle, which in the poet's mind symbolized New England Calvinism, was so well built that without repair
or defect it ran for exactly one hundred years when at
once every part went to pieces in complete dissolution.
Though the wish may have been father to the thought,
there is enough truth in such a conception to justify
the poet; still, in the interest of accuracy, the historian
must modify the picture. The youth growing up between 1800 and 1830 were indeed exhilarated by the
breaking of barriers to thought and the wide new world
of speculation; but the discipline of Calvinism was left,
with its social order and habits of orthodoxy. However
wild the views accepted, the habits of the newly liberated
stood in this generation comparatively unchanged, and
as this movement centered in the intellectual middle
class, these were the habits of "plain living and high
thinking." Each new view, moreover, became for its
disciples "the" gospel, and the advocacy of "causes" became the chief object of their lives.[1] The author has
seen one of their descendants preaching football with a
spiritual force worthy of Jonathan Edwards.

What Emerson and the others got from Kant was the
supreme importance of the ideal as contrasted with the
apparently real, and this led to something of a schism
between them and their elder contemporaries in that its
temporary effect, at least, was to stay the advance of
scholarship laboriously accumulating details and let the
mind flow into expression in prose and verse. The
American Academy of Lorenzo de' Medici was the
democratic and parsimonious Brook Farm. This was

[1] T. W. Higginson, *Cheerful Yesterdays* (Boston, 1901), 167-195.

Above: Hiram Powers'
"Greek Slave."

Below: Brook Farm, West
Roxbury, Massachusetts.

Thomas Sully's portrait of Fanny
Kemble as "Beatrice."

"Berry Hill," a Parthenon house in
Halifax County, Virginia.

Classicism and Transcendentalism

a communistic experiment, the outgrowth of the Transcendentalist movement and started by George Ripley in 1841. Beginning as the "Brook Farm Institute of Agriculture and Education," it turned into a "phalanx" on the principles of the French philosopher, Charles Fourier, and in 1846 it failed. While it existed, however, it was the controversial and joyous meeting place of many members of the rising generation where they associated on terms of equality regardless of social origin and of sex.[1]

The greatest of this new group was, as we have seen, Ralph Waldo Emerson. After Emerson, the reputation which has best lasted is that of Nathaniel Hawthorne. While identified with Brook Farm, Hawthorne was more a literary man and less a reformer than most of the rest. He first came conspicuously before the public in his *Twice Told Tales*, published in 1837, but soon turned to subjects purely American. In his *Scarlet Letter*, published in 1850, he produced a work that blended romance with deep psychological study. To him again, the period did not afford support, and petty political offices kept the wolf from the door.

The Quaker, John Greenleaf Whittier, was the outstanding poet among the reformers. As with Hawthorne, his dominant tendency was undoubtedly literary, but a deep interest in causes and principles affected much of his writing, and he was active in the movements for peace and against slavery. In his *Legends of New England* (1831) is the "King's Missive," a stern attack upon the Puritan traditions of Massachusetts; and his *Ichabod* in 1850, an attack on Webster for supporting the Compromise of that year, was among the half-dozen most potent political documents of the period. The younger poet, James Russell Lowell, first became prominent through his *Biglow Papers* (1846-1848). He followed

[1] Lindsay Swift, *Brook Farm* (N. Y., 1900).

an old tradition, and one particularly prevalent at the time in America, of putting his wisdom into the vulgate of local dialect and into the mouths of the lowly. With a satire biting yet frolicsome, he attacked the conservatives of his day, and with a strong note of patriotic pride, espoused the new causes, such as peace and the rights of the Negro. In his later career poetry, criticism, a Harvard professorship and the ministry to England blended to identify him with the best in American effort. The interest excited by these new writers attracted Horace Greeley, who was editing the *Tribune* in New York. He became closely allied with them. Margaret Fuller he employed as a special writer to visit and report on the West—a sensational employment for a woman at the time. In 1848 he made Charles A. Dana managing editor of the *Tribune,* and that paper became to a degree the popular vehicle of the new lights, although it would have been quite different in many respects had it been edited in Boston.

As literature was expected to justify itself by a purpose besides that of art, so purposes were expected to be set forth with some attention to literary effect. Daniel Webster revised his orations with scrupulous care, and they were read by many more than ever heard them. The sermons of William Ellery Channing were finished literary productions. The grand style was affected by most of those who appeared before the public, and the Fourth of July reverberated with periods most unfairly fathered upon Cicero and Demosthenes. With some apology, however, many listened to and read the racy speeches and memoirs of "Davy" Crockett, and the humorous political skits of "Major Jack Downing," the Maine Yankee character presented by Seba Smith and his imitators. In Georgia a group of writers were producing studies of American character: A. B. Longstreet, *Georgia Scenes;* W. T. Thompson, *Major Jones's Court-*

ship; and J. B. Baldwin, *Flush Times in Alabama and Mississippi.*[1]   Beneath the surface was produced and circulated a ribald literature.

On the whole, the aristocratic tradition persisted more strongly in literature than in most other fields of life. It adapted itself to changing ideas and conditions with commendable vigor.   Standards were maintained with some effect, and influenced the form even of the more radical school.   There was still reverence for that which was not understood, and millions boasted of books they had never read, because the authors were Americans. By the end of the period writers had become almost as numerous as politicians.   As in England and France, the public taste had changed from poetry and didactic essays to romances and stories of adventure and travel. It is not too much to say that, as in those countries, fiction had by 1850 triumphed over all other forms of writing in the United States.

[1] J. D. Wade, *Augustus Baldwin Longstreet* (N. Y., 1924), chaps. v-xii.

CHAPTER XII

REFORM AND SLAVERY

THE word "reform" played much the same part in the life of the thirties and forties that "progressive" does today. It was a touchstone which differentiated people more incisively than did party allegiance. It was something rather felt by instinct than defined by reason. There was something fortuitous about it. If one succeeded in getting his particular hobby labeled a "reform," it received the support of certain classes and encountered the opposition of others regardless of its real classification. In general, however, political reforms may be excluded; they were regarded as a mere extension and application of principles already accepted and proved. "Reform" had usually some social implications.

Most reformers were interested in all reforms while specializing on some of their own. The histories of the different movements were differentiated by the reactions which they caused rather than by their internal character, their support or the methods by which they were promoted. Public education was perhaps the most successful of them all during this period, and one reason was that it aroused little opposition, except that of the taxpayers and private-school interests which was so demonstrably based on selfish motives that it was forced gradually to yield before public opinion.

An outstanding reformer was Samuel Gridley Howe.[1]

[1] Laura E. Richards and Maud H. Elliott, *Julia Ward Howe, 1819-1910* (Boston, 1915), I, chaps. iv-vi; S. G. Howe, *Letters and Journals* (Laura E. Richards, ed., Boston, 1906-1909), I, 389-419; II, 96-166, 237-272.

Son of a wealthy Boston merchant, after a frolicsome career at Brown University he studied medicine at Harvard. Caught by enthusiasm for the cause of Greek independence, by dint of persistence he collected funds from Boston friends and devoted seven years of active service to that land. After the Greek cause triumphed, he lingered on the continent to study his particular medical interest, blindness. Back in Boston he installed several blind patients in the home of his father whose reputation for crabbedness must have been somewhat fictitious. With his ever compelling charm he won support for the establishment in 1832 of the famous Perkins Institution for the Blind, of which he became superintendent. At one fair in Boston the ladies raised over fourteen thousand dollars for this philanthropy. Here Howe made his most striking contribution, the opening of the world to Laura Bridgman who was blind, deaf and dumb.

In 1843 he won in marriage Julia Ward, a beautiful and vivacious New York heiress, of a family which has contributed many of our leading artists and novelists. Already she was remarked as an illustration of the new type of woman in American life. Together the Howes created a home through which most of the reformer group passed, renewed in their good works and generally unaffected by the counsels of moderation with which their more balanced host endeavored to temper them. Other centers through which most reformers passed were the homes of Arthur Tappan in New York City and Gerrit Smith in central New York, where they received a support more lavish, as accorded with the means of the hosts, and advice perhaps more sympathetic and somewhat less tinctured by wisdom.[1]

[1] O. B. Frothingham, *Gerrit Smith* (N. Y., 1879), 137-144; Lewis Tappan, *The Life of Arthur Tappan* (N. Y., 1870), chaps. ix-x, xiii, xv-xvi.

Somewhat older than Howe, Dorothea L. Dix was later in appearing on the stage of public life. From her Quaker associations she received a sound education and an unconsciousness of sex inequalities. For many years she supported herself by teaching, her ability enabling her early to secure a school of her own. Meanwhile she was studying the world about her. What most affected her was the inhumane treatment of dependents. Her daily task took her by the prison of Charlestown, Massachusetts. The indifference of the public to the treatment of prisoners and of paupers, and particularly the unthinking inhumanity toward the insane, aroused her pity and indignation. From 1841 she devoted her principal attention to the relief of these classes.[1] Her chief method was public speaking. With stern, commanding determination she set forth the situation and demanded that it be changed. Like Howe, she aroused the generosity of the wealthy. As a result, numbers of insane asylums were reorganized, as the Lunatic Hospital of Boston in 1839, and new ones of high character were established, as Butler Asylum at Providence, Rhode Island.

Before many years she began to appear before legislative bodies, which disapproved of being addressed by a woman but knew not how to get rid of her except by heeding the appeal she made, an appeal which by all the canons of the time touched subjects quite properly within woman's province. She was so successful in securing grants from neighboring states that she was called to Kentucky, where her New England angularity, however it may have failed to charm the gentlemen of the South, did not prevent their yielding to her solicitations. During the last years of the period she was devoting much attention to Congress, from which she ultimately se-

[1] Francis Tiffany, *Life of Dorothea Lynde Dix* (Boston, 1890), chaps. viii-xv.

cured a grant of over ten million acres for the indigent insane, only to have it snatched away by the United States Constitution as interpreted by President Pierce.

Miss Dix was not so much the originator of ideas as their advocate. In fact, most of the reforms she urged had long been advocated by the Quakers and by European philanthropists. The actual carrying out of these ideas into practice was the work of many men and many years. The period of the thirties and forties neither sowed the seed nor reaped the full fruit. As in so many lines, however, it was the period of experimentation and of the acceptance of certain reforms as desirable and needing only development. During these years imprisonment for debt practically disappeared,[1] the number of crimes for which the death penalty was exacted diminished, and the idea of abolishing that penalty entirely began to be strongly advocated, although it nowhere gained sufficient legislative support. Everyone accepted the principle that men and women should be separated in prison, but it was not everywhere carried out. In general, the idea of cells, instead of one common room, was accepted, but this plan was too costly for universal use. Practical reformers were much divided between the Pennsylvania or solitary system, in which the outstanding feature was solitary confinement at hard labor, and the New York or silent system, adopted by the Auburn State Prison, in which the cell was used but the prisoners were employed by day in large workshops without being allowed to speak to one another.[2] In Massachusetts and New York prison associations were

[1] H. E. Barnes, *The Repression of Crime* (N. Y., 1926), 203-205.

[2] O. F. Lewis, *Development of American Prisons and Prison Customs, 1776-1845* (N. Y., 1922), chap. xxv; Gustave de Beaumont and Alexis de Tocqueville, *On the Penitentiary System in the United States* (Francis Lieber, tr., Phila., 1833); Dorothea L. Dix, *Remarks on Prisons and Prison Discipline in the United States* (Phila., 1845); F. C. Gray, *Prison Discipline in America* (Boston, 1847); G. W. Smith, *Defence of the System of Solitary Confinement* (Phila., 1833).

formed, and the study of imprisonment as a reforming as well as a punishing measure began to be widely discussed.

The improvement in the condition of the ordinary poor was still less definitive, as it was most largely a matter of local action. In general, the problem of pauperism was much less important than in most countries, for the poor were fewer, though the Irish immigrant wave, for all its value to the country, brought many without means or much ambition who became a burden to the public. Stories were told of poor old Irishwomen in Philadelphia, who in their letters home chiefly recommended the United States because of its palatial almshouses. On the whole, the treatment of paupers, even at the beginning of the period, was rather better than elsewhere, owing to the very fact that the customary "poor farm" was better situated than the English "workhouse." For the most part, however, such farms were let on contract, and much depended on the character of the contractors, who were seldom philanthropists. During the period there was a gradual improvement, and foreigners generally commented very favorably upon conditions. The real change, however, consisted in the withdrawal of the insane poor to asylums for their special care. In fact, the treatment of the insane, in this separation and the beginning of the differentiation of the curable from the incurable, showed more general improvement than that of either prisoners or paupers.

A more spectacular reform was that which went under the general designation of temperance. The success of this movement involved a drastic change in the long established habits of the people, and also a disturbance of the business interests concerned in the liquor traffic, though these latter were not so well organized as in later times. In other words, the reform meant, instead of a mere arousing of the conscience, a conflict of enmity and bitterness. When this generation was in its youth, intoxicating drinks were habitual and excited no moral reaction whatever; even occasional drunkenness, particularly if the occasion were good, scarcely came within the moral catalogue. As we have seen in earlier volumes of this series, at the ordination of a New England clergyman the town or congregation was expected to provide enough to make all present merry. Oliver Wendell Holmes casually describes the perils of driving home after such an event. In a Southern election it was the custom for the candidates to provide the means for similar results. In New York, open house was maintained on New Year's day by all those with social pretensions, and the debutantes not unsuccessfully urged the young men to take, at each house, quite as much as they could well manage, though well aware of the round of homes that they would make thereafter. Widows and maiden ladies felt embarrassed if they had no sherry to serve the clergyman when he called.

On the other hand, while practically all women drank, none who were respectable were supposed to become drunk; and they rarely did. Moreover, it was coming to be disapproved for the men to become seriously intoxicated in mixed parties, until the dancing was over—a point on which the preceding generation had been less particular. The limits of less polite drinking were determined chiefly by opportunity. The differences between sections of the country were those of the beverage locally produced. In general, the Americans drank spirits, except the rich who could afford also imported wines. The tradition of the old English ales had almost passed away, their place being taken, perhaps, in the apple-growing districts by cider. In the Ohio Valley the Germans during this period introduced lager beer and, as has been seen, domestic wine.

Whether conditions were worse in America than in northern Europe it is difficult to say. Statistics are absent, and there were not enough American travelers abroad to set against the European comments on American conditions. In fact, the small amount of comment indicates conditions not very dissimilar; Europeans were more shocked at the American consumption of ice water than of spirits. It was a native instinct, and not comparison, that made this generation from its youth dissatisfied with conditions and determined to reform them.

The movement was well under way by 1830, but it had expressed itself largely in mild criticism of excesses.[1] Recently the evangelical churches had taken it up with constantly growing enthusiasm, though they had the opposition of some thorough predestinarians like the Primitive Baptists and the sacerdotalists among the Episcopalians, especially clergymen like Bishop John H. Hopkins of Vermont. It was widely alleged that the reform was a New England enterprise, and it was true that one third of the societies and membership in 1831 were concentrated east of the Hudson, while most of the remainder were to be found in regions settled by that stock. The seven hundred societies in the banner state of New York constituted half of the total of the country, but the majority of those were located in counties peopled largely from the Eastern states. In order to give the crusade more of a national character a convention was held at Philadelphia in 1833 with more than four hundred representatives from twenty-one states in attendance. Here the United States Temperance Union was formed on a federation basis, an organization to be known three years later, after the inclusion of Cana-

[1] The following account of the temperance movement is based largely upon J. A. Krout, *Origins of Prohibition* (N. Y., 1925), 119-186. 208-252; but see also H. W. Blair, *The Temperance Movement* (Boston, 1888), chaps. xx-xxiv, and John Marsh, *Temperance Recollections* (N. Y., 1866), chap. ii.

dians, as the American Temperance Union, and destined to be far more effective than the American Temperance Society it superseded. The deep interest of politicians in the movement, if not in its principles, was evidenced in the American Congressional Temperance Society under the presidency of Lewis Cass in 1833.

Women were admitted to the societies, later to conventions, and finally many, like Lucretia Mott, Elizabeth Cady Stanton, Abby Kelley and others, to the lecture platform, on an equality with men; but they had to overcome strong disapproval as to their modesty in thus leaving their own hearths to attend to other people's business, and it may be said that the movement remained chiefly a man's concern throughout the first half of the nineteenth century. There were also hundreds of clubs for children, especially those of the "Cold Water Army" which attracted so much attention in the parades at temperance celebrations. Later there were the Sons of Temperance formed in Teetotalers' Hall, 71 Division Street, New York City, in September, 1842, whose local lodges, each performing its ritual under a Worthy Patriarch, spread over much of the United States. The old prudential argument that alcohol destroyed the human system was vigorously exploited and, about 1830, another, that it reduced industrial efficiency, which was ultimately to tell so strongly in a country where everyone worked; in connection with the building of the Baltimore and Ohio Railroad in that year, for instance, the superintendent of construction prohibited all use of spirits. Such considerations, however, were little stressed. People were called upon to reform by releasing themselves from habits that shackled them to a life of sin.

In the last of the thirties there arose a dissension within the ranks. The older advocates had been content to abstain from spirituous liquors, but the extremists now gained more and more support for total abstinence from all that could intoxicate, including, of course, wine and malt beverages. Many thought this impracticable. Then, too, a generation trained to respect so deeply the letter of the Scriptures had difficulty in reconciling such a stigma upon wine with Christ's use of it for the sacred purpose of the Last Supper. But some were ready to match against this the warning that wine was a "mocker"; others with fearless exegesis explained quite seriously that the Master sanctioned only pure wine, which was now so rare an article of commerce that its use could hardly be considered mandatory. A growing number of church congregations were persuaded by Dr. Eliphalet Nott and other scholars to believe that the wine which Christ had used must have been the unfermented juice of the grape. Among the many temperance periodicals, some were established especially to argue out this "communion question." Under the lead of Edward C. Delavan, of Albany, whose zeal, personal fortune and organizing power made him perhaps the most effective temperance man of his time, the radicals in 1836 were able to carry the general convention at Saratoga Springs for total abstinence. There ensued a bitter pamphlet warfare, and for a time societies which took this stand lost heavily in membership, but the outcome seemed to prove its wisdom. Governor Allen Trimble of Ohio wrote in 1837: "The societies that have adopted the total abstinence pledge are active and increasing their numbers. Those societies that go upon the principle that distilled spirits alone should be excluded, are dragging heavily, and I think retrograding, rather than advancing." [1]

For a period after 1840 the leadership was taken by those who were themselves reformed. The agitation in

---

[1] *Journal of the American Temperance Union, Tenth Rep.* (Boston, March, 1837), 39.

its new phase was known as the Washingtonian movement, and it had its inception in a small group of hard
drinkers in Baltimore in 1840 who had been shown the
error of their ways by the exhortation of an evangelist.
These men set themselves to reforming other tipplers, and
the latter in turn took up the work. Soon the movement
infected many parts of the country; everywhere meetings were held, addressed by reformed drunkards, and
new recruits from the gutter pushed forward to tell their
experiences to an admiring public. Perhaps most of the
new evangelists were mere swaggering autobiographers,
eager for the chance to enjoy a momentary notoriety,
and in the long run their influence was distinctly demoralizing. Nevertheless, among the redeemed drunkards
were some individuals of great eloquence and genuine
force of character. For example, men like John Hawkins
and John B. Gough added greatly to the effectiveness of
the temperance agitation and never deserted the cause.[1]
Among the outside speakers Father Theobald Matthew,
who divided his time between Ireland and America, was
one of the most influential.

Literature, also, was laid under heavy contribution in
the propaganda. Holmes, Willis and many less distinguished poets brought their muse to embellish the
temperance "gift books"; *The Fountain* (1847) had
offerings in prose and verse by such writers as John G.
Whittier, Lydia H. Sigourney, Horace Greeley, Bayard
Taylor, Fanny Forrester and T. S. Arthur. The six
volumes of *Temperance Tales* by Lucius M. Sargent had
an immense popularity throughout the country. Mrs.
Sigourney wrote unnumbered sentimental temperance
stories defending the American home in a somewhat

[1] J. B. Gough, *Platform Echoes, or Leaves from My Note-Book of
Forty Years* (Hartford, 1884); Carlos Martyn, *John B. Gough* (Carlos
Martyn, ed., *American Reformers*, N. Y., 1893); Charles Jewett,
Speeches, Poems, . . . on Temperance and the Liquor Traffic (Boston,
1849).

stilted style. Timothy Shay Arthur, a native of New-burgh, New York, living in Philadelphia, devoted such talent as he possessed almost exclusively to the subject. In this period he published *Six Nights with the Washingtonians* (1842), and just after it, in 1854, the most famous of the temperance works, *Ten Nights in a Bar-Room*, which was quickly dramatized and had a vogue and influence little less than that of *Uncle Tom's Cabin* in later years. To these instruments was added the still more universal appeal of the cartoon, or at least of the picture with a moral, which somehow managed to leave a vivid impression on many a youthful mind.

The change of emphasis from temperance to total abstinence was logical and appropriate to the philosophy of the time. Much more difficult to grasp is the development in the forties of the movement for prohibition.[1] Such a program seems to fly directly into the face of the individualism of the period and that conception of governmental functions which was being reënforced by the *laissez faire* doctrine of the only group of British thinkers whose influence reached America. Three considerations help somewhat to clarify the inconsistency, though it may be a hopeless enterprise to seek logic in a generation so chaotic. The primary aim of reform was to release the individual, to secure a real freedom. It is not surprising that the active minds of enthusiasts came to regard many things as servitudes which the state should end in order to liberate the human soul. To extend this to habits was indeed to lose the general principle in the particular case; but such twists are not unhuman. In the second place, they were under the spell of the millenarian conception, which led them to

---

[1] Neal Dow, *Reminiscences* (Portland, Me., 1898), chaps. vi, viii-xi, xiv-xvii; Krout, *Origins of Prohibition*, chap. xi; Gallus Thomann, *Liquor Laws of the United States* (N. Y., 1885), chaps. viii-ix.

TEMPERANCE PIC NIC

Father, don't send me after whiskey, to-day!—See p. 26.

Gleanings from the Temperance Literature, 1830-1850

expect their reforms to be complete in their own lifetime. Their horror was of failing to do their full duty, and they were moved by the spirit of that most self-confident exhortation ever delivered, which was voiced later by one of their distinguished sons, when Edward Everett Hale said: "When in doubt, do it." More important is the third consideration. The prohibition movement was to all intents and purposes a New England movement, and in New England the current philosophies swayed public opinion but within narrow limits. From the beginning to the present, New England, except Rhode Island, has believed in community responsibility.

The lead for prohibition was taken by Neal Dow, a political leader in Maine, which state was both radical and also radically New England. Here, just at the close of the generation, in 1851, he obtained a prohibition law, which, excepting during the years 1856-1858, withstood all buffets of reaction, until swallowed up by the Eighteenth Amendment. In the first years of the new generation, the movement was to spread rapidly, carrying other New England states, and urged upon the new states of the West by their increasing population of New England extraction.

While the millennium did not arrive, the results of this moral reform were not to be despised; in fact, they more nearly justified the hopes of its advocates than the slurs of its foes. In the first place, it almost destroyed drinking among women. It still remained good form in the "society" of the larger cities, and in the South, but here good manners prevented excess. In middle-class America and generally on the frontier women did not drink. The drunken woman was practically unknown, and came to be one of the novel sights recorded by Americans traveling in certain countries abroad. Among men the results were more marked in the number who drank not at all than in the number who moderated their drinking. At no time during this generation did occasional drunkenness offer a bar to political preferment, though later among the children of the generation, in certain localities, it came to do so. Brilliant lawyers could, at least in the West, appear drunk in court and keep their practice. More often such habits might stand between a young man and the girl of his desire, although the majority of girls were willing to take the risk, with the purpose of "reforming" the man after marriage. Still, the number of young men who had never tasted alcohol was probably larger than in any previous place or time, unless in some Mohammedan countries at periods of religious revival. The number of older men who had changed the habits of their youth was really incredible, and perhaps greater than it would have been had they not, for the most part innocently, mitigated their reform in the spring of the year by patent medicines, which began to appear, whose effects were due rather to their forty per cent of the anathematized liquor than to the herb extracts which they advertised. Whereas a large proportion of men of a typical Maine village were in the youth of this generation occasionally drunk, in its old age the town drunkard was an object of curiosity and rather reprobated than laughed at by the boys. In diminishing measure similar results extended southward and westward until the Potomac and the Ohio were reached, beyond which a change of habits was much less noticeable, though existing in varying degree.

The most important moral change of the time, however, was not American, but general in the European world. This was the continued progress and exceptional accomplishment of the humanitarian movement,[1] which began among the Quakers and became general in the

[1] F. P. Robinson, *Reform Movements of the Thirties and Forties* (unpublished thesis, Univ. of Wis., 1925).

eighteenth century. In colonial Massachusetts John Winthrop gave up shooting for pleasure, but none of the reasons which he carefully enumerates includes the cruelty of the practice. Representative boys growing up in the thirties and forties, like Abraham Lincoln and U. S. Grant, objected to hunting because they did not like killing animals. While individuals took this extreme view, and fanatics extended their tenderness to fish and even trees, the crowd revolted from many of the brutalities of the preceding generation, such as animal baiting, cock fighting and the human gouging matches of the frontier described by Thomas Ashe in 1806.[1] Horace Mann even advocated the disuse of corporal punishment in the schools.

While the individual conditions of the time permitted glaring exceptions which shocked visitors and, in the case of the Indians, extended to public practice, it remains true that the Americans on the whole were distinguished by their kindness of heart. This was, however, so dominant a feature of the period, and was so varied in its manifestations, that in this chapter it can only be referred to as one of the moral accomplishments of the time.

A striking anachronism of American life was the legal and political position of woman. Nowhere was she accorded a higher place in so far as lip service went, and this attitude was not a tribute to particular women but to the sex. Genuine Southern gentlemen extended even to female slaves the ordinary courtesies of social intercourse. European travelers universally commented upon the deferential attitude of American men toward women, even in the more primitive communities. Nevertheless, by law women were given a distinctly in-

[1] Allan Nevins, ed., *American Social History as Recorded by British Travellers* (N. Y., 1923), 58-60.

ferior place to men in the social organization.[1] Indeed, in the new democracy they seemed actually to play a smaller part than in the old days of aristocratic dominance. Politics was more distinctly a man's business than in Great Britain or France. As in earlier times, married women had no control, that is, legal control, over their property or children. In no state or locality did they possess the right to vote. These contrasts were especially noticeable to women who came from abroad with glowing ideas of the position their sex would occupy. Frances Kemble, an English actress who married Pierce Butler, a Georgia planter, could not long endure the life. Frances Wright, who came over from Scotland in 1818, soon began to devote herself to improving woman's position. Ernestine Rose, a Polish Jewess, had the same reaction, and became a speaker in the cause.

Naturally American women were not behindhand.[2] Their interest was first generally aroused by their desire to coöperate in other movements of general reform. They soon discovered that they were not wanted, but before their persistence the male reformers, representing of course liberal opinion generally, were powerless. In 1840 eight were sent as delegates to a World's Anti-slavery Convention in London. With debate and commotion they were excluded therefrom, and agreed among themselves that the position of women was pivotal to other measures and that they would devote themselves to it as a cause. The leader was Lucretia Mott, a middle-aged Quaker preacher of Philadelphia. With her was

[1] A. W. Calhoun, *A Social History of the American Family* (Cleveland, 1917-1919), II, chaps. iv-v; M. J. McIntosh, *Women in America* (N. Y., 1850).

[2] Sarah M. Grimké, *Letters on the Equality of the Sexes* (Boston, 1838); Anna D. Hallowell, *Life and Letters of James and Lucretia Mott* (Boston, 1884), chaps. vi-xiii; Elizabeth C. Stanton, Susan B. Anthony and Matilda J. Gage, eds., *History of Woman Suffrage* (N. Y., 1881-1922), I, chaps. iv, v-vii and *passim*; Theodore Stanton and Harriet S. Blatch, *Elizabeth Cady Stanton* (N. Y., 1922), I, 125-150.

Elizabeth Cady Stanton, a bride of twenty-five. Keenly interested in the movement also was Margaret Fuller, who was already exemplifying the possibilities of women in varied fields of work.[1]

The main object at first was the securing of civil rights for women. Of these the first to win support was the rectification of laws regarding property; and some progress was made. In 1839 Mississippi granted to married women the control over their own property, and similar laws were enacted in the next decade by Texas, Indiana, Pennsylvania, New York, California and Wisconsin. Encouraged by these successes, a younger group of women began to press the less popular issue of equal suffrage. Thus, in 1847, Lucy Stone graduated from Oberlin at the age of twenty-nine and began at once to fight for the vote. In 1848 a woman's-rights convention was held at Seneca Falls, New York, the first in the history of the world. The delegates drew up an impressive declaration of sentiments patterned closely upon the Declaration of Independence. They asserted that "all men and women are created equal," and demanded equality with the men before the law, in educational and economic opportunities and in the suffrage.[2] Though greeted by the ridicule and condemnation of press and pulpit, the gathering was to have almost yearly successors until the outbreak of the Civil War diverted the attention of the feminist leaders for a time to other matters.

The condition of wage-earners during these years differed from that of women in that they had no system of laws to batter down but new economic conditions to contend with. In so far as they wished legal changes,

[1] Augusta G. Violette, *Economic Feminism in American Literature Prior to 1848* (Univ. of Maine, *Studies*, ser. 2, XXVII, no. 2), chaps. v-ix.
[2] A. M. Schlesinger, *New Viewpoints in American History* (N. Y., 1922), 137-140.

this desire was for new protective measures, to pass which was contrary to the spirit of the time. The number of wage-earners was continually increasing with the new tasks of engineering and the factories. They included women as well as men, and many children.[1] The employment of children in factories gave no severe shock to the public sentiment of the generation, for children had always been expected to work. Few realized the difference of work at home and on the farm, and work in the rising factories.

The chief objective which the laboring men strove for was the ten-hour day (instead of the prevalent twelve or thirteen),[2] though they never lost sight of their program announced at the end of the twenties, especially the demands for free tax-supported schools and for the abolition of all monopolies such as banks and other chartered corporations. From 1828 to 1832 they sought such reforms through political action, but between 1832 and 1836 they contented themselves with agitating strongly by means of organization and strikes, and many labor papers were published. Among their leaders was George H. Evans who published at New York the *Working Man's Advocate*. In 1836 the union membership of the country numbered nearly 300,000. The movement looked like one of the most promising of the reform agitations of the time, and one might have predicted that within a short period it would achieve reasonable success. The trade societies received a serious blow, however, in 1835 by reason of certain common-law decisions beginning with People *v.* Fisher, in New

[1] Edith Abbott, *Women in Industry* (N. Y., 1919), 158-166, 192, 248-253.
[2] This account is based very largely on Mary R. Beard, *A Short History of the American Labor Movement* (N. Y., 1920), chaps. iv-vii; J. R. Commons and others, *History of Labour in the United States* (N. Y., 1918), I, pts. iii-iv; Selig Perlman, *History of Trade Unionism in the United States* (N. Y., 1922), 18-39.

York, which declared strikes illegal, and during the period of depression which began in 1837 they would have been, in any case, useless. The competition for jobs became so keen that wage-earners could not exact conditions. Standards of hours and wages which had been won by organized efforts were sacrificed; leaders were discouraged; Evans, for example, retired to a farm.

Some impression had been made, however. In 1840 President Van Buren declared ten hours a legal day's work on government undertakings, and private employers adopted the same policy in the important business of shipbuilding. Chief Justice Shaw of Massachusetts, in the same year, reinterpreted the common law in such a way that strikes were no longer banned as a combination in restraint of trade. In 1843 that state, which had never entirely dropped her colonial habit of controlling the lives of her inhabitants, forbade the employment of children under twelve for more than ten hours. With the return of prosperity one finds in 1845 strikes for an eleven-hour day. The movement revived. Evans returned to New York, after an experience in the West, imbued with one of those simple solutions for man's woes which were so apt to outcrop in a frontier environment. He asserted the right of every man to an equal portion of the earth's surface and believed that the recognition of this right would adjust the principal difficulties of labor. Such an agrarian solution received the support of Andrew Johnson who appeared in Congress in 1843 as member from Tennessee, and made the passage of a homestead law one of the chief objects of his public life. Meantime Greeley in the *Tribune* was doing much to interest the reform group in general in the problem of labor. The period ended with no such definite accomplishment, or even program, as in the case of the other reforms that have been treated, but the workingman's condition was much better in 1850 than it had been twenty years before.[1]

The belief in the perfectibility of man which pervaded men's thinking shaded off quite easily into a belief in the perfectibility of nations. The founding of the American Peace Society in 1828 had given a national support to the cause of world peace, and the enthusiasms of this period made possible the creation of an international basis of support. The constructive program of the American Peace Society provided for the formation of a congress of nations, meeting periodically, and further, for the establishment of a high court of arbitration for the adjustment of international controversies. In 1835 the Massachusetts legislature was induced to indorse this plan, but persistent petitions sent to Congress brought no response during these years. The American peace advocates, however, joined hands with some European societies, and in 1843 took part in a world peace congress in London. Four years later Elihu Burritt, one of the foremost American leaders, went to Europe, and succeeded in persuading the international congress held at Brussels in 1848 to ratify the American peace proposal. In 1849 Richard Cobden submitted to the House of Commons a proposal that Britain should enter into communication with other powers for the purpose of referring questions in dispute to arbitration; but the proposition was rejected by a vote of 176 to 79. By mid-century the friends of peace felt that definite progress had been made in educating peoples on the subject of peace, and even took credit for the failure of Great Britain to go to war over the Oregon boundary dispute in 1846.[2] The events of the next decade, however, were to erase most of the gain they had made, and deal

---

[1] D. R. Fox, *The Decline of Aristocracy in the Politics of New York* (Columbia Univ., *Studies*, LXXXVI), 381-399.

[2] A. D. Call, "The Will to End War," *Advocate of Peace*, LXXXVI (1924), 228-240.

almost a body blow to the American Peace Society itself.

Three elements are to be observed in the various reform movements. In the first place, there was the part played by those hereditary reformers, the Quakers. Nearly always there was a Quaker at the start, but the leadership seldom remained with them. The second element was the action and reaction between Europe and America. This was particularly marked in the case of Great Britain. The foreign missionary movement there stimulated that of the United States. American women lectured on women's rights in England, and British temperance workers in America. Prussian education was drawn on for American use, and before the end of the period German and American reformers were fraternizing The whole movement was presided over by the *Egalité* and the *Fraternité* of the French Revolution. Charles Sumner, the beautiful youth, who was developing into the St. George destined by all reformers to kill all dragons, was equally welcome on both sides of the Atlantic.

The third element was the relentless driving power given by the New England renaissance, curiously like and yet differing from the dominant Jacksonian democracy. As with Jackson, universality was of the essence of their thought. It would be unfair to say that they were in such a hurry to convert the world that they did not worry over converting themselves; certainly, however, they were much less self-searching than their ancestors. Confident of themselves, they devoted their attention to their neighbors with all the intrusive power developed by two centuries of prying village life. As individuals and as a group, they were exceptional for high mindedness and propriety of habits. One is, however, forever wishing to preach to them from the text: "And why beholdest thou the mote that is in thy brother's eye, but perceivest not the beam that is in thine own eye?"

Embodying all these three elements, the movement for the abolition of slavery encountered special conditions which made it the most interesting of all both to contemporaries and to posterity. Long continued development of European practice hastened by the earlier humanitarian movement of the eighteenth century had created a general sentiment of disapproval in the European world. The idealism of the Revolutionary period had been sufficient to abolish the institution in those parts of the United States where the disturbance of property rights and the social problem of the freed Negro were not too embarrassing. Before this generation appeared, slavery had ceased, or was in legal process of disappearance, in all states north of the southern boundary of Pennsylvania, which was known as the Mason and Dixon line, and of the Ohio. Moreover, the demarcation line had been extended, omitting the jog made by the slave state of Missouri, to prohibit slavery in the territory north of the parallel of 36° 30' to the Rocky Mountains, then the western limits of the United States.

While there was a general belief that this was a temporary division and that slavery would ultimately be eliminated, the only serious movement to bring this about was among the Quakers. Having declared against slavery, they had early adopted a discipline excluding members who held slaves. They continued to work against it, chiefly in the piedmont regions to the east and west of the Alleghanies where they had settlements. Some among them objected so strongly that they migrated to the north of the Ohio, forming a strong center in Indiana. Among the leaders was Benjamin Lundy, who from 1812 to 1836 published a periodical entitled *The Genius of Universal Emancipation*. Beginning his work in Ohio, he moved his headquarters in 1824 to the slave city of Baltimore.

In the meantime the spirit of the French Revolution was sweeping slavery from its last recesses in the Christian portions of Europe and from the Latin-American republics, and was buffeting it in the European colonies. Between 1800 and 1815 the slave trade had ceased to be a reputable source of income, and became a discredited and illegal occupation in all the more advanced countries. The Pope added his disapproval, and to these combined forces Spain and Portugal were forced to yield. The United States had prohibited the importation of slaves in 1808, and in 1819 declared the trade piracy. In England the brilliant Wilberforce devoted his remarkable energies to the cause, inducing the government to make a major issue of the suppression of the trade everywhere. Gradually he succeeded in creating a sentiment that in 1833 legally initiated the gradual extinction of slavery itself in the English colonies, England, as is her habit, compensating the proprietors of an ancient custom, newly recognized as vicious, for their losses. Throughout our period the agitation for abolition in the colonies of other countries was in full swing. In 1840, as has been noticed, a world's antislavery convention met in London, and by 1850 slavery had ceased throughout the European world except in the colonies of Spain, in Brazil and in the Southern states of the American Union.

As slavery in the United States became more and more an isolated anachronism, pride added fuel to the zeal of those who aimed at its extinction here. The slow process of persuasion by example and mild sermonizing no longer sufficed the souls of those interested. To many it became no longer merely an undesirable habit or a political inconsistency but a crime to allow, a sin to practise. To Benjamin Lundy came in 1829 the twenty-

four-year-old William Lloyd Garrison, a printer of Newburyport, Massachusetts.   Garrison had had few conventional educational advantages, but at that time a
printing shop was a university to the printer's devil who
knew how to take advantage of his opportunities.   Garrison, like Franklin and Greeley, became a cultured man
—more so than Greeley, less than Franklin.   His particular talent was as editor, and in this respect he has
had few equals in American.   Later he developed a
capacity for public speaking, but his eloquence was
rather an intimate appeal to the few than the swaying of
great masses.[1]

Quickly Garrison found the methods of Lundy too
slow and compromising.   Unable to work under restrictions, he returned to the North, and in 1831 set up a
paper of his own, the *Liberator*.   In this he adapted the
antislavery cause to the new spirit of the time.   "I will
be harsh as truth, as uncompromising as justice;" slavery
was not an evolutionary economic institution but an immorality.   He would have naught to do with expediency.   With Edwardean logic, every slaveholder became to him a sinner.   The United States Constitution,
by recognizing slavery, became a compact with hell;
he would not recognize it until slavery was eliminated.
Abolition must be immediate; it must be without compensation.   The idea of removing the freed Negro from
the country—a favorite project of Henry Clay and many
others—was as sinful as slavery itself.   The freed Negro
must be admitted at once to full equality; equal, he
would make his own place in society.   Garrison's mot-
toes were: "I will not retreat one inch," and "I will be
heard."

Bred in a strong Quaker tradition, Garrison was more

[1] F. J. and W. P. Garrison, *William Lloyd Garrison, 1805-1879:
the Story of His Life Told by His Children* (N. Y., 1885-1889), I.
chaps. vii-xii; II, chaps. i, iii-v; III, chaps. ii, ix.

keenly interested in the cause of universal peace than in anything except slavery. He would not, therefore, proceed against that institution by force. His interpretation of force, however, was distinctly limited. He encouraged the Negroes to run away, using the cartoon to reach their illiterate minds. He promoted the formation of what was known as the "Underground Railroad," a series of secret stopping places for the escaped slaves arranged to protect them on their way to freedom across the Canadian border.[1] To stir the latent disapproval of the North to action, he lashed his audiences with tales of the injustices and atrocities of slavery, and eulogies of the Negro and of humanity. One of his earliest converts was the son of an aristocratic Boston family, Wendell Phillips, who became perhaps the greatest of our emotional orators after Patrick Henry.[2] The gradually gathering band of his supporters Garrison organized after the custom of the time. The first association was formed in 1831. In 1832 the New England society was organized, and then, in 1833, the American Anti-Slavery Society.

At first antislavery meetings were attacked by mobs of the conservatives.[3] During 1833 and 1834 Prudence Crandall, for undertaking a school for Negro girls at Canterbury, Connecticut, was ostracized by her neighbors, abused, and prosecuted by town and legislature. In 1833 Elijah P. Lovejoy established the antislavery *Observer* in St. Louis and in 1836 he removed his paper to Alton, Illinois. Here his office was mobbed, and he

[1] W. H. Siebert, *The Underground Railroad* (N. Y., 1898), chaps. iv-viii, x-xi; B. T. Washington, *Frederick Douglass* (E. P. Oberholtzer, ed., *American Crisis Biographies*, Phila., 1906), chaps. iii-viii.

[2] Carlos Martyn, *Wendell Phillips: the Agitator* (Carlos Martyn, ed., *American Reformers*, N. Y., 1890), I, chap. v; II, chaps. i, vi-viii, x, xiv; Wendell Phillips, *Speeches, Lectures and Letters* (Boston, 1891), 1-39.

[3] William Birney, *James G. Birney and His Times* (N. Y., 1890), chaps. xxi, xxiii.

and one of his attackers were killed. This phase, however, quickly passed, and Garrison was more disturbed by the spread of his campaign to a more moderate element, which was unwilling to go to his extremes. The fact was that many abolitionists wished to pursue the more usual American method of political effort. Such a group separated from Garrison, and in 1840 ran James G. Birney of Kentucky, editor of the *Philanthropist*, for the presidency.

No movement of the time attracted so much attention, engaged so many active workers, or, with the exception of public education, won by the end of the period so wide a range of really interested support in the North. In legislative achievement, however, none seemed in 1850 more futile, nor was this because there were no small preliminary steps to take. In 1850 as in 1830, the Negro nowhere lived under the same laws as the white, except in New England. In New York some voted, but beyond that state they were debarred from the suffrage. In cities and on all routes of travel, slaves, personal servants of traveling masters, were a familiar sight, and were nearly everywhere held to their service by the law. Aside from a few state laws to protect their free Negro populations from claims of Southerners under the fugitive slave act of 1792 and a thriving colony of escaped Negroes in Ontario, there was no apparent legal gain from the movement.[1] Privately, however, something had been done in the way of greater care and better educational opportunity for the negro in the North.

This relative lack of accomplishment was due to the special conditions of slavery. In the first place, slavery

[1] Emil Olbrich, *The Development of Sentiment on Negro Suffrage to 1860* (Univ. of Wis., *Bull.*, no. 477), chaps. ii-iv; C. G. Woodson, *The Education of the Negro Prior to 1861* (N. Y., 1915), 162-228, 232-295; D. R. Fox, "The Negro Vote in New York," *Pol. Sci. Quar.*, XXXII, 252-275.

in America was a question of race; this of itself differentiated it from the other reforms. With convinced reformers this had no weight, for to them all races were born equal in possibilities, and differences in condition could be obliterated by equality in law. Their view would have been more widely accepted, had they admitted a period of tutelage, but their insistence on immediate recognition added to the opposition the agnostics as well as the confirmed believers in racial differences. In this respect the movement rested on a far more debatable foundation than that for education.

More important was the fact that slavery was sectional, and that the new movement came from the region in which it did not exist. This meant that the attackers had a simplicity of vision which ignored the difficulties of the situation, and that the attacked were not unnaturally stirred to high resentment. All this was in marked contrast with the temperance movement where the work was done among neighbors and, to a large extent, by reformed drunkards—like appealing to like. The earlier movement for the general extinction of slavery had indeed been widespread in the South, and never disappeared. Some Southerners even took part in the new movement of violence. The Grimké sisters of South Carolina joined it; but they came North. In the border state of Kentucky, Cassius M. Clay was able to carry on his activities at home. In overwhelming proportion, however, the new denunciatory campaign was carried on by Northerners in the North, but the effect of the campaign was immediately evident in the South.

The Garrisonian attack hit the South on four points on which it was most sensitive and at a time when the tariff controversy had begun to emphasize to Southerners how much they had in common. In the first place, it was directed against the greatest Southern economic interest, the foundation of her whole industrial system.

There had been a period when slavery had been felt to be a detriment, but with the extension of cotton growing, this condition had changed, and with the change had come an almost imperceptible shift of attitude. By 1820 the rising generation of Southerners was ceasing to think of slavery in terms of a dying institution, but rather as a necessary evil. No student of the Southern people can suppose that they would have forever supported an evil on such grounds, and there are strong reasons for the belief that when the virgin cotton soil had been exhausted, the earlier conditions and attitude would have revived. It was a fact, however, that in 1830 slavery was working well from the economic point of view and that it could not have been suddenly extinguished without wrecking the Southern industrial machine.

Garrison, however, was not merely an economic theorist whose view was dangerous to a vested interest; he was an advocate of direct action. While slavery was still legal, he organized to the limit of his capacity a system of stealing slaves and carrying them beyond the reach of law. The demand of the South that the national government and the Northern states protect its property from the machinations of these raiders who were legally criminal, found a natural response in the minds of the more balanced Northerners, and accounts to some extent for the well-dressed mobs who, illogically meeting direct action by direct action, broke up the gatherings of the abolitionists in the early stages of their campaign.

Nor was the fear of property loss the only or the greatest of Southern apprehensions. One of the strongest points in Southern culture was its acquaintance with the elements of classical literature. To them the history of the servile wars in Rome was a familiar topic. Nor was it ancient history alone which alarmed them. Fresh in their memory were the horrors of the Negro revolu-

tions in Haiti.   Toussaint L'Ouverture, who to Wendell
Phillips was an apostle of liberty, was to them a demon
of cruelty.   How far the Negroes who surrounded them,
who cooked their food and nursed their children, had
been affected by civilization, and how far they retained
the primitive savagery they were presumed to have
brought from Africa, they did not learn until the Civil
War.   It so happened that one of the few Negro insur-
rections in the South, that of Nat Turner in which fifty-
five whites were killed, occurred in 1831, just after Garrison began his campaign.[1]   While no connection was
proved it is not surprising that many believed it existed
and that continued propaganda would continue to produce similar results.

To these main tangible causes were added certain
strong psychological tendencies.   In the first place, the
whole Southern mode and habit of life and consequent
conception of government emphasized individual freedom.   The prying ways of a New England community
shocked their sense of good breeding and true neighbor-
liness.   In general, a large part of the New England program of reform struck the Southerners as meddling and
ungentlemanly as well as dangerous.   Much more important was the second reaction.   The South was proud
of its religious life.   Southerners felt very strongly that,
however undesirable slaveholding might be, the practice
did not constitute a sin, and they resented being told that
they were sinners, especially by New England "Come
Outers" such as Unitarians, whom most of them believed
to have rejected the fundamental tenets of Christianity.

It was this reaction that gave the South its basic defense.   Too high-strung to fight merely for a material
cause, they sought a religious and moral banner.   To this
they were driven and assisted by the strong strain of
Scotch blood, which, having descended from the moun-

[1] G. R. Gray, *Nat Turner's Insurrection of 1831* (Balt., 1831).

tains, rose at this time to leadership. Under such men as Calhoun and McDuffie in South Carolina, the Polks in the West and a host of able and powerful clergy, there was being evolved in this period a religious and moral counterargument, which was accepted in the South more quickly and completely than was Garrisonianism in the North. Slavery ceased for them to be a necessary evil. It became the divine system sanctioned by the Scriptures as well as the classical philosophers, by which alone different races could live together in peace; its merits were insisted upon by statistical comparisons with the conditions produced by the Industrial Revolution in England and New England; for the Negro it was a means of salvation by bringing him into the care of Christian masters and Christian teachings.

Nor can it be claimed that this was merely a dry and cynical attempt to obtain a sanction for a profitable anachronistic immorality. It warmed the attitude of many toward the slave. While in most states the teaching of the slave to read was prohibited by law after 1830, the teaching and preaching of the Christian religion to them were in every way encouraged.[1] Between 1830 and 1850 much thought was given to the methods best suited to them, and many experiments were tried, with a growing tendency in favor of separate congregations. The Methodists were most successful in this work, with the Baptists a close second. The Presbyterians and Episcopalians studied the problem, and leaders of those faiths were not unwilling to assist Negro congregations of other denominations. By 1850 South Carolina was fairly dotted with Negro chapels, and it was usual for the Negro children of a plantation to be brought together on Sunday for instruction by some member of the family. Between a fifth and a sixth

[1] C. G. Woodson, *History of the Negro Church* (Wash., 1921), 100-120, 123-166.

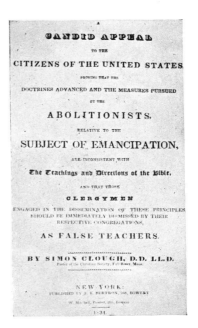

Proslavery men claimed that their institution was authorized by Nature and the Bible;

But even they deplored the necessity of the slave trade, as shown, for example, in this march of a gang to market.

of the Negroes of that state were in 1850 church members.

This new advocacy of slavery was not confined to the comparatively small slaveholding class. By 1835 the main controversies in the South between the slaveholders and nonslaveholders over suffrage and representation had been quieted by the general adoption of manhood suffrage and by compromises on representation. The planters, too, were, during this period, the genuine leaders of the people, a real aristocracy of the strongest to which economic opportunity, at least down to 1840, made admission so easy that there was little excuse for failure to become a member of the governing class, except inability. Still more powerful a consideration was the fact that for the poor white in the South the chief solace to his pride was the superiority of the free man over the slave. This was in most cases a consideration stronger than economic jealousy, and reduced differences on the subject of slavery to a minimum.

The first action resulting from Garrison's campaign was taken in the South. In the thirties North Carolina and Tennessee reflected the tendency to make the question one of race instead of status by excluding free Negroes from the suffrage which they had previously enjoyed. Laws prohibiting, or making difficult, the private emancipation of slaves were passed, and far more effective police control of the Negro population was provided. Much attention and some financial support were given to the American Colonization Society with the object of removing from the country the anomalous free Negro. The attempt to bar free Negroes of the North from Southern states led to a picturesque encounter between Massachusetts and South Carolina in 1844 when the former sent Samuel Hoar to defend the rights of its colored sailors, and the gentry of Charleston politely expelled him from that city.[1] The powerful force of social ostracism, exercised according to the representative manners of the various localities, made the discussion of emancipation, at least in the Lower South, practically impossible.[2] By various laws the writing and circulation of abolitionist literature were made illegal. In 1835 when the people of Charleston invoked federal aid to prevent the use of the post office for such purposes, President Jackson endorsed such local control of its functions, and in spite of action by Congress in 1836, the mails remained practically closed. The South was thus able to a considerable extent to exclude the agitation from its borders. When, however, in the early forties, the governor of Alabama sought to use the power of extradition to secure and punish Northern writers of dangerous literature which found its way into his state despite all precautions, he met firm and successful opposition from Governor Seward of New York, who so handled the controversy as to arouse a wider support for the antislavery cause in the North than it had previously received.[3]

A gap in the dike the South was thus building existed in the discussions in Congress. The abolitionists resorted, among other methods, to that of petition and found many signatures for some of the less drastic of their proposals, such as that of prohibiting slavery in the District of Columbia; which would indicate national disapprobation of slavery without interfering with the rights of the states. In 1836 the House of Representatives voted to lay all such petitions on the table without debate. This created an issue of freedom of speech which immediately engaged the attention of the most

[1] *Niles' Register*, LXII (1844), 226; Horace Greeley, *American Conflict* (Chicago, 1864-1866), I, 180-185.

[2] A. B. Hart, *Slavery and Abolition* (A. B. Hart, ed., *The American Nation, a History*, N. Y., 1904-1918, XVI), chap. xvi.

[3] Frederic Bancroft, *Life of William H. Seward* (N. Y., 1900), I, 101-104.

adroit and skillful of the House leaders, John Quincy Adams, now rounding out his astonishing political career by eighteen years of service in the body where most leaders begin theirs. With every art of the parliamentarian he kept the discussion alive before the country, and he succeeded in large measure in identifying the campaign against slavery with the general cause of political liberty and freedom of speech. In 1844 he was finally successful in reopening the House of Representatives to such petitions.[1]

This failure of the South to compel the silence of the national organs of government was emphasized by the fact that questions of foreign relations were continually occurring in which slavery was an issue. Here the South was more fortunate, for the most continuous of such problems arose from the desire of Great Britain to secure our support in suppressing the ocean slave trade by allowing a mutual right of search. In this case the traditional American distrust of the British navy and memories of how that right had been exercised during the Napoleonic wars caused the Southern insistence on the immunity of the American flag on the high seas to be the attitude generally considered patriotic. For his influence in impressing this view upon the court of France, Lewis Cass of Michigan was made Democratic candidate for the presidency in 1848. On the whole, the South was able to direct national policy on this point, though in the Webster-Ashburton treaty of 1842 we agreed to maintain a squadron off the coast of Africa to police our own merchant marine.[2]

[1] T. H. Benton, *Thirty Years' View* (N. Y., 1854-1856), I, 609-624; II, 130-143, 150-154, 409-412, 696-698, 711-713, 729-733; W. H. Seward, *Life and Public Services of John Quincy Adams* (Auburn, N. Y., 1849), chaps. xii-xiii.
[2] W. E. B. DuBois, *The Suppression of the Slave-Trade, 1638-1870* (*Harvard Hist. Studies*, I), 141-149, 151-167; A. C. McLaughlin, *Lewis Cass* (J. T. Morse, jr., ed., *American Statesmen*, Boston, 1891), chaps. vi-viii.

Less conspicuous but difficult cases arose in the coastwise carrying of American slaves from one American port to another. One case was that of the *Creole,* on which a few slaves mutinied, killed one of the owners and took the vessel into the British West India port of Nassau. Here the murderers were held for trial, and the remainder of the slaves liberated, on the principle that slavery disappeared on British soil. The South may well have been dissatisfied with the handling of this case by Daniel Webster, who was then secretary of state and whose rather perfunctory attitude brought from Lord Ashburton merely the promise that there would be in the future no "officious interference" in such instances. More important was the principle evolved by Calhoun to meet the situation.[1] He argued that as the states had granted to the national government all their powers of foreign diplomacy, it was the bounden duty of that government to defend all the interests and institutions of each state, regardless of whether such interests and institutions were approved by the majority; in other words, that its function was that of attorney, not principal. While this principle seems essentially sound, Calhoun failed in his presentation by not recognizing that the national government must possess discretion as to means. His view is important as an indication that he foresaw in 1840 what twenty years later became a glaring fact, that the Southern policy of defense could not be complete without a sympathetic national administration.

By 1840 the sectional cohesion of the South was fairly evident. It was to some degree, however, disguised from the eye, and was for twenty years prevented from the full exercise of its power by divergent views on matters of policy. One group of Southern leaders, distinguished

[1] J. C. Calhoun, *Works* (R. R. Cralle, ed., N. Y., 1853-1855), III, 462-487.

by such figures as Calhoun and his youthful disciple, Jefferson Davis, followed the practice of Jefferson in relying upon the noninterference policy of the Democratic party for protection to their institutions. Another group, among whom the brilliant Georgians, Alexander H. Stephens and Robert Toombs, were during the forties becoming conspicuous, relied rather upon the class sympathy and the general desire for stability which they found among the Northern Whigs. This division of Southern leaders as to the better course with reference to political alliances tended to diminish for a time the full force of the new sectionalism and to keep the political parties national throughout the period.[1]

It was natural that party leaders should exert their full influence to keep questions of slavery out of politics. Thus, in 1847, when John G. Palfrey, a Whig from Massachusetts, refused to vote for John C. Winthrop as speaker because he suspected that certain committee appointments would quash slavery discussion, there was an outburst of partisan wrath that the young James Russell Lowell satirized in a poem beginning

> No? Hez he? He haint, though? Wut?
> Voted agin him?
> Ef the bird of our country could ketch him,
> she'd skin him.[2]

The more sensitive organizations of the religious bodies were less able to resist.[3] In 1844 and 1845 the more democratic bodies, the Baptists and the Methodists, split on the subject, and there were organized a Southern Baptist Church and a Methodist Episcopal Church,

[1] A. C. Cole, *The Whig Party in the South* (Wash., 1913), chaps. ii-v.
[2] J. R. Lowell, *Writings* (Boston, 1848), VIII, 76; see also the *Anti-Slavery Papers* of James Russell Lowell (Boston, 1902).
[3] C. H. Ambler, *Sectionalism in Virginia from 1776 to 1861* (Chicago, 1910), chap. ix; J. N. Norwood, *The Schism in the Methodist Episcopal Church, 1844* (Alfred Univ., *Studies*, I).

South. The Presbyterians, with their stronger system, prevented separation for the time by agreeing not to meet. In a similar way periodicals became sectional or abstained fom reference to sectional differences.

CHAPTER XIII

MANIFEST DESTINY

THROUGHOUT the period there was a general determination not only to reform American civilization and plant it firmly in the Valley of the Mississippi but, in addition, to secure for it those other regions assigned to it by a "Manifest Destiny." There was, moreover, throughout the period a fairly definite conception as to what these boundaries should be. When in 1819 John Quincy Adams secured the Floridas and a line zigzagging across the continent to a point on the Pacific, he considered that he had performed his greatest task, but he considered it merely a step. Like Jefferson he believed that Cuba was to become part of the United States. He merely suspended our claim to Texas, and he foresaw a Pacific frontage. Webster long had his eye on the Bay of San Francisco and declared Hawaii within the range of our interests; Calhoun included the Columbia Valley and Puget Sound in his vision; and Lower California, it was generally thought, would round out a satisfactory whole. This the American people believed to be theirs, and for it a majority were prepared to fight when nations they considered rivals seemed likely to anticipate them.

Beyond this to the north lay Canada. With regard to that region this generation inherited and passed on the belief that, in due course of time, it would naturally be added to the national body. They found it difficult to believe that the Canadians would remain in their Arctic seclusion when the warm sun of American democracy beckoned, except by compulsion.   On the other hand, there was a growing acceptance of the fact that combination would take place only by action of the Canadians themselves.   Henry Clay tempered the views of forcible annexation which had urged him to the War of 1812, and they remained only with a diminishing number of border enthusiasts.   This hope rose to some importance during the Canadian insurrection of 1837, organized itself into a league of "Hunters' Lodges," influenced politics, and was thought in 1841 to threaten war.[1]   Nevertheless the annexation of Canada was felt by the majority to be her business rather than ours.

It was generally recognized that another type of civilization existed to the south.   Except at one moment of heat forcible acquisition was not sought.   In fact, the optimistic views of the genial Seward that these countries, cleansed and stabilized by adopting our institutions, would ultimately join our union in equal sisterhood never produced a profound response.   More popular was the idea of Clay of coöperation based on their continued independence.

The older statesmen of the generation had held that there was no cause for hurry; in fact, that delay was a distinct advantage to a nation yearly growing, as was the United States, into a position of greater relative strength.   The arrangement made with Great Britain in 1818, with regard to the territory claimed by both nations on the northwest coast, was in exact harmony with their policy.   The territory was to be held in joint occupancy for ten years, neither nation within that time to acquire new rights.   In 1828 this was renewed in-

[1] Paul Knaplund, "James Stephens and British North American Problems," *Canadian Hist. Rev.*, V, 21-41; Charles Lindsay, *William Lyon MacKenzie* (Toronto, 1908), 440-443; W. L. MacKenzie, *Life and Times of Martin Van Buren* (Boston, 1846), 282-291; E. M. Shepard, *Martin Van Buren* (J. T. Morse, jr., ed., *American Statesmen*, N. Y., 1888), 300-306.

definitely with a mutual power of annulment on one year's notice. It was the general belief in the United States that, when we chose to bring the matter to a determination, we would be able to bring greater forces to the argument and that active American settlers, while not changing the legal status, would form a factor not negligible. This policy was perhaps continued the longer since it was in harmony with the Jacksonian conception that government should leave everything possible to individual initiative.

Throughout the period this initiative was ready. The adventurer was as characteristic of the generation as the reformer. In fact one may consider that two elements, always present in any civilization but brought to America in unusual proportion by the selective processes of migration, came simultaneously to full flower. One was that of the utopians who sought to realize their plans on the virgin soil of America, and the other, the adventurer type, seeking varied fortunes but at heart more interested in the exciting process than the attainment.

There were adventurers of every kind. The business-like Austins, Moses and Stephen, sought an estate in Texas and found it necessary to found a state. There were missionaries, like Marcus Whitman, who wove the Christianizing of the Indians, agricultural colonization in Oregon and international politics into a fascinating mysterious web. There were poets of action, like Samuel Houston, moved by romance and sentiment, attracting attention by mystery and mannerisms, and developing through necessity the capacity of statesmen. There was the knightly Crittenden, who gave his life for Cuban freedom. There was the eccentric David Crockett, who was equally at home fighting Indians or Mexicans, speaking on the stump or platform or presenting the claims of his constituents as a member of Congress; and there was the fantastic William Walker whose filibustering in Nicaragua made him to many the "grey-eyed man of destiny." The opportunities for daring enterprise afield attracted individuals who under normal circumstances would have been quiet and usual citizens. So we have seen that young aristocrats like Francis Parkman were drawn adventurously to the wilds, and quiet scholars like Draper and Audubon sought their material in the woods. Similar spirits from other lands yielded to the fascination of America.

It was typical of the time that in 1836 a mysterious gentleman named James Dickson was leading an army of sixty Canadians across Minnesota, with the ostensible purpose of liberating and organizing the Indians, and with the expectation of falling upon the flank of the Mexicans and liberating Texas. One of his majors, Martin McLeod, confided to his diary: "As yet I know little of this man, but if I may judge from so short an acquaintance, he is somewhat visionary in his views—N'importe I wish to go North and Westward and will embrace the opportunity." Through the incredible hardships of the futile winter trudge, McLeod was studying Spanish, he met Polish refugees, he read *The Lady of the Lake, Scottish Chiefs* and *Thaddeus of Warsaw.* Of the object of the expedition he wrote: "How noble and truly philanthropic the attempt of regenerating these people [the Indians]. They are, I feel confident, susceptible of all the refinements of civilized life. Still, perhaps, they would not be so happy.

> "If ignorance is bliss
> " 'Tis folly to be wise." [1]

The desire for adventure, the belief that it was manly

[1] MS. Diary of Martin McLeod in Minnesota Historical Society. See also Grace L. Nute, "James Dickson," *Miss. Valley Hist. Rev.,* X, 127-140.

for a youth to fare forth after his fortune, the conviction that there was some Holy Grail to reward the disinterested, were in this period touching actually a larger percentage of Americans than at any other time. The strongest altruistic motive was the patriotic—either the concrete idea of opening territory to settlement by exploration, or of spreading American institutions. This gave a particular prestige to projects beyond the national boundaries. In carrying out such undertakings the interest and agency of the national government had eventually to be sought, and so ultimately the question of national adventure was raised.

To altruism were added more practical considerations. First was land hunger, which spurred different men differently. Some it caused to push out from settled areas to ranges just beyond while acting under the legal institutions of the time. Others were impelled to a far distant leap by a vision of lands under other flags, but of fabulous fertility, free in exhaustless quantities. Every leader of adventure added to his prospectus freeholds of enticing size to be the reward of his coöperators. To the liberators of Canada and Texas, farms and ranches were promised; to the emancipators of Cuba, plantation estates. Mere general publicity induced in 1843 a thousand seekers, mostly farmers, to undertake the overland trail to Oregon to save that region to the nation, and to secure new farms pictured to their trusting imagination by missionaries and politicians.[1] With similar trust thousands of Mormons plunged into the desert.

During the period also there revived the lure of metal which had for so long been dead in the United States. Coal mining was, of course, steadily growing but with-

---

[1] Francis Parkman, *The Oregon Trail* (N. Y., 1849) ; an illustrative body of documents is *The Austin Papers*, edited by E. C. Barker, of which two parts were published in the Am. Hist. Assoc., *Rep. for 1919*, II.

out excitement. Except for inconsiderable deposits of gold in North Carolina and Georgia, the first interest was excited by the discovery of the baser metals along the Mississippi in northern Illinois and southwestern Wisconsin. Thither in the twenties and thirties the "Suckers," as they were called after the river fish of the same habit, came up river in the spring by the thousands, to return home in the fall. By lake route came others, the "Badgers," who dug themselves into the hillside mines and kept their homes in the region the year around. Rumor crossed the Atlantic and sturdy Cornish miners came to ply their ancient art in this new region.[1] The discovery of gold in California in 1848 made the United States the focus of adventure for all the world.

Throughout the period, while such schemes were chiefly occupied with the frontier, they drew their support from all regions. Naturally, however, the nearer one came to the scene of proposed action, the greater the proportion of the population interested. Tennessee, with its population derived from the rough stock of the mountain and with its fresh experience in frontiering and Indian fighting, stood foremost. When it was a question of advance into Texas, the greater number of the pioneers were from the South, and New Orleans was the center of their activities. The Oregon movement drew chiefly from the region about the Missouri, the gateway to the promised land. Filibusters, however, with their visions shading from haloed glory to empire and loot, were most numerous about the seaports; and New York vied with New Orleans. Not entirely divorced from these were the traders and whalers and the missionaries who set out prayerfully from such New England ports as New Bedford, Boston and Nantucket.

Of all these movements, that into Texas was the most

[1] O. G. Libby, "Significance of the Lead and Shot Trade in Early Wisconsin History," Wis. Hist. Soc., *Colls.*, XIII, 293-334.

inevitable and the most interrelated with the other currents of the time. Its foundation lay in the treaty ratified in 1821, which cleared the national title to that region by assigning it to Spain whose position was soon taken over by independent Mexico. Its second foundation lay in the land policy of Spain, followed by Mexico, which was based on the idea of large free grants to enterprising men on condition of securing settlers—a contrast to the United States policy of charging for all land. Numbers of Americans obtained such grants; and in order to secure settlers they advertised land in their several zones at very low rates, intending, as did the Mexican government, to compensate themselves by the increment of value which would come to the portions they reserved. Thus they offered land at twelve and a half cents an acre when the United States government was selling at a minimum of a dollar and a quarter. This appeal made an impression particularly on those who wished to take advantage of the boom in cotton growing and yet had small capital. The majority of those who came to Texas, therefore, were from the Southern states, and while they brought but small numbers of slaves, they hoped to acquire the possession of great numbers.[1] As an incident of acquiring their land title, these settlers were obliged formally to accept Mexican citizenship and the Roman Catholic faith. It seems unlikely, however, that many of them expected to die in the Mexican republic or the Roman Catholic Church.

That the situation was not stable was recognized on both sides. Lucas Alaman, the brilliant Mexican secretary of foreign affairs, studying the process of United States expansion into Indian country and into the

[1] G. P. Garrison, *Texas, A Contest of Civilization* (H. E. Scudder, ed., *American Commonwealths*, Boston, 1903), chaps. xiii, xvi-xxi; G. P. Garrison, ed., *Diplomatic Correspondence of Texas*, Am. Hist. Assoc., *Reps. for 1907* and *1908, passim.*

Floridas, saw in Texas a new manifestation of a subtle method of advance and acquisition which he believed to be as purposeful as it was powerful. He induced his government to adopt a series of counteracting measures. Many among the settlers, perceiving the approach of a crisis and dissatisfied with the conservative measures of their leader Stephen F. Austin, sought to import a leader. Dr. Branch Y. Archer of Virginia was offered the opportunity, and declined it. Living among the frontier Indians, as was his occasional habit, was Samuel Houston who had abandoned the governorship of Tennessee because of blighted love. His grief assuaged, he appeared, picturesque and mysterious, in Washington, an intimate of his old patron President Jackson. What they talked of no man knows, but it is hard to believe that, when Jackson appointed him commissioner to certain Indian tribes on the Texas border, the desirability of a strong man in a region of approaching storm was overlooked.

The storm broke in 1833, but the Texan revolt happening to coincide with one of the habitual Mexican revolutions, the two were united by the astute Mexican leader Santa Anna, and Texas remained Mexican. The lull was but temporary. In 1835 a new Mexican revolution left Texas as the sole region supporting the old Mexican constitution. The strain upon loyalty was too great. Texas seceded and in March, 1836, declared her independence.[1] Promptly Santa Anna sought to reduce the revolting territory. The new Texan government at once offered extensive land grants to volunteers who would come from the United States, and at the same time asked for annexation. Patriotism and free land, adventure and revenge, opportunity for distinction, and even religious hostility, all combined to fire American enthusiasm. From New England west and southward the answer came. Its intensity, however, was in marked

[1] J. H. Smith, *The Annexation of Texas* (N. Y., 1911).

relationship to propinquity. New England sent subscriptions, not large; Cincinnati sent a battery; Kentucky, men. A Georgia editor apologized to his readers
for the meagerness of his paper by stating that all his
staff had left for Texas; a planter of Mississippi gave his
fortune.

The government, officially neutral, could not have prevented the organization of these forces had it wished;
and it probably did not wish to. When Houston, commander of the Texan forces, won at San Jacinto a sensational victory over Santa Anna, whom he captured,
the event was applauded as a national victory. Annexation by the United States was now to have been expected; nor after a decent interval could it have been
considered objectionable since the population and institutions of Texas were American.

Two things, however, stood in the way. The first
was, or was represented by, John Quincy Adams. His
brilliant talent, his experience and his enormous capacity
for work, which had until 1830 been devoted to advancing the international interests of the United States, were
becoming concentrated upon the cause of antislavery.
In a devastating speech, lasting one hour a day for a
month, he created the terrifying bogie of a slavocracy or
Slave Power, sleepless and malevolent, which was to become one of the forces rallying the North to the antislavery banner in the fifties, and which, exploited by
Von Holst, dominated the accepted view of American
history for many years.[1] With a wealth of information
and an oversubtle synthesis of facts, actually related only
by unconscious tendencies, he made the whole movement
into Texas a conspiracy to create new slave states in the
Union. His speech made a deep and lasting impression
on the public mind—in the North, a growing fear of

[1] W. H. Seward, *Life and Public Services of John Quincy Adams*
(Auburn, N. Y., 1851), 272-292.

Southern power and motives; in the South, a hatred such as is felt by one who, unjustly attacked, forgets all his real sins; and among all the moderate-minded, an alarm at the disruptive power of the slavery issue.

Had the Texans still remained in danger from Mexico, it is improbable that the movement in their favor would have been stayed. As it was, the disruptive qualities of the question cooled the enthusiasm of those politically minded and gave unusual strength to the small class, strongest in New England but existing also throughout the seaboard South, who were habitually opposed to expansion. The consequence was that the question played no part in the campaign of 1840 and that, as has been seen, the leaders of both political parties agreed to keep it out of the campaign of 1844.

This deadlock was the first created by the conflict of the two leading tendencies of the period, the love of the Union and the belief in Manifest Destiny. It was broken by the force of two arguments. First was the appeal to the patriotic spirit based on the claim that, should America prove recreant to her Destiny, other nations would step in and reap the harvest.[1] Second was the fact that Destiny began to point northwestward and to offer the North compensation for the strength Texas would give the South.

A succession of treaties had left on the Pacific Coast a region between the parallels of 42° and 54° 40' which was open to the joint occupation of the United States and Great Britain. When Jackson became president, the actual enjoyment of the territory was with the British Hudson's Bay Company, whose factor Dr. John McLoughlin maintained such order as existed. After 1835, as has already been pointed out, a missionary movement introduced an American element. The

[1] E. D. Adams, *British Interests in Texas* (Balt., 1910) ; same author, "English Interests in California," *Am. Hist. Rev.*, XIV, 744-763.

reports of these missionaries and of members of Congress such as Lewis F. Linn and Thomas Hart Benton, both of Missouri, aroused the popular imagination both as to the desirability of Oregon and the necessity of forestalling Great Britain.

In 1842 President Tyler sent an agent to the district to treat with the Indians. As he passed through the Northwest many prospective settlers joined him. In 1843 a widespread popular movement brought a thousand people with two hundred wagons from Missouri, Arkansas, Tennessee and Illinois to Westport, Missouri, with the intention of crossing the plains and reaching Oregon.[1] With the ready adaptation of Americans they organized into two bands with chosen leaders. In rude order, sleeping in camps fortified by a circle of their wagons, slowly, with toil and suffering but not without the pleasure of intercourse, new sights and adventure, they pushed northwest. Previously wagons had been abandoned at the mountains, but Dr. Marcus Whitman, who had been over the route, now found passage for them. Early in September the van of the column reached Walla Walla. Planting and building began simultaneously, and in the next year, unwilling to accept the rule of Dr. McLoughlin, the settlers organized a provisional government. New recruits continued to arrive by the route now broken, the Oregon Trail, which continued to be trodden into convenience until railroads arrived.

The exponents of Manifest Destiny took advantage of this situation and captured the Democratic party for expansion. They hoped to avoid the bitterness of the slavery conflict by joining Oregon with Texas, and to reassure the conservative by basing their program on

[1] Robert Greenhow, *The History of Oregon and California* (Boston, 1845), chap. xvii; Joseph Schafer, *The Pacific Northwest* (N. Y., 1905), chaps. xi-xiii; J. C. Bell, jr., *Opening a Gateway to the Pacific* (Columbia Univ., *Studies*, XCVI).

what were represented as historic rights: the "re-annexation of Texas and the re-occupation of Oregon." They presented as their candidate in 1844 James K. Polk of Tennessee, whose slight reputation made it appropriate to give added emphasis to this platform. The Whigs followed their preconceived plans, and chose Clay who endeavored to minimize the issue of expansion. Nevertheless, Manifest Destiny dominated the campaign, and the election of Polk was properly interpreted by President Tyler as a verdict in its favor. By securing the consent of Congress to the admission of Texas to the circle of the states, the outgoing president was able to give some traces of a sunset glory to the expiring months of his administration.[1]

Not only did the new president, Polk, believe in Manifest Destiny but he believed it was the finger of God that pointed it out. With but moderate intellectual powers, he had an unbending purpose and an iron will. He determined not merely to complete the Democratic platform but to realize the popular conception of our future by securing California and the land between that province and Texas. The means by which he pushed this purpose belong more particularly to political history. By the spring of 1846 he had come to a compromise agreement with Great Britain in regard to a boundary for the Oregon country and had brought on a war with Mexico.[2]

In the eyes of most American citizens it was Manifest Destiny which thus brought this generation into a war —to be fought, for the most part, by members of the coming generation. Little as the nation was organized for national effort, it nevertheless did somewhat better, even considering the disparity of the opposing forces,

[1] J. S. Reeves, *American Diplomacy under Tyler and Polk* (Balt., 1907), chaps. v-vii; G. L. Rives, *The United States and Mexico, 1821 to 1848* (N. Y., 1913), I, chaps. xx, xxiii-xxiv.

[2] E. I. McCormac, *James K. Polk* (Berkeley, 1922), chaps. xvii-xxi.

than in the War of 1812. This seems to have been due
not so much to a general ability to pull together in an
emergency as to the fact that this war was among the
things that could be accomplished by a partial effort,
and that, in the confusion of simultaneous tendencies
which was characteristic of its life, there really were tendencies toward efficiency and order. The country was
fortunate in the possession, in General Winfield Scott,
of a veteran of the War of 1812 who was a man of no
mean abilities and great experience. General Zachary
Taylor, another veteran of 1812, was an ideal leader of
small, hard-fighting expeditions. About them were
many of the ablest young men of the country, like
Grant, Davis, Lee, McClellan and Joseph E. Johnston,
who had been drawn to West Point. They had received
there an education, which, however defective it may
have been from the point of view of military science,
produced remarkable results in developing effective
leaders. These leaders, with a regular army increased
for the emergency to a total of thirty-one thousand men,
fought a brilliant and successful war.[1] When on September 14, 1847, an army under General Scott captured
Mexico City, the whole republic was in a state of de-
moralization; the United States had won a complete
victory.

Meantime, at home, there swirled about this efficient
undertaking a tumult of popular excitement. No American citizen, except in the army, was in danger; no
American vessel was incurring risks; no American territory saw the enemy's flag except captive. Even American trade with Mexico across the plains by the famous
Santa Fé trail was not entirely interrupted. There was,
therefore, no such distress as there had been in the Revolution and the War of 1812. Still less was opposition
counted treason. James Russell Lowell expressed a

[1] J. H. Smith, *The War with Mexico* (2 vols., N. Y., 1919).

fairly widespread pacifist idea in one of the *Biglow Papers:*[1]

> Ez fer war, I call it murder,—
> There you hev it plain an' flat;
> I don't want to go no furder
> Than my Testyment fer that.

Nor did he hesitate to write:

> Thet air flag's a leetle rotten,
> Hope it aint your Sunday's best.

With a humor rare among the reformers, he ridiculed the arguments of oratorical patriotism:

> The side of our country must ollers be took,
>   An' Presidunt Polk, you know, *he* is our country.
> An' the angel thet writes all our sins in a book
>   Puts the *debit* to him, an' to us the *per contry.*

He did not hesitate to discourage enlistments.

> Parson Wilbur sez *he* never heerd in his life
>   Thet th' Apostles rigged out in their swaller-tail coats,
> An' marched round in front of a drum an' a fife,
>   To git some on 'em office, an' some on 'em votes:
>   But John P.
>   Robinson he
> Sez they didn't know everythin' down in Judee.

While the reformers raged, the responsible opposition, the leaders of the Whig party, played their part with skill. They avoided the absolute hostility of the Loyalists of the Revolution, the attempt to dictate ultimatums to the government which had killed the Federalist party in the War of 1812, and even the lack of coöperation which the extreme wing of the Democrats showed sub-

---

[1] J. R. Lowell, *Writings* (Boston, 1890), VIII, 45-46, 67-68.

sequently in the Civil War. They voted supplies and supported the conduct of the war. They "pointed with pride" to the fact that it was being conducted by the Whig General Scott and the whiggish General Taylor. This they did with some loss of the extremists, the "Conscience Whigs," of their own party. On the other hand, they attacked the war as unnecessary and demoralizing. By what was known as the "Spot Resolution," some of them sought to bring home to the people the fact that the place where President Polk declared in his war message:[1] "Mexico has passed the boundary of the United States, has invaded our territory and shed American blood upon American soil," was actually soil which we had as late as 1845 acknowledged to be in dispute.

The administration, meantime, was endeavoring to organize the war upon the usual American basis; a temporary army of volunteers was to furnish the bulk of the invading army. Enthusiasm for service was hardly greater than it had been in 1836 in the case of the Texan Revolution; as at that time, it grew in effectiveness and spontaneity as one went West and South. In Ohio opinion was such that some felt that a war record would be of later political advantage, but others believed equally firmly that failure to respond to the call would be of an advantage. In the South enthusiasm was genuine, and enlistment went forward with all the usual warmth of popular support customary in a national war.

The Democrats naturally regretted that the conduct of the war was in the hands of generals of the opposing faith. An attempt was made to obviate this by creating anew the office of lieutenant general, with the idea of appointing thereto Thomas H. Benton. This

[1] J. D. Richardson, *Messages and Papers of the Presidents* (Wash., 1896-1908), IV, 442.

scheme failed, and on the whole the volunteer army played small part in the war, less than in any other. The organization of the volunteers was left most largely to the states, and the men chose their own line officers.[1] The initiative was frequently taken by those who hoped to be officers. General Lew Wallace in Indianapolis hung out a transparency: "For Mexico; fall in." In three days he had a company. Fourteen regiments were offered in Illinois, which was to provide only four. In Tennessee thirty thousand volunteered. Along the Gulf the question was raised of how many could safely leave for the battlefield in view of the presence of the Negro population.

No provision was made for officer training, no instructions were given with regard to health, and discipline was dependent largely upon the personal character of the officers. Of the volunteers about fifty-nine thousand actually served. As contrasted with the regulars, three of the latter in each hundred died in battle or of wounds, while only one in a hundred of the volunteers was so lost. Disease and such causes, on the other hand, took eight in one hundred of the regulars, and twelve in one hundred of the volunteers.[2] The latter's lack of discipline was particularly obvious in the invasion of a foreign country, and one to whose religion the invaders were opposed. It was with difficulty that brutality was suppressed.

While the war lasted, its excitement and spirit grew. It nationalized the zest for adventure which up to this time had been individual. A faction developed on the opposite wing from the Lowell type of reformers, who saw the nation engaged in a great national adventure and believed that the hour for the complete realization

[1] Smith, *War with Mexico*, I, 537-538; II, 74-76.
[2] Smith, *War with Mexico*, II, 318-319, 511-512; L. P. Ayres, *War with Germany* (Wash., 1919), 124.

of our Manifest Destiny had struck. Most vocal of this faction was Senator E. A. Hannegan of Indiana. The dominant "Hard" faction of the New York Democracy adopted resolutions for the annexation of all Mexico. "Shall we occupy it?" they asked. "Shall we now run with manly vigor the race that is set before us? Or shall we yield to the suggestions of a sickly fanaticism, or sink into an enervating slumber? . . . We feel no emotion but pity for those whose philanthropy, or patriotism, or religion, have led them to believe that they can prescribe a better course of duty than that of the God who made us all." Nor was the sentiment confined to Democratic organs; an antislavery paper, the *National Era*, favored the absorption of Mexico state by state. From England George Bancroft reported that the prevailing sentiment favored United States control of Mexico in the interests of civilization.[1]

Polk kept steady amid this maelstrom of conflicting forces. With the expedition against central Mexico he had sent Nicholas P. Trist, chief clerk of the state department, an eccentric well-meaning Virginian, connected with many of the reformer group. Trist became involved in a conflict of stronger personalities and was recalled. Ignoring this summons, he remained and negotiated at Guadalupe-Hidalgo a treaty signed on February 2, 1848, which deviated from his instructions, among other things, in failing to secure for the United States the peninsula of Lower California. Polk, however, concluded to submit it to the Senate, probably because of the fear that a delay might prevent the accomplishment of his great task within the set limits of his own administration.

Despite his firm stand against the absorption of all Mexico, he countenanced other schemes which reflected

[1] M. A. DeW. Howe, *Life and Letters of George Bancroft* (N. Y., 1908), II, 5-28.

the popular zest for expansion.   The secretary of state, James Buchanan, was authorized to offer Spain a price for Cuba.   This government action, which was met by a prompt refusal, was immediately followed up by a vigorous campaign of denunciation of Spanish tyranny which fired many generous hearts and some ambitious minds with the dream of freeing that island so long regarded as a proper pendant to our territory.   In April, 1848, Polk submitted to Congress a request of the Mexican state of Yucatan for aid against the Indians, which was coupled with an offer to accept annexation and a statement that similar requests had been sent to Great Britain and France.   Polk made no direct recommendation but favored aid, and quoted Monroe's message of 1823 to the effect that we should consider any attempt of a European power to extend the European "system to any portion of this hemisphere as dangerous to our peace and safety." [1]   It is not without significance that Polk's secretary of war, William L. Marcy, when a few years later he became secretary of state, concluded a treaty of annexation with the Kingdom of Hawaii, the first of such attempts.

The government was but just ahead of the emigrant. Thousands now went each year over the long trail to Oregon.   The trader anticipated the migrant, and booths offered refreshment at intervals on its long expanse.   On January 10, 1848, James W. Marshall discovered placer gold in the San Joaquin Valley of California.   By autumn of that year four thousand Mexicans had reached the San Francisco Bay region.   On the slow wings of sailing vessels the news was brought to the East.   On September 16 it was first mentioned by the New York press.   Soon it was confirmed and spread by telegraph throughout the settled portions of the country.   President Polk in his December message gave

[1] Richardson, *Messages and Papers*, IV, 582.

CARAVAN OF EMIGRANTS FOR CALIFORNIA.
(Crossing the Great American Desert in Nebraska.)

INDIAN ALARM ON THE CIMARRON RIVER.

The Covered Wagon.

the story official sanction. Youth took fire. In the West, whether north or south, and in fairly uniform proportion, young men of a neighborhood met, talked, organized and started across the continent, using the trails of which they had read in the popular tales of frontier adventurers and official explorers.[1] Many went with little forethought and scant equipment, but even for those who prepared themselves best the expense was necessarily limited by the lack of transportation facilities. In caravans and troops they worked up the Platte through the "Great American Desert," now the fertile plains of Nebraska, and then into the mountains and across the arid wastes, of whose sparse water they found little and where many halted, some to return and some to die. About July of 1849 they began to debouch into the Sacramento Valley.

Already there had arrived thousands from the coast districts who, having sufficient money to pay their fare, embarked in the vessels of the Pacific Mail Steamship Company, which had just been established. The necessity of linking the newly added Pacific Coast to the rest of the United States had been felt even before gold was discovered, and Congress had in 1847 authorized a mail contract, amounting to a subsidy, to be bid for by those interested. In April, 1848, the Pacific Mail was incorporated with the purpose of making use of the route across the Isthmus of Panama, and opportunity was thus ready for some of those seeking California, soon known by the classic title of Argonauts. On February 28, 1849, the *California* with the first shipload of such passengers arrived in San Francisco.

This regular provision was far from adequate for the thousands seeking California. On February 25, 1849, William H. Seward wrote to his wife from New York:

[1] O. T. Howe, *Argonauts of 1849* (Cambridge, Mass., 1923) ; Edward Channing, *History of the United States* (N. Y., 1905-), VI, 40-52.

"Thus far on my way to Washington, I find myself floating on a strongly-increasing tide of people, who hinder, annoy, and embarrass each other. The world seems almost divided into two classes, both of which are moving in the same direction; those who are going to California in search of gold, and those going to Washington in quest of office. How many adventurers are preparing themselves for disappointment, revenge, and misanthropy." [1]

In seacoast towns young men banded themselves together, formed gold-mining companies, chartered ships, and started forth on the long voyage about Cape Horn or through the Straits of Magellan. In Massachusetts alone there is record of one hundred and twenty-four such companies. Sixty-five vessels are reported to have made the voyage from that state in 1849, the quickest taking one hundred and forty-three days, the longest voyage lasting two hundred and sixty-seven. The *Leonore* was the first to reach San Francisco, on July 5, 1849.

California drew the adventurous from all the world. In the summer of 1849 several hundred vessels, of many nations, were in San Francisco Bay, many abandoned by crews who had sought the gold fields. By the middle of January, 1849, five California mining companies had been organized in London with an aggregate capital of £1,275,000. The islands of the Pacific began at once to send their quota, and the Chinese were roused to action. H. H. Bancroft, whose means of information give credibility to his conjectures, estimates that by the end of 1849 the total number of arrivals was nearly one hundred thousand. On the basis of records, he finds thirty-nine thousand arriving by sea, including twenty-three thousand Americans. By land he counts fifty-two thousand, including nine thousand from Mexico,

[1] F. W. Seward, *Seward at Washington* (N. Y., 1891), I, 100.

eight thousand of the newcomers from the southern, New Mexico route, and twenty-five thousand by the more usual South Pass and Humboldt River trail. This was a movement of population larger than the war had drawn out. Like the volunteers and unlike the Mormons, the majority were in intention adventurers rather than migrants. They planned to return home, and, with their nuggets, realize dreams of place and purpose. The charm of California and the absence of a rival civilization firmly established as in Mexico caused large numbers to change their minds and to make their settlement final.[1]

Except in the case of Texas, the authorities at Washington had kept ahead of the frontier advance in extinguishing the title of foreign governments. No one could doubt that it would compel a lagging government to hasten. In 1830 men felt fairly certain that the course of empire lay westward between limits fixed by climate and soil. In the glare of the later forties few felt so certain of its direction; and its speed, far excelling that predicted for it by Jefferson, seemed almost to justify the millenarian conception.

The outward rush of Americanism did not escape the attention of the world. In December, 1848, Eugene Guillemot, the representative of the new French Republic to Uruguay, reported home: "Two opposed elements contend at present in all South America, the local element and the European . . . around the first group all the tendencies, stationary and retrograde. . . . Around the other colonization, expansion, in all good senses, agricultural, industrial, and commercial. But let the local element prevail, and a new element, influence and perhaps control, the Anglo-American, will not be

[1] R. G. Cleland, *History of California: the American Period* (N. Y., 1922), chaps. vii-ix, xv-xviii; Cardinal Goodwin, *The Establishment of State Government in California* (N. Y., 1914), chaps. ii, xvii-xix; Bayard Taylor, *Eldorado* (N. Y., 1850), chaps. xxviii, xxix-xxx.

long in appearing in the midst of the social torpor if not anarchy, and will produce a complete and without doubt violent renovation, and more or less our exclusion as well as that of Europe." He advised that "A fruitful germ of our nation ought to be deposited among them, and if some day the Anglo-Americans pretend to pass over Panama and descend toward Cape Horn, it is well that they find at least on the route a people of our race, not less hardy than theirs, which may serve to head the column of the others." [1]

[1] Eugene Guillemot, *Affaires de la Plata* (Paris, 1849), 6-7.

CHAPTER XIV

THE END OF AN ERA

EIGHTEEN hundred and forty-eight indeed opened as a wonder year for this generation. Not only was the Manifest Destiny of the United States being fulfilled with regard to its territorial heritage but also in respect to its spiritual. Throughout the spring every returning liner brought from Europe news of the approaching triumphs of what were considered American ideas.[1] The "system" of Metternich against which the Monroe Doctrine had been directly launched was toppling to a fall. In Hungary Louis Kossuth, a little later to become for a moment the most popular man in America, led the way. In France the kingdom fell; in the German states constitutions arose; in England the Chartist movement seemed on the point of establishing equality. At Rome the new Pope Pius IX exhibited sympathy for this liberal movement.

As was usually the case in the event of such revolutionary movements in Europe, the first reaction in the United States was one of pleasure touched with pride at what was considered an appreciation of that example which so many Americans from the days of Winthrop had believed we were presenting to the world.[2] It was only later, when the news of the methods so often

[1] James Buchanan, *Works* (J. B. Moore, ed., Phila., 1908-1911), VIII, 32-46; George Ticknor, *Life and Letters* (G. S. Hilliard and others, eds., Boston, 1876), II, 230-242.
[2] E. N. Curtis, "American Opinion of the French Nineteenth-Century Revolutions," *Am. Hist. Rev.*, XXIX, 249-270; J. G. Gazley, *American Opinion of German Unification, 1848-1871* (Columbia Univ., *Studies,* CXII), 17-49, 233-274, 453-460.

employed by the revolutionists began to cloud the first message, that the reaction began which invariably divided the more conservative from the more ardent, usually along the traditional party lines. At this time the Democrats clung to the advocacy of the new movements, the Whigs became skeptical. The Democratic convention meeting at Baltimore in May congratulated the people of France, and resolved "that with the recent development of this grand political truth,—of the sovereignty of the people and their capacity and power for self-government, which is prostrating thrones and erecting republics on the ruins of despotism in the Old World,—we feel that a high and sacred duty is devolved, with increasing responsibility, upon the Democratic party of this country . . ., to sustain and advance among us constitutional liberty, . . . and uphold the Union as it was, the Union as it is, and the Union as it shall be. . . ." [1]

The high elation which these European uprisings excited in America was quickly tempered by a grave questioning as to the durability of the system that was being held up for foreign imitation. On August 8, 1846, President Polk had sent a special message to Congress requesting a vote of money "for the adjustment of a boundary with Mexico." A bill to appropriate two million dollars was promptly introduced into the House. When it was brought forward, David Wilmot, a young Democrat from Pennsylvania, proposed as an amendment a proviso "that neither slavery nor involuntary servitude shall ever exist in any part of said territory, except for crime, whereof the party shall first be duly convicted." [2]

[1] Edward Stanwood, *A History of the Presidency* (Boston, 1898), 235.
[2] C. B. Going, *David Wilmot, Free Soiler* (N. Y., 1924), chaps. ix, xi-xiv, xvii.

This Wilmot Proviso may be said to mark the point where the happy progress of this generation, up till then proceeding with undisciplined force, with splendid altruism and abundance of comic relief, turns into tragedy. The generation had attempted to free itself of politics by trying to minimize the functions of government. Two of its main interests, reform and expansion, had gradually become political; and now they had clashed, irrevocably as it proved, bitterly and dangerously as all thinking people at once realized.

The immediate effect was to check the movement for expansion. Conservatives in both North and South united to oppose all thought of additions of territory which produced so violent an internal reaction. The force was taken out of the popular demand for Cuba. In 1852 the Democratic party considered, but rejected, the idea of another campaign for expansion, based on another alliterative slogan, "Cuba or Canada." Even in domestic affairs the line of demarcation between the organized states of Arkansas, Missouri and Iowa and the unorganized Indian territory to the West was firmly held against the increasingly restless frontiersmen, whose cause was being championed by the rising young Stephen A. Douglas of Illinois.

Though checked, the spirit of Manifest Destiny smoldered and occasionally flared. The adventurous continued to fare forth within and without the accepted boundaries of the United States. To land hunger, patriotism and excitement were in fact added the zeal for sectional advantage. As opportunity now lay to the south, such adventures originated mostly in the slave states, and then and for many decades later, the expansionist movement was believed by many who should have known better to have been a Southern extravagance.[1] Not so, thought the optimistic Seward, who never lost his vision of a United States of the Americas, confident that time and reason would cause slavery to be abolished as the flag progressed.[2] To such genuine expansionists were added numbers who believed that a campaign of external glory would, in the end, do much to unite the country. Powerful among them was James Buchanan, Polk's secretary of state, later to be president.[3] To the verge of the Civil War he sought to quiet the conflagration at home by pointing the Stars and Stripes toward external dominion. To the majority, however, expansion seemed most calculated of all things to fan the flames at home and they preferred peace to more adventure in Manifest Destiny. That such Destiny had been in fact practically accomplished, few realized.

If reform had dealt a staggering blow to adventure, it was by no means certain that adventure had not equally brought reform to a standstill, at least in so far as it affected slavery. Both the antislavery movement in the North and the proslavery movement of the South experienced a distinct shock. That this shock was less than that on expansion was due to the fact that the latter movement had clearly brought into the country vast regions, adding about fifty per cent to the national territory where the status of slavery was as yet unsettled. Minds set to work upon solutions.

Probably a majority expected an extension of the line of 1820.[4] Northern extremists embraced the concep-

[3] Robert Toombs, Alexander H. Stephens and Howell Cobb, Correspondence (U. B. Phillips, ed., Am. Hist. Assoc., Rep. for 1911, II), 80-218; C. S. Boucher, "In Re That Aggressive Slavocracy," Miss. Valley Hist. Rev., VIII, 13-79; Buchanan, Works, VIII, 381-392; Horace Greeley, The Life and Public Services of Henry Clay (Auburn, N. Y., 1854), 283-292.

[2] W. H. Seward, Works (G. E. Baker, ed., Boston, 1853-1884), III, 605-618.

[3] Buchanan, Works, VIII, 90-101.

[4] E. I. McCormac, James K. Polk (Berkeley, 1922), 612-655.

tion of the Wilmot Proviso, excluding slavery from all
new territory;[1] Abraham Lincoln, member of Congress
from 1847 to 1849, said later that he voted for it forty-
seven times.   Calhoun countered for the Southern extremists by claiming that the Constitution protected
slavery in all United States territory.[2] Lewis Cass, to
remove the question from the halls of Congress, endorsed the proposal that the settlers in the territories
answer the question for themselves.[3]

To have organized the campaign of 1848 on the issue
would have been to dissolve the existing national parties.   The party leaders, therefore, exerted their best
efforts to eliminate it from politics.   In so doing they
were inspired not merely by desire for party cohesion
but also by the firm belief that the sectionalization of
the parties would be followed by division of the Union.
This attempt to remove the sectional question from
public debate no longer had the success it had secured a
decade before because there was now a fundamental question that must be settled.   The South felt fairly safe.
After a bitter factional fight among the Democrats in
New York, the "Hard" group, favorable to expansion
and to the South, had won, and that party seemed unlikely to attempt legislation unfriendly to slavery; the
Whigs selected a candidate, Zachary Taylor, whose inheritance and interests made appreciation of the Southern
position probable.   It was, therefore, the extreme wing
in the North which was most dissatisfied.   The reformers met in convention at Buffalo, and with them joined
the New York "Soft" Democratic supporters of Van
Buren, who resented his rejection by the party in 1844

---

[1] A. B. Hart, *Salmon P. Chase* (J. T. Morse, jr., ed., *American
Statesmen*, Boston, 1899), chaps. iv-v.

[2] W. M. Meigs, *The Life of John C. Calhoun* (N. Y., 1917), II,
394-437.

[3] A. C. McLaughlin, *Lewis Cass* (J. T. Morse, jr., ed., *American
Statesmen*, Boston, 1891), chap. viii.

and the introduction of the issue of expansion, which they believed was the source of all our troubles. Combined, they chose Van Buren as candidate for president, and the young Charles Francis Adams for the vice-presidency. They declared in favor of the principles of the Wilmot Proviso and for other cognate policies.[1]

The result of the election showed that this "Free Soil" element throughout the North held the balance between the two major parties. The membership of the new party having been drawn from both the old parties, it was in a good position to bargain, and consequently was able to win a number of senators, as Salmon P. Chase of Ohio and John P. Hale of New Hampshire. This result, while more evident, was not more significant than that in the South. There the vote showed that Taylor, as a Southern man, was more trusted than Cass, winning a popular majority and eight states out of fourteen, where in the preceding campaign the Whigs had been in the popular minority and won only six states to six. In elections to Congress, however, they were less successful. Taylor was elected but without a majority in Congress.

In a position thus poised between principle and policy, chance was free to play an unusual part. First came the sudden Minerva-like birth of California, a child of the Union as a whole. Its population of nearly a hundred thousand males sought immediate statehood, and, drawn in fairly even proportions from all parts of the country, the majority of them voted for a free constitution. To admit her thus would destroy in practice the Compromise line of 1820, and would immediately unsettle the balance between free and slave states, the importance of which had just been illustrated. In the second place came the unexpected development that

---

[1] T. C. Smith, *The Liberty and Free Soil Parties in the Northwest* (*Harvard Hist. Studies*, VI), chap. iii.

the new president found his chief advisers in Thurlow Weed, who had been responsible for his nomination, and William H. Seward, newly elected senator from New York and the leading antislavery man of high political importance. Under their guidance the president favored not only the immediate admission of California but the organization of all the disputed territory into states, which at this stage of their existence meant with free constitutions.[1]

Thus, suddenly and unexpectedly, the South was confronted for the first time by an unfriendly administration. Its cohesion was for the moment accomplished. Everywhere was protest, mingled with threats of separation. The state of Mississippi, as a result of deliberations on the part of the more extreme leaders, called a convention to meet at Nashville to consider Southern interests. Its date was finally fixed to follow the impending session of Congress; and its purpose, in the minds of some, was to review the situation in which the session would leave the South, in the minds of others, to serve as a sword of Damocles to hang over that session and induce favorable action to the South.[2]

Congress came together in more gloom than any which had as yet assembled. The brilliant optimism with which this generation had begun life was to be found now only in the younger leaders whose careers really belong to the next period. It is easy to dismiss such a change and contrast as an effect of age, but to do so is to lose the essential facts. Most of the younger leaders were surcharged with enthusiasm for some cause which they had, in their several communities, seen rising—Chase, the opposition to human slavery; Jefferson

[1] J. F. Rhodes, A History of the United States from the Compromise of 1850 (N. Y., 1884-1913), I, chap. ii.
[2] P. M. Hamer, The Secession Movement in South Carolina, 1847-1852 (Allentown, Pa., 1918); M. J. White, The Secession Movement in the United States, 1847-1852 (New Orleans, 1918).

Davis, the cohesion of Southern sentiment; [1] Douglas, the prosperity of the frontier. The older leaders had conceived a more comprehensive vision. To them the Union was the center of all things, a union growing larger and better, to serve as an example to other nations of the inevitable success of our institutions. This perfect fabric of a great free democratic nation, so nearly realized in many respects, seemed now in danger of being rent in twain by a division, not unforeseen, but which it was thought had been provided against. Seasoned and refined by the most adventurous political life in American history, Henry Clay came to Washington to repair the damage, neither optimistic nor pessimistic, but like a good workman ready to try anew where his previous efforts had failed of success. With finesse and labor he compiled a plan, later embodied in an "Omnibus" bill, in which he sought to reach a solution fair to all parties.[2]

This compromise became at once the center of the greatest debate of the generation. The spirit in which the problem was regarded by the men of the thirties and forties is revealed in the attitude of Webster. Upon Webster hung the sole possibility of success. With a physical and mental vitality too vigorous to admit of permanent pessimism, he had developed, as a result of the increasing reliance upon him of strong men, a sense of responsibility equally phenomenal. He held to the full the aristocratic view of leadership and believed that upon him, his wisdom and his health depended the fate of the nation—a view which he shared with many others. That with this weight upon him he was moved by personal ambition unassociated with the opportunity

[1] Jefferson Davis, *His Letters, Papers, and Speeches* (Dunbar Rowland, ed., Jackson, Miss., 1923), I-II, *passim;* N. W. Stephenson, "A Theory of Jefferson Davis," *Am. Hist. Rev.,* XXI, 73-90.

[2] Carl Schurz, *Henry Clay* (J. T. Morse, jr., ed., *American Statesmen,* Boston, 1887), II, chap. xxvi.

of performing the greatest national service, as Whittier alleged in his poem *Ichabod,* is inconceivable. His correspondence reveals that he took care to investigate the state of the Southern mind and came deliberately to the opinion that failure to soothe the South would result in secession.

Webster had first appeared in national politics as the champion of his section. His greatest speech had been a defense of New England against the attacks of his senatorial colleagues from the West and South. This speech against Hayne, however, marks a turning point in his interests. What is remembered about it is not his eulogy of his section but his insistence on union. He had come to the primary loyalty of Clay and Jackson. He passed, moving in the opposite direction, Calhoun who was changing from national to sectional loyalty. The year 1850 found Calhoun facing the dissolution of the Union to save his section, Webster ready to make sectional sacrifices to save the Union.

On March 7, 1850, in the most heralded speech ever made in America, Webster declared in favor of Clay's proposals, and the compromise was given a chance of life.[1] In a close balance, luck, skill and the atmosphere of the time combined to turn the tide. Early in July President Taylor died, to be succeeded by the vice-president, Millard Fillmore, a pupil of the elder statesmen, who appointed Webster secretary of state and threw the support of the administration to moderation. Clay, perceiving that his "Omnibus" bill would fail by combining the extremists of both sides against it, divided it into its several sections, each one of which commanded the united support of the section it favored and that of the compromisers of the other sections. As the months passed, moreover, the blazing splendor to which the

[1] H. D. Foster, "Webster's Seventh of March Speech, and the Secession Movement, 1850," *Am. Hist. Rev.,* XXVII, 245-270.

material progress of the last two decades had risen proved a conservative and mollifying influence. The Compromise finally passed, the Nashville convention proved harmless, and the supporters of compromise were, for the most part, endorsed by the people, who hoped that once more a way had been found to preserve their unity for the task of continued development and for the enjoyment of the very considerable results they had achieved.

The Compromise of 1850 may reasonably be taken as the end of an era. History, of course, does not lend itself to division and all attempts are arbitrary; convenience, however, demands it, and from the point of view of presentation there is the justification that it renders possible a certain emphasis on forces which rise to dominance and fade. Eighteen hundred and fifty is least satisfactory from the material point of view, for the new economic forces continued with acceleration until 1857, when they encountered a debacle from which recovery was slow. The reform movements continue beyond 1850 with no conspicuous change until the organization of the Republican party, in 1854, when they merged for a time with general politics. The striking change of 1850 is in the controlling leadership. A few years before and after mark the passing of the group of men who emerged into national politics with the War of 1812, who assumed control in 1829, and who kept their grip on national affairs until they died. Jackson died in 1846, Calhoun in 1850, Clay and Webster in 1852. In the small span of life left the last two after the Compromise, all thought of their earlier constructive program had vanished and all their efforts were directed to maintaining their last work.

Their last work was in no sense the culmination to which they had looked forward. Certainly the brash young men who had taken it on themselves to run the nation in 1830 did not expect that the final work required of them would be the sacrifice of their ideals. It may be held, indeed, that in accepting this necessity they showed spiritual growth, but their sacrifice lacked the inspiring quality of finality. It is arguable that the Compromise saved the Union, but certainly not in the sense in which they conceived it.

There died, then, with its political leaders something of that geniality and universality that had characterized the optimism of this generation in its youth. There remained among the reformer element a sufficiency of *élan*, confidence in still obtaining their hopes in their own day, but more bitterness and hysteria. The conservatives gave over their struggle for a program and pessimistically tried to decide which was the lesser of two evils. They gave little evidence even of the catastrophic philosophy of Hamilton and George Cabot, that by hastening evils to run their full course they would promote the return of sanity. After 1850 one seems to be in a nation held together in part at least by reticence and restraint instead of by the free and trusting belief of 1830 that all good could be simultaneously pushed to rapid accomplishment.

CHAPTER XV

THE BALANCE SHEET

IN contrasting the picture of the United States at the beginning and at the end of the thirties and forties it is important to differentiate between the changes which had been made and those which were in process. The greatest change of all was the increase of diversity. It had not been an age of striking originality or of complete realization; it was—and this was inherent in its philosophy and its politics—an age of experimentation. Ideas which had long been formulated were taken into the laboratory and workshop and put into usable form. Not many of them were put into general use but they were made ready for use.

In brief comparison with the analysis of conditions in 1830 it may be said that no substantial change had been made in ideals. There had been some hammering into practical shape, some rise of skepticism; but no new elements had seriously entered into American thought. Population had increased from 12,866,020 to 23,191,876.[1] The material inheritance now passed on represented a substantial accumulation The majority of the people were better housed and had more domestic conveniences; roads of all kinds had remarkably

---

[1] Between 1830 and 1850 the population of the Atlantic seaboard increased from 8,633,632 to 12,729,859; that of the Mississippi Valley and Gulf from 4,232,388 to 10,344,746. The trans-Missouri region to the Rocky Mountains remained Indian country. J. D. De Bow, comp., *Statistical View of the United States . . . Compendium . . . Seventh Census* (Wash., 1854), 41.

improved;[1] manufacturing equipment incomparably advanced and extended; luxuries had been turned into necessities; public institutions multiplied.[2] With the exception of some use of water and steam power, this had been accomplished by concentration on work and by labor-saving devices rather than by exploitation of natural resources, which remained as vast and now even more obvious than in 1830.

With regard to social inheritance the case was different. It had been one of the purposes of the generation to break the aristocracy which had been so powerful in its youth and which so contrived to influence its taste. In this it had to a considerable extent succeeded. At least, the aristocracy was driven from power, except in the South, and its alliance with the rising moneyed class had not created a new body able to set standards of conduct. The provincial middle-class cultures had proved more stubborn; many of their props, however, had been torn from them. The Dutch, "Pennsylvania Dutch" and Quakers had distinctly lost ground. New England was expanding its influence, but was suffering dilution. The creation of a general American culture was lagging though it was in process of formation. Its mandates were felt by those who violated its sensibilities, but it was as yet impossible to define its code or to separate the essential from the trivial in its habits.

In the matter of getting an education the change was one of the greatest in our history, and yet its effect may easily be exaggerated. The new thing was the evolution of a system. As, however, this began to develop only in the late thirties it had not been sufficiently carried into effect to have greatly influenced the education of

[1] A graphic history of the improvements in transportation is given in J. L. Ringwalt, *Development of the Transportation System in the United States* (Phila., 1888), 73-91, 103-106, 115-119.
[2] In 1850 there were in the entire country 38,183 churches with property valued at $87,983,028. *Compendium, . . . Seventh Census,* 133.

those who were to receive the torch when this generation passed it on.   Indeed, owing to the large influx of foreigners, the percentage of adult white persons who could not read and write increased from 3.77 to 5.03 in the two decades from 1830 to 1850.[1]   Spasmodically, in certain districts, the rising generation were more ready with the pen and in handling books than their parents, but one could not yet predicate of the average American that he would know certain things, as was later to be the case.   In higher education the change was not one of system but of development.   Here and there young Americans were receiving in college an inspiration that twenty years earlier they had to bring to college with them.   The foundation of small colleges had, too, run ahead of the increase of population, and a larger proportion of the people were receiving a college education. New ideas and methods of higher education, however, were still a whole generation away.   Of an importance perhaps more immediate than any of these things was the spread of the means of adult education through all the new paraphernalia of publicity, which was making it increasingly difficult for the average citizen to escape some knowledge of things that the earnest had previously labored to secure.[2]

In the matter of making a living two striking changes had taken place.   In agriculture a new era was beginning with the introduction of machinery.   This, however, was of the things which as yet affected but a small proportion of the population.   The important fact was that the chaotic agriculture of the West had taken form, or, rather, two forms.   The frontier which had united to elect Andrew Jackson was in the process of division into the Northwest and Southwest, which were soon to

[1] *Compendium   .   .   .   Seventh Census*, 153.

[2] The annual circulation of newspapers alone increased from an average, in 1828, of about six to the individual to about twenty-two to the individual in 1850.   *Compendium   .   .   .   Seventh Census*, 158.

fight each other, and the Ohio Valley, which this fight was to rend. Of all the forces making for this division none was more powerful than that of agricultural institutions. Into the Southwest had entered the plantation system of industrialized cultivation based on slavery, not indeed everywhere dominant in practice but universally dominant as an aim and hope. In the Northwest the scattered frontier farms had developed according to the model set by the Northeast: small farms cultivated by the owners with a minimum of hired help, each forming part of a community centering in a village. In the whole West there was, however, a common difference from the parent institutions of the East in that the aim was less to be self-sustaining and more to produce a selling crop. This meant that transportation was of fundamental importance. The South was a little better served by its river system, but this was not satisfactory. By 1850 the idea of canals had been dropped and all were looking with confidence to the railroads.

The other change in means of livelihood was that a continuously increasing number of Americans were relying upon wages, and that the community was accepting the idea of a permanent wage-earning class. Pick-and-shovel jobs were everywhere laying the material foundations of a new kind of civilization. Wage-earners increased also in the rapidly expanding business of internal transportation, and particularly in the developing factory system, which was not only steadily diminishing the dependence of Americans upon imports but, within the United States, displacing the hand-made goods that had supplied most of the needs of 1830. Craftsmen were disappearing, but from the best among them was arising a class of skilled mechanics, who continued to exhibit standards of fine workmanship as well as an aptitude for invention.

Industry was obviously producing so much more

wealth than had heretofore existed that there was comparatively little dissatisfaction.   Several tendencies did, however, deserve attention.   For one thing American prosperity was becoming more involved with that of Europe.   As a crude index of this, it may be noted that American imports were valued at $70,876,920 in 1830, and at $178,138,318 twenty years later.   In the same period the export trade of the United States grew in value from $73,849,508 to $151,898,720.[1]   The increased consumption of American-grown cotton and the new demand for American-grown food products were the key to the rising high wages and profits.   Again, the distribution of wealth was becoming more unequal. There was no decline in the general minimum, although, owing to causes social rather than economic, slums were becoming a problem in the large cities.   The fortunes of the rich, however, were beyond anything previously dreamed of in America.

In the third place, this new wealth was beginning to exercise a control in the free states which the old aristocracy had not possessed.[2]   The attack on banking had displaced the old aristocracy only to substitute another, a moneyed class.   In the Northeast the relative desirability of well-located city land had created for certain families, such as the Astors, fortunes which aroused the emulation of speculators in the West.   The development of the transportation system, chiefly by private corporations, gave small groups of directors a hold upon the fortunes of communities which had previously been unknown in this country.   Most important of all, the factory system, as yet practically unchecked by legislation or by the organization of labor, made a few the arbiters of destiny for the many.

[1] *Compendium* . . . *Seventh Census,* 184.
[2] Gustavus Myers, *History of the Great American Fortunes* (Chicago, 1910), esp. II, *passim.*

Among specific achievements, probably the greatest was the realization of Manifest Destiny in the rounding out of the territory of the United States. To the 1,787,159 square miles held in 1830 had been added 1,194,007.[1] With very slight exceptions the area over which the American people have chosen, or been able, to expand their civilization was in 1850 under the American flag. Little as this was accepted in 1850 as final, it corresponds in the main with the original ideas of the generation.

Next in importance, among material things, was the actual occupation of the Mississippi Valley and the establishment of far flung posts in Oregon, Texas, Utah and California. By 1850 the people had run their first plow over the colossal region that Jefferson had thought would occupy them for a thousand generations, had advanced beyond it, and were actually being held back from certain portions by the law rather than by lack of vitality for the work.

An accomplishment of a different kind was the completion of the railroad system, which had reached a point where it could, and soon would, be spun like a web over the vast expanse of the nation. In 1830 the steam railroad could hardly be said to exist; by 1850 it had attained a mileage of more than nine thousand.[2] If after 1850 no improvements had been made, the railroad would nevertheless be one of the greatest factors in the life of today. The same may be said of its handmaid, the telegraph. Less progress, however, was made in the case of the other great utilities. Agricultural machinery was well started, but did not yet constitute

[1] In 1850 about one half of the national area was organized into states. Of the state area, a total of 851,508 square miles was slaveholding, and 612,597 free soil with slavery forbidden or in course of extinction.

[2] The mileage of railroads in use increased from 32 in 1830 to 9021 in 1850. U. S. Bureau of Census, *Statistical Abstract* (Wash., 1921), 376.

a system. The sewing machine was invented, but still needed to be applied to leather. The ocean-going steamship reached a high point of usefulness, but was rather a gift to America than a native production. In fact, the lavishness of American productivity at this time is evinced by the fact that, at the very period when steam was beginning to rule the ocean, our shipwrights were sending out the most superb wind-driven craft the world has ever seen, the Baltimore clippers.[1]

Already in 1850 the railroad, the telegraph and the ocean steamship were affecting the life of practically every American home. Just over the line, in 1851, letter postage was made three cents for three thousand miles instead of five cents for three hundred miles. Whatever may be its effect, it is at least a change to have news promptly, and news of Paris could reach New Orleans in less than half the time possible in 1830, and did so more regularly.[2] Owing to the general economic situation of the day these new instruments reduced the prices of things dealers bought, and increased them for things they sold.

Without notable change in methods of construction the population was nevertheless better housed than twenty years before. In the Northwest but few years elapsed before the original log cabin became a corncrib, pigpen or kitchen and a first real house arose. While, therefore, there was no marked change in the character of the American house, fewer Americans were living in temporary structures.

Inside the house the amount of furniture had considerably increased, but its character had already begun to deteriorate with the employment of factory-made

[1] A. H. Clark, *The Clipper Ship Era* (N. Y., 1911), chaps. iv, ix.

[2] J. B. McMaster, *A History of the People of the United States* (N. Y., 1884-1927), VIII, 106-120; Otis Clapp, "The Post-Office as It Has Been, Is, and Should Be; as a Means of Modern Civilization," *Hunt's Merchants' Mag.*, XXXV (1856), 680-697.

products. There was some increase in gayety; more floors were covered with carpets instead of rag rugs; more rooms were decorated with wallpaper, which began to blossom into wilder colors; while lithographs and process-produced chromos spotted the wall spaces. Lighting had generally improved. While gas was rare and poor, lamps were common, and there was more effort to light rooms instead of to light merely one's work or book. While lamps did little to diminish the labor of the housewife, matches almost universally removed one long-standing source of ill-temper.

The most important change in living conditions, however, was to be found almost solely in cities, and that was the running of water out of faucets from city mains and the draining of sewage into central systems. From these already began, for the more well-to-do, the blessings of indoor toilets and baths. Indeed, the effect of such changes was more widespread than one might suppose. One could hardly imagine in 1830 what happened in 1851, when two students of the pioneer Lawrence College at Appleton, Wisconsin, rigged up a shower bath of perforated tin through which they doused each other with water ice-cold from frozen pails. One certainly reads also of more enjoyment of open-air bathing, not only on the beaches of the East but in the forest streams and lakes of the West, and one gathers that Americans began to be somewhat cleaner than heretofore.

In the whole matter of food and clothes changes were rather in the nature of fashions than of methods. Food indeed changed little except for the gradual increase of coffee drinking. This new habit may have been the result of South American independence or of the temperance movement, or perhaps merely the discovery of an agreeable aroma. Stoves, however, were better and more common. Dress became less distinguishing as to class, though it still marked city or country origin. The women of the cities followed with increasing nervous pleasure the changes of fashion, the standards shifting during the period from London to Paris.[1] Not yet were the originals chosen in the foreign capital by their wearers. Dressmakers constructed the first examples from models and plates and, with a skill of eye and finger which seems to have been universal among American women, they were cheapened and multiplied until American city crowds were already among the most uniformly and fashionably dressed in the world. For men and women all this was still the result of the hard-driven needle of housewife, dressmaker or tailor. Such clothes were more substantial than those of today and intended for longer wear. It is only in comparison with 1830 that the changes were quicker, and the most noticeable thing is the democratic spread of fashion over a larger portion of the population.

Americans were somewhat more gregarious in habit than they had been, which was obviously due, in large part, to the improvement in the means of transportation. There is evidence also that a larger number of them had some leisure time and energy. In both cases instinct was still controlled by past conditions and habits. Except for the small group of city rich, they were apt to spend their leisure on production, such as fancywork, rather than on cards or sport, and to assemble for some useful and convenient purpose. On the frontier a house-raising was still a social event. Increasingly the church social gave the odor of sanctity, and the convenience of a necessary meal, to pleasant gatherings. Idling was still unpopular and was possible only to those who could set others to work for them.

[1] See, for example, Meade Minnigerode, *The Fabulous Forties* (N. Y., 1924), chap. ix; Eliza Ripley, *Social Life in Old New Orleans* (N. Y., 1912), chap. viii; and any of the women's fashion magazines during these years.

Fashions for 1844.

Smart gentlemen of the period not only learned the Polka, but began to grow beards.

The art and science of the period had as yet little effect on the life of the community. They were generally respected in the abstract, but appreciation and support for them came almost entirely from the discredited aristocracy which thus found a new field for the activity previously given to politics. In music there was some improvement in the popular taste, but this was confined for the most part to such forms as hymns and songs suited to parlor use, in which many could take part. The literature produced by the generation, if inferior to that of England or France, was certainly far superior to anything produced in America before; and the foundations were laid for something of choice and lasting value.

Foreign travel for pleasure, on a considerable scale, began about the middle of the forties. Perhaps the founding of the Collins Line in 1847 with a subsidy from the United States government may be taken as the beginning.[1] Foreigners in America were a much more common sight in 1840 than in 1830, and at the very end of the period they became a factor and a problem. While they were soon to create one of those violent reactions of nativism which have from time to time occurred in the United States, there seems in this generation little foundation on which to build an expectation of such a movement. Violent feeling against them was confined to a few large cities. On the whole the attitude toward them seems to have been condescending and kindly.

In few periods of American history did conscious borrowing of European ideas, as in the case of education and communistic experiments, excite so little hostility. The temporary and fading superiority of the material civilization of Europe and the fact that in political mat-

[1] W. L. Marvin, *The American Merchant Marine* (N. Y., 1902), chap. xii.

ters that continent would ultimately sit at the feet of the American Gamaliel were accepted by the majority as axioms. Equally axiomatic was the belief that for the United States to assume what garb of Europe it wished and for Europe to digest the American political system would both be easy tasks.

While laying the foundations for the industrial America that was to come, this generation showed that it had not lost that genius for constructive political practice which had characterized their ancestors. Far less versed in political thought than their forebears and less able to concentrate on such problems, they nevertheless effected, in the convention system, a compromise between pure democracy and representative government, which must be considered as among the real contributions to the forms of government, and which, while it became later clogged in some of its main manifestations, still operates with an efficiency so smooth that it is seldom recognized.

Equally important, though not so new, was the evolution of the business corporation in such a form as to secure capital from one district to spend in another under a central control. In fact, no decision of the generation was probably so important as that limitation of the functions of government which forced the development of this machinery. In 1850 the corporation stood almost as complete as the railroad system, ready to assume the gigantic tasks the next two generations would thrust upon it.

With less evidence of result, this generation was attempting to solve the problems, always joined in the American mind, of a circulating medium and of a banking system. On the surface its accomplishments were destructive. Taking advantage of the federal system of an Independent Treasury, however, men of affairs in the states were trying out ideas and conducting experiments.

As practical ideas there were worked out the licensing and inspection of banking institutions, the clearing-house method of quickly detecting a lack of solvency, and the plan of a paper currency resting upon publicly controlled funds. It was on these foundations that a satisfactory national system was ultimately constructed in the sixties.

Perhaps more amazing than these contributions to material life and to organization was what the generation did to its character—the traits which it acquired and passed on to its descendants. It is not necessary to assume that human nature changed; it was rather that blindness in certain directions was rendered longer impossible. At any rate one becomes conscious of a certain general humaneness to a degree not previously observable. In part this was, like the progress of invention, a world movement. It had, however, certain characteristics distinctively American. The most remarkable demonstration was to be given when the Civil War came on and was fought in an atmosphere of thoughtfulness which had been unknown in all previous wars.

Kindred to this was the ability which large numbers of the generation showed to change their own habits. Particularly, the adoption of total abstinence was a striking illustration of a power of self-control, which would not have been expected by the casual observer, but which the student must have predicted for a generation which reduced government to a skeleton and yet ran to construction rather than to anarchy.

Among the conscious purposes of the generation was the preservation and strengthening of the Union. In the development of its material program and of new organizations, it was spinning a web which seemed to render separation more and more difficult and was actually to prove the foundation of a much closer national life. It must be remembered, however, that closer contacts and intimacies may mean fiercer disagreement instead of harmony. Increasing communication might in time smooth away some of the provincial differences, but was more apt immediately to intensify them. It would certainly be long before it could blend the rival material interests of the physiographic sections into a whole conscious of the mutual dependence of their several prosperities. It was certainly these more disastrous immediate results of the more closely knit life of the nation that became more obvious as the decades waned.

More striking was the change in the larger sectionalism based on a combination of elements material and immaterial. In 1830 the outstanding sectionalism of the country was that between the East and the West, the old and the new, the parent section and the colony, whose divergencies were at the root of so many of the problems of party politics and the main issues of political campaigns. The development of the period decidedly lessened these antagonisms, which indeed the American colonial system and the Jeffersonian code of politics tended to reduce to a minimum. By 1850 the Mississippi Valley was ceasing to be frontier, and was settling into a consciousness of its more permanent interests based on its nature and the characteristics of its population.

Meantime a new sectionalism, of which much slighter evidences had previously existed, was coming to the forefront of politics and of American life with such momentous steps that as many of the patriotic were endeavoring to be deaf to its advance as were racking their brains for a way to stop it. This was, of course, that of the North and South, with the issue of slavery as the chief, though not the only, irritant. Still held apart by a middle region of doubt and of mediation, the extremes were approaching each other with hostile mien, and the Mason and Dixon line was becoming a division between two purposes apparently more permanent, and infinitely more bitterly opposed, than had been the East and West in 1830.

When one considers the tendencies working through this period and its genuine accomplishments, one must rise from its study with a feeling very different from that of the travelers who hastily observed a cross section of all these slightly bound and so greatly different movements, or from that of the reader of the newspaper who read each day what was sensational and picturesque. Never was the surface of American life so chaotic; seldom has a nation been more absurd, and the absurdity was part of the reality. One could walk up Broadway and visit Barnum's Museum, and that was America. One could, if one had permission, visit the machine shops of the Stevens family across the river, and that was America. One could spend a day at Concord and talk philosophy with Emerson and visit Agassiz's laboratory on the way, and that was America. One could drink a mint julep with Robert Toombs of Georgia and damn New England, or 'midst the splashing of ink, hear from Garrison a logical demonstration that the difference between the slaveholding Bishop Polk of Louisiana and the inmates of the penitentiary at Auburn was all in favor of the latter; and both were evidences of America. Of course, such contrasts may be found at all times and places; but in this period their existence denoted the lack of a common standard by which to evaluate these differences. They were equal contemporaries in a life that recognized all as equal—whatever they might think of each other.

The generation of the thirties and forties did not evaluate, it destroyed taste: it produced, and let time value its products. It saw the acme of a particular development of individualism which had for some time been gaining ground and from which there was to be a rapid change to a more rigid system of community control. It presents one of the outstanding instances in history of the working of individuals trammeled by a minimum of law and convention. Its accomplishments were almost unprecedentedly the work of individuals, for leaders had little to enforce their leadership; they were the result of the independent work of more individuals than had ever before been free to work by and for themselves, at what they chose, and how they pleased.

CHAPTER XVI

CRITICAL ESSAY ON AUTHORITIES

PHYSICAL SURVIVALS

THE nonliterary sources of the period exist in abundance, but for the most part in attics and other places inaccessible to the public. In the older portions of the country architectural development can be easily traced owing to the general practice of dating public buildings, business blocks and sometimes even private dwellings. Since this period of American history possessed no special gift of design or construction and has, as yet, acquired small halo of antiquity, its buildings are being rapidly destroyed. Specimens of the houses of the period may be found through the guidance of Howard Major, *The Domestic Architecture of the Early American Republic: the Greek Revival* (Phila., 1926). Of distinguished structures the Croton Aqueduct across the Harlem River (J. B. Jervis, chief engineer), perhaps the greatest work of the time, is threatened, while Trinity Church in New York City (Richard Upjohn, architect) is apt to be preserved. The reproduction of such material in engravings and lithographs, while superior both in abundance and quality to that for any preceding period, has not been collected or arranged. Though the first daguerreotype taken in America was of a building, it was not until after the period that the photograph was generally used for such purposes. The illustrated periodical was born in the period, but did not outgrow its infancy.

Furniture and costumes, being more perishable and equally undeserving, have fared even worse. Such "parlor magazines" as *Godey's Lady's Book* and *Peterson's Magazine* are an important visual aid. While their illustrations show the mode of life of but a small section of the population, yet

339

there was probably no other country where so large a proportion aimed to be fashionable. In most matters respecting the common life of the time, important pictorial source material can be found in R. H. Gabriel, ed., *The Pageant of America* (15 vols., of which seven have appeared, New Haven, 1926-   ).

The best general museum collection is that of the United States National Museum, under direction of the Smithsonian Institution at Washington. Of very great value to the social historian, also, is the Essex Institute at Salem, Massachusetts, containing collections of daguerreotypes, silhouettes, household utensils, bonnets, shoes, dresses, toys and other articles illustrative of the period. The Peabody Museum in the same city has probably the finest collection of ship models, nautical instruments and portraits of Salem shipmasters of the period. Whaling days may be vividly recalled in the Old Dartmouth Historical Society Museum in New Bedford, Massachusetts. On invention the collection of the Patent Office at Washington will never be equaled. Destroyed by fire in the thirties, the commissioners of the forties with commendable energy restored it in form not quite so complete but with better models. Similar material is held by other institutions and by certain railroad companies. The locks and other works along the canals of Pennsylvania, Virginia and Ohio exhibit the state of engineering in the thirties. The collection on transportation, now being amassed at Dearborn, Michigan, by Henry Ford, bids fair to surpass all others in comprehensiveness and extent. Agricultural apparatus is preserved in the museum of the Bucks County Historical Society at Doylestown, Pennsylvania. A union catalogue of the machinery lists in the principal historical society collections and other museums is greatly to be desired. At Harvard, Massachusetts, the old farmhouse of Fruitlands, Bronson Alcott's colony, has been restored and is open to the public.

Coins are naturally less important than for less documented times, but, with paper currency and all kinds of financial tokens issued under all sorts of auspices, they would form a valuable fund of illustration of the chaotic finance of the times. There can never be a complete *corpus*. but all important museums, such as that of the Numismatic Society in New York, collect, and many private collections will in time add to their richness. Postage stamps, again, came into use through many agencies in the forties, being first issued semiofficially by the postmasters of the large cities. Collections reasonably complete are fairly common.

Art divides itself into two classes. Of these the products of fancywork have not been organized. A good collection is that of the Sawyer Museum of Oshkosh, Wisconsin. Of painting, and in a less degree of sculpture, illustrations are to be found in all important galleries. The best collections for purposes of appreciation and study are those of the Metropolitan Art Museum of New York and the Corcoran Art Gallery at Washington. The Massachusetts, New York and other historical societies have collections containing examples of most of the leading portrait painters and many others which illustrate the prevalence of portrait painting as a handicraft before the introduction of machine-made likenesses. The Hudson River School is represented in most large galleries.

PUBLIC DOCUMENTS

Official documentary sources are voluminous, but widely scattered and of uneven quality. Among federal documents, the statutes form an important source, but, owing to the dearth of national legislation, are of less value than for any other period. As this was an age of oratory, the reports of public addresses are of greater significance than at any other time since Cicero. Although the reports were not so accurate as at present, they were more so than Johnson's debates of Parliament. A correlation of the *Register of Debates* and the *Congressional Globe* for that portion of the thirties where they overlap would be desirable. The reports of departments and of committees vary widely in quality. The most perfect are those emanating from the federal courts and from the United States Patent Office. The reports of the secretary of the treasury are valuable for finance and also for the development of state banking. The decennial census reports are of first importance despite the fact that the material available was not well developed in publication. For example, the best of the census reports for the period, that of 1850, is excellent for agriculture but very defective for manufacturing. Notwithstanding the abundance of the materials in print, the amount as yet unpublished is very great and of decided, though not sensational, value. Its character is described in C. H. Van Tyne and W. G. Leland, comps., *Guide to the Archives of the Government of the United States in Washington* (Wash., 1907). Work at that capital is still necessary for the writing of monographs on many subjects.

The importance of state governments renders their documents even more essential than for later periods. Access to them is facilitated by R. R. Bowker, comp., *State Publications* (4 pts., New York, 1899-1908), and by Adelaide R. Hasse's successive indexes to *Economic Material in the Documents of the States* (Carnegie Inst., *Publs.*, no. 85, Washington, 1907-   , in progress). The state archives are described, more or less fully as they stood from ten to twenty years ago, in the successive reports of the Public Archives Commission of the American Historical Association, which are published in the *Annual Reports* of that body. All states have now been so covered, some with supplementary and correcting studies. Aside from the laws, the most important state documents are the *Journals* of the various constitutional conventions. The greatest *lacuna*, as compared with the documents of the national government, is in the almost total absence of records of debates, which have to be filled in from the public press and private correspondence. Reports of state executive officers vary greatly, the most complete being the messages of the governors. Here and there others of great importance are to be found, as those of Horace Mann as secretary of the Massachusetts board of education.

The records of local governments are still more chaotic. It is possible, however, to reconstruct the course of events in such large cities as Boston and New York from printed documents, and manuscript archives exist from which a history of many others could be worked out by students having local access to the materials. Great possibilities exist, for instance, in the records of the courts.

PERSONAL MATERIAL

A mass of autobiographic and reminiscent writing sheds much light on the social and intellectual conditions of the period. Among the more important of such works, and representative of this type of literature, are S. G. Goodrich, *Recollections of a Lifetime* (2 vols., N. Y., 1856) ; Lyman Beecher, *Autobiography* (Charles Beecher, ed., 2 vols., London, 1863-1865) ; Ben. Perley Poore, *Perley's Reminiscences of Sixty Years* (2 vols., Phila., 1886) ; Horace Greeley, *Recollections of a Busy Life* (N. Y., 1868) ; Josiah Quincy, *Figures of the Past* (Boston, 1883) ; Nathan Sargent, *Public Men and Events* (2 vols., Phila., 1875) ; John Trumbull, *Autobiography, Reminiscences and Letters* (N. Y., 1841) ; Reuben Davis, *Recollections of Mississippi and Mississippians* (Boston, 1891) ; Frederick Douglass, *Life and Times, Written by Himself* (Hartford, 1881) ; J. H. Fairchild, *Oberlin, the Colony and the College* (Oberlin, 1883) ; T. W. Higginson, *Cheerful Yesterdays* (Boston, 1898) ; S. J. May, *Memoir, Consisting of Autobiography and Selections from His Diary and Correspondence* (Boston, 1873) ; J. B. Gough, *Sunlight and Shadow* (Hartford, 1881) ; J. T. Fields, *Biographical Notes* (Boston, 1881) ; Samuel F. B. Morse, *Letters and Journals* (E. L. Morse, ed., 2 vols., Boston, 1914) ; G. S. Hilliard and others, eds., *Life, Letters, and Journals of George Ticknor* (2 vols., Boston, 1876) ; W. H. Milburn, *Rifle, Axe, and Saddle-Bags, Symbols of Western Character and Civilization* (N. Y., 1856) ; Peter Cartwright, *Autobiography* (N. Y., 1856) ; Philander Chase, *Reminiscences of Bishop Chase* (N. Y., 1844) ; John Hughes, *Complete Works* (Lawrence Kehoe, ed., 2 vols., N. Y., 1866) [Roman Catholic bishop of New York]. John Quincy Adams, *Memoirs, Comprising Portions of His Diary from 1785 to 1846* (C. F. Adams, ed., 12 vols., Phila., 1874-1877), stands in a class by itself. Emerson,

Bronson Alcott, Margaret Fuller and others of the Transcendentalist group are represented with extraordinary fullness. A satisfactory bibliography of their writings (and of works about them) may be found in W. P. Trent and others, eds., *The Cambridge History of American Literature* (4 vols., N. Y., 1917-1921), I, 546-566. *The Heart of Emerson's Journals* (Bliss Perry, ed., Boston, 1926) is a useful abridgment of an indispensable intellectual document of the times.

The letters, diaries and account books of secondary and of obscure individuals are gradually finding their way into print, which is particularly important in a period, such as this, when individual initiative played so important a part. Trinity College (now Duke University), the Historical Commission of North Carolina and the historical societies of Wisconsin and Minnesota have been particularly active in such publication, for the most part in their magazines. The amount of manuscript material of this description already gathered by these and other agencies and by the Library of Congress is colossal. Facilities for investigation by means of catalogues, inventories, calendars and photostatic reproduction are constantly increasing; but it is probable that travel will remain a necessity for the student of this period.

The biographical literature is extensive. Most of the major political figures of the time are included in J. T. Morse, jr., ed., *American Statesmen* (rev. edn., ser. 1, Boston, 1899), and E. P. Oberholtzer, ed., *The American Crisis Biographies* (Phila., 1904-1915 [?]). Excellent biographies of leaders in certain other fields of American life may be found in Carlos Martyn, ed., *American Reformers* (N. Y., 1890-1894 [?]); C. D. Warner, ed., *American Men of Letters* (Boston, 1881-1906 [?]); and Laurence Hutton, ed., *American Actor Series* (Boston, 1881-1882). In many cases, however, a better life of a particular man or woman can be found apart from any of the standard series. A selective list of such works, including the men of this period, is given in Edward Channing, A. B. Hart and F. J. Turner, *Guide to the Study and Reading of American History* (Boston, 1912), 102-121. Some other biographies

published since the appearance of the *Guide* are cited later
in this chapter.

GENERAL PERIODICALS

The magazine era, in the modern sense, had scarcely begun
by the end of the period; and those magazines that existed
contained a disproportionate amount of material reprinted
from European journals. The most generally useful are
Niles' Weekly Register (76 vols., Balt., 1811-1849); *Hunt's
Merchants' Magazine* (63 vols., N. Y., 1839-1870); *De
Bow's Commercial Review of the South and West* (39 vols.,
1846-1870); *North American Review* (Boston, 1815-
1877; N. Y., 1878-   ); the *Southern Literary Messenger*
(29 vols., Richmond, 1835-1859); and the *Democratic Review* (43 vols., N. Y., 1838-1859). The scope of the last
named was much greater than its name indicates. Though
general magazines were few, it needs to be remembered that
the religious press was at the height of its activity during
these years, and that through this vehicle most Americans
gained their knowledge of the world in which they lived. It
is also true that many other periodicals of a specialized kind
were published. Thus, as will be shown later, every reform
movement of importance maintained one or more organs,
whose altruistic appeal made it possible for them to attract
writers far beyond their financial capacities; and there also
began to be important at this time technical journals relating
to the various industries. The *American Almanac* (33 vols.,
1830-1862) is a mine of social and political information for
the student of American life. Children's magazines also
began to be widely published in this period.

More important than the magazines were the newspapers
which, for the first time, sought to make a special appeal to
the less literate sections of the population. Comment on this
body of material may be found in chapter vii of this work.
In general, the varied life of the day was less fully presented
than in present-day newspapers; but, on the other hand,
public opinion was perhaps better expressed. In order to

gain such a knowledge, however, it is necessary to survey the press with some completeness, for its merit consisted in the ease with which new journals were founded to represent each shifting plane of opinion. The critique of such material is rapidly assuming form. Lucy M. Salmon has treated such literature as a whole in *The Newspaper and the Historian* (N. Y., 1923). Of particular importance, in view of their respective places of publication, were the *National Intelligencer* (Washington, 1800-1870), *The Enquirer* (Richmond, 1804-   ), the *Evening Post* (N. Y., 1801-   ), the *New York Tribune* (1841-1924), and the *Courier-Journal* (Louisville, 1831-   ).

PROFESSIONAL AND TECHNICAL WRITINGS; BROADSIDES

Books published in the thirties and forties on professional and technical subjects have, for the most part, lost their original use, or have been so revised as to have lost their original appearance, as in the case of Webster's *Dictionaries*, Gray's botanies and the McGuffey *Readers*—whose evolution is traced in H. H. Vail, *A History of the McGuffey Readers* (Cleveland, 1911). But as a record of the state of knowledge both of the erudite and the masses, they remain of great value to the historian. The most important are the school textbooks and the medical works. The value of the former has begun to be appreciated in recent years, and special collections of them may be found at the American Antiquarian Society, the University of Wisconsin and Harvard University. Of music the best collections are that in the Library of Congress and the Lowell Mason collection in the Yale University library.

The pamphlets of the period are, in large part, reprints of articles and addresses which may be found in larger works. Therefore, pamphlet literature forms a less important source for the historian than in earlier times. On the other hand, broadsides assume a greater importance, and excellently reflect the spirit of the time. The best arranged collection of broadsides, if not the most complete, is that in the Library of Congress.

TRAVEL ACCOUNTS

A general estimate of the value of descriptive works on travel has been given in chapter vii of the text. The most complete list of British travel accounts is to be found in the appendix of Allan Nevins, ed., *American Social History as Recorded by British Travellers* (N. Y., 1923), a volume which reprints long excerpts from a number of the travelers of this period. The most complete general list for the period 1763-1846 is in the *Cambridge History of American Literature*, I, 468-490. The following narratives of travel are of unusual importance for the thirties and forties: M. Beyer and L. Koch, *Amerikanische Reisen* [1834] (2 vols., Leipzig, 1839); Michel Chevalier, *Lettres sur l'Amérique du Nord* [1833-1835] 2 vols., Paris, 1837); George Combe, *Notes on the United States* [1838-1840] (2 vols., Phila., 1841); George Lewis, *Impression of America and the American Churches* (Edinburgh, 1845); Francis Lieber, *The Stranger in America* (2 vols., London, 1835); Sir Charles Lyell, *Travels in North America* [1841-1842] (2 vols., London, 1845); Alexander Mackay, *The Western World* [1846-1847] (3 vols., London, 1849); Harriet Martineau, *Society in America* [1834-1836] (3 vols., London, 1838); Captain Marryat, *A Diary in America* [1837-1838] (3 vols., London, 1839); J. Salzbacher, *Meine Reise nach Nord-Amerika* [1842] (Wien, 1845)—reporting on the condition of the Roman Catholics; Frances M. Trollope, *Domestic Manners of the Americans* [1827-1831] (2 vols., London, 1832); Francis Wyse, *America, Its Realities and Resources* (3 vols., London, 1846); J. S. Buckingham, *The Eastern and Western States of America* (3 vols., London, 1842); same author, *The Slave States of America* (2 vols., London, 1842).

GENERAL SECONDARY WORKS

In the last year of the period was published the first work which may be classed as a systematic historical account of

American life in its many aspects. This is Emerson Davis, *The Half Century* (Boston, 1850), treating educational, scientific, religious, humanitarian and economic developments in the years after 1800. Of similar scope as to subject matter are *The First Century of the Republic: a Review of American Progress* (N. Y., 1876), a composite work written by T. D. Woolsey, F. A. P. Barnard, D. A. Wells and others, and N. S. Shaler, ed., *The United States of America* (2 vols., N. Y., 1894). These are all valuable for a large view of the social and intellectual life of the times.

The comprehensive histories should not be ignored notwithstanding the preoccupation of the authors with political and constitutional events. The first important general history covering the period, Hermann von Holst, *Constitutional and Political History of the United States* (J. J. Lalor, tr., 8 vols., Chicago, 1876-1892), II-III, contains a certain amount on the history of civilization, but, though scholarly in treatment, the whole is violently colored by an antislavery bias. The first volume of J. F. Rhodes, *History of the United States from the Compromise of 1850* (8 vols., N. Y., 1893-1919), contains an admirable study of the Compromise of 1850 and a well-balanced account of slavery conditions. Edward Channing, *A History of the United States* (6 vols. in progress, 1905-   ), V, is an original study embracing many of the elements of civilization. The greatest attention to social history, however, has been paid by J. B. McMaster, *History of the People of the United States* (9 vols., N. Y., 1883-1927), a work based largely upon newspapers, of which the sixth and seventh volumes bear upon the period. Albert Bushnell Hart, ed., *The American Nation: a History* (28 vols., N. Y., 1904-1918), treats of this period, largely from a political point of view, in volumes xv-xvii, written respectively by William MacDonald, Albert Bushnell Hart and G. P. Garrison. Allen Johnson, ed., *The Chronicles of America Series* (50 vols., New Haven, 1918-1921), deals with social and intellectual developments in the thirties and forties in the volumes by A. B. Hulbert (XXI), Constance L. Skinner (XXII), H. E. Bolton (XXIII), N. W. Stephenson (XXIV), S. E. White (XXV), Jesse

Macy (XXVIII), E. E. Slosson (XXXIII), Bliss Perry (XXXIV), S. P. Orth (XXXV), R. D. Paine (XXXVI), Holland Thompson (XXXVII) and John Moody (XXXVIII). J. T. Adams, *New England in the Republic, 1776-1850* (Boston, 1926), the last volume of a trilogy on New England history, devotes attention to intellectual and social forces.

INDUSTRY, FINANCE AND INVENTION

Of the numerous short manuals on American economic development that have appeared in recent years H. U. Faulkner, *American Economic History* (N. Y., 1924), is perhaps the best, and is reasonably full on the thirties and forties. Of greater use to the student of these years, however, are the earlier and more detailed works: C. L. Flint and others, *Eighty Years' Progress of the United States* (Hartford, 1866), and C. M. Depew, ed., *One Hundred Years of American Commerce* (2 vols., N. Y., 1895). These deal not only with manufacturing but also with business, transportation and agriculture.

The best study of manufacturing during the period is V. S. Clark, *History of Manufactures in the United States, 1607-1860* (Carnegie Inst., *Contribs. to Am. Econ. History,* Wash., 1916). Much information not easily obtainable elsewhere, however, is packed into J. L. Bishop, *A History of American Manufactures from 1608-1860* (3 vols., Phila., 1866), and A. S. Bolles, *Industrial History of the United States* (N. Y., 1878). R. M. Tryon, *Household Manufactures in the United States, 1640-1860* (Chicago, 1917), should also be consulted. Certain industries have received careful historical study, notably A. H. Cole, *The American Wool Manufacture* (2 vols., Cambridge, 1926); J. E. Defebaugh, *History of the Lumber Industry of America* (2 vols., Chicago 1906-1907); J. M. Swank, *History of the Manufacture of Iron in All Ages* (Phila., 1892). The records of business organizations have never received proper attention in America either from historians or librarians. For this period they have been used to some small extent for the preparation of histories of particular corporations that have recognized the advertising value of such enterprises, but they have not been published as documents. One may expect valuable contributions from the ever growing archives and manuscripts in the collection of the Business Historical Society deposited in the Harvard Business Library.

On banking and finance the most satisfactory book for the general student is D. R. Dewey, *Financial History of the United States* (5th edn., N. Y., 1922). Certain phases of the subject, of special importance to this period, have been given close study in R. C. H. Catterall, *The Second Bank of the United States* (Chicago, 1903); D. R. Dewey, *State Banking before the Civil War* (Wash., 1910); R. C. McGrane, *The Panic of 1837* (Chicago, 1924); and E. G. Bourne, *History of the Surplus Revenue of 1837* (N. Y., 1885). In F. W. Taussig, *Tariff History of the United States* (7th edn., N. Y., 1923), will be found excellent concise analyses of the tariff acts of the period.

Despite the increasing number of historical accounts of invention E. W. Byrn, *The Progress of Invention in the Nineteenth Century* (N. Y., 1900), remains one of the most satisfactory discussions for the period. George Iles, *Leading American Inventors* (N. Y., 1912), affords a biographical approach. Waldemar Kaempffert, ed., *A Popular History of American Invention* (2 vols., N. Y., 1924), is a composite work of uneven merit. For particular inventions the following should be consulted: M. F. Miller, *Evolution of Reaping Machines* (U. S. Experiment Station Office, *Bull.*, no. 103, Wash., 1902); S. F. B. Morse, *Modern Telegraphy* (Paris, 1867); Robert Hoe, *A Short History of the Printing Press and of the Improvements in Printing Machinery* (N. Y., 1902); Charles Goodyear, *Gum Elastic and Its Varieties* (N. Y., 1853); Joseph Torey and A. S. Manders, *The Rubber Industry* (International Rubber Congress, *Rep.*, 1911); J. V. Woodworth, *American Tool Making and Interchangeable Manufacturing* (N. Y., 1911); J. W. Roe, *English and American Tool Builders* (New Haven, 1916);

and R. H. Thurston, *The Messrs. Stevens, of Hoboken, as Engineers, Naval Architects and Philanthropists* (Phila., 1874).

TRANSPORTATION AND SHIPPING

Much information and a good bibliography on the subject of transportation can be found in C. E. MacGill, *History of Transportation in the United States before 1860* (Carnegie Inst., *Contribs. to Am. Econ. History*, Wash., 1917). Seymour Dunbar, *A History of Travel in America* (4 vols., Indianapolis, 1915), contains many rare prints. Probably the best outline of early railway development as a whole is still A. T. Hadley, *Railroad Transportation, Its History and Its Laws* (N. Y., 1885). Brief historical discussions are included in E. R. Johnson and T. W. Van Metre, *Principles of Railway Transportation* (N. Y., 1922), and Eliot Jones, *Principles of Railway Transportation* (N. Y., 1924). R. E. Riegel, *The Story of the Western Railroads* (N. Y., 1926), and U. B. Phillips, *Transportation in the Eastern Cotton Belt to 1860* (N. Y., 1913), treat special areas. C. F. Carter, *When Railroads Were New* (N. Y., 1909), is popular and interesting. A valuable work offering a comprehensive picture of railroad building and expansion prior to the Civil War is W. P. Smith, *The Book of the Great Railway Celebration of 1857* (N. Y., 1858). On particular railways the following are helpful: W. B. Wilson, *Pennsylvania Railroad Company* (2 vols., Phila., 1899); Milton Reizenstein, *The Baltimore and Ohio Railroad* (Johns Hopkins Univ., *Studies*, XV, 1897, pts. 7 and 8); E. H. Mott, *Between the Ocean and the Lakes: the Story of Erie* (N. Y., 1899); and W. K. Ackerman, *The Illinois Central Railroad* (Chicago, 1890). The closely related express business is studied in P. A. Stimson, *History of the Express Business* (N. Y., 1881). See also H. G. Tyrrell, *History of Bridge Engineering* (Chicago, 1911).

The original material on early railway history consists almost entirely of official reports, railroad and financial periodicals and state documents. The best collections may be found in the Bureau of Railway Economics in Washington, in the Harvard Business Library, in the Scudder Financial Library at Columbia University, and in the Wharton School of the University of Pennsylvania. The J. J. Hill collection at the University of Wisconsin is also important in this connection. Of railroad periodicals the most valuable is the *American Railroad Journal* (ser. 1, 1832-1871).

The standard history of American commerce is E. R. Johnson and others, *History of Domestic and Foreign Commerce of the United States* (Carnegie Inst., *Contribs. to Am. Econ. History*, 2 vols., Wash., 1915), which contains the most complete bibliography available on the subject. The various historical works on the merchant marine all pay particular attention to this period, notably W. W. Bates, *American Marine* (Boston, 1897); W. L. Marvin, *The American Merchant Marine* (N. Y., 1902); and J. R. Spears, *The Story of the American Merchant Marine* (N. Y., 1910). A. H. Clark, *The Clipper Ship Era, 1843-1869* (N. Y., 1911), and S. E. Morison, *Maritime History of Massachusetts, 1783-1860* (Boston, 1921), are valuable for their respective subjects. The general story of the canal era is told with many illustrations in A. F. Harlow, *Old Towpaths* (N. Y., 1926). Canal development in nearly every state has received separate study.

LABOR

The labor movement of the period is thoroughly discussed by Helen L. Sumner, E. B. Mittelman and Henry Hoagland in the first volume of J. R. Commons and Associates, *History of Labour in the United States* (2 vols., N. Y., 1918). More concise treatments may be found in Selig Perlman, *A History of Trade Unionism in the United States* (N. Y., 1922), and Mary R. Beard, *A Short History of the American Labor Movement* (N. Y., 1920). A specialized study is Norman Ware, *The Industrial Worker, 1840-1860* (Boston, 1924). Edith Abbott, *Women in Industry* (N. Y., 1910), contains much on the period. Sydney and Beatrice

Webb, *History of Trade Unionism* (London, 1911), chap. ii, affords an opportunity for comparison with the contemporaneous movement in England. Two books which throw light on the influence of labor in local politics in the thirties are A. B. Darling, *Political Changes in Massachusetts, 1824-1848* (New Haven, 1925), and D. R. Fox, *The Decline of Aristocracy in the Politics of New York* (Columbia Univ., *Studies*, LXXXVI, 1918).

The only published collections of source materials are J. R. Commons, ed., *A Documentary History of American Industrial Society* (10 vols., Cleveland, 1909-1911), IV-VIII, and Ethelbert Stewart, *Documentary History of Early Organizations of Printers* (U. S. Dept. Labor, *Bull.*, XI, Wash., 1905). Something over seventy-five labor papers in many parts of the country began publication during the period, most of them short-lived. The best collections of such periodicals are to be found at the University of Wisconsin and in the John Crerar Library in Chicago.

AGRICULTURE AND THE PUBLIC LANDS

The main primary and secondary authorities for an understanding of these subjects are listed in the following manuals: W. J. Trimble, *Introductory Manual for the Study and Reading of Agrarian History* (Fargo, 1917); F. J. Turner and Frederick Merk, *List of References on the History of the West* (rev. ed., Cambridge, 1922); and L. B. Schmidt, *Topical Studies and References on the Economic History of American Agriculture* (rev. ed., Phila., 1923). Useful historical summaries of agricultural progress are often included in government publications, such as D. J. Browne, "Progress of Agriculture," Commissioner of Patents, *Annual Report, Agriculture, 1857*, 1-50; B. P. Poore, "History of Agriculture in the United States," Commissioner of Agriculture, *Ann. Rep. for 1866*, 498-527; and G. K. Holmes, "Progress of Agriculture in the United States," U. S. Department of Agriculture, *Yearbook for 1899*, 307-334. A. H. Sanford, *The Story of Agriculture in the United States* (Boston,

1916), is a brief popular treatment. The best study for a section, containing valuable data on the thirties and forties, is P. W. Bidwell and J. I. Falconer, *A History of Agriculture in the Northern United States, 1620-1860* (Wash., 1925). The ablest account of the Southern farming system is found in U. B. Phillips, *American Negro Slavery* (N. Y., 1918). M. B. Hammond, *The Cotton Industry* (Am. Econ. Assoc., *Publs.*, new ser., I, 1897), continues to be distinctly valuable; and A. O. Craven, *Soil Exhaustion as a Factor in the Agricultural History of Virginia and Maryland, 1606-1860* (Univ. of Ill., *Studies*, XIII, no. 1, 1925), throws much light upon general farming conditions.

The rapid expansion of agriculture led to the establishment of a number of farm journals, the files of which form a rich mine of information. Of first importance are the *American Agriculturist* (1842-   ), the *Prairie Farmer* (1840-   ), and *The Cultivator* (Albany, 1834-   ). On the general subject see G. M. Tucker, *American Agricultural Periodicals, an Historical Sketch* (Albany, 1909). Significant source records pertaining to Southern agriculture are printed in U. B. Phillips, *The Plantation and Frontier* (*Documentary History of American Industrial Society*, I-II, Cleveland, 1910). The McCormick Agricultural Library in Chicago is engaged in amassing a great collection of manuscripts, pamphlets and reports relating to American agricultural history.

F. L. Paxson, *History of the American Frontier, 1763-1893* (Boston, 1924), is the standard work on that subject, and provides a good background for an understanding of the evolution of the public-land policy. The influence of sectional rivalries in shaping federal land legislation is studied in R. G. Wellington, *The Political and Sectional Influence of the Public Lands, 1828-1842* (Cambridge, 1914), and G. M. Stephenson, *The Political History of the Public Lands from 1840 to 1862* (Boston, 1917). The trend and scope of such legislation are subjected to careful analysis in B. H. Hibbard, *A History of Public Land Policies* (N. Y., 1924).

IMMIGRATION

The contemporaneous writings on immigration fall into four classes: guidebooks, of which Calvin Colton, *Manual for Emigrants to America* (London, 1832), is a good example; nativist propaganda, best illustrated perhaps by the often reprinted S. F. B. Morse, *Imminent Dangers to the Free Institutions of the United States through Foreign Immigration* (N. Y., 1835); official reports, such as the *Annual Reports* of the Commissioners of Emigration of New York from 1847 to 1860; and general accounts. Of the last named class the most important works are W. J. Bromwell, *History of Immigration into the United States, 1819-1855* (N. Y., 1856); Jesse Chickering, *Emigration into the United States* (Boston, 1848); and Louis Schade, *The Immigration into the United States of America* (Wash., 1856).

Many of the later treatises on immigration deal with developments in the thirties and forties, notably H. P. Fairchild, *Immigration* (rev. ed., N. Y., 1924), chap. iv; F. J. Warne, *The Tide of Immigration* (N. Y., 1916), chap. xii; S. P. Orth, *Our Foreigners* (*Chronicles of America Series*, XXXV), chaps. v-vii; and G. M. Stephenson, *A History of American Immigration* (Boston, 1926), chaps. x-xi. There is an extensive and growing literature, much of it untrustworthy, on the history of different racial stocks in the population. Some of the more scholarly works, of particular value for the period, are A. B. Faust, *The German Element in the United States* (2 vols., Boston, 1909); S. C. Johnson, *History of Emigration from the United Kingdom to North America* (N. Y., 1914); R. B. Anderson, *Norwegian Immigration to 1848* (Madison, 1895); G. T. Flom, *A History of Norwegian Immigration to the United States* (Iowa City, 1909); and Amandus Johnson, *The Swedes in America, 1638-1900* (Phila., 1914). The Know-Nothing movement as a whole is without an adequate history although many special studies of particular phases have been worked out. Among the more important of these are L. D. Scisco, *Political Nativism in New York State* (Columbia Univ., *Studies*, XIII, no. 2, 1901); L. F. Schmeckebier, *History of the Know Nothing Party in Maryland* (Johns Hopkins Univ., *Studies*, XVII, 1899); Joseph Schafer, "Know-Nothingism in Wisconsin," *Wis. Mag. of Hist.*, VII, 3-21; Carl Brand, "The Know Nothing Party in Indiana," *Ind. Mag. of Hist.*, XVIII, 47-81, 177-206, 266-306; G. M. Stephenson, "Nativism in the Forties and Fifties, with Special Reference to the Mississippi Valley," *Miss. Valley Hist. Rev.*, IX, 185-202; and A. C. Cole, "Nativism in the Lower Mississippi Valley," *Miss. Valley Hist. Assoc., Proceeds.*, VI, 258-272. An excellent "Select Bibliography" on immigration in American history may be found in Stephenson, *History of American Immigration* (already cited), pt. 4. Edith Abbott, ed., *Historical Aspects of the Immigration Problem* (Chicago, 1925), contains source documents of importance.

LITERATURE AND THOUGHT

The great work on the subject is *The Cambridge History of American Literature* (cited earlier under Personal Material), which envisages literature in a broad way, and includes essays by specialists on such subjects as book publishing, journalism, speech, religion, scholarship, historiography and philosophy. The wealth of bibliography contained in these volumes makes it unnecessary to go into the matter in any detail here. Hervey Allen, *Israfel, the Life and Times of Edgar Allan Poe* (N. Y., 1926), may stand as an example of how very useful a literary biography may be to the social historian. Several special studies of Southern literature give attention to this period, notably M. J. Moses, *The Literature of the South* (N. Y., 1910); Carl Holliday, *A History of Southern Literature* (N. Y., 1906); and W. M. Baskervill, *Southern Writers* (2 vols., Nashville, 1898-1903). J. D. Wade, *Augustus Baldwin Longstreet* (N. Y., 1924), sheds light upon intellectual conditions in the Lower South. R. L. Rusk, *The Literature of the Middle Western*

Frontier (2 vols., N. Y., 1926), which carries the story to 1840, has nearly a volume of bibliography as well. A similarly useful work for the period is Dorothy A. Dondore, *The Prairie and the Making of Middle America* (Cedar Rapids, 1926), which may serve as a reading guide as well as an exposition of the subject. The humorous writings of the thirties and forties are treated in Jeannette Tandy, *Crackerbox Philosophers in American Humor and Satire* (N. Y., 1925). The growth of the American-English tongue during the period can best be followed in G. P. Krapp, *The English Language in America* (2 vols., N. Y., 1925), and H. L. Mencken, *The American Language* (2d edn., N. Y., 1921). On philosophic tendencies O. B. Frothingham, *Transcendentalism in New England* (N. Y., 1876), and Woodbridge Riley, *American Thought* (N. Y., 1915), are valuable.

Algernon Tassin, *The Magazine in America* (N. Y., 1916), gives an inadequate account of the situation in this period. More studies are needed like A. H. Smyth, *The Philadelphia Magazines and Their Contributors, 1741-1850* (Phila., 1892), and B. B. Minor, *The Southern Literary Messenger, 1834-1864* (N. Y., 1905). E. L. Bradsher, *Mathew Carey, Editor, Author and Publisher* (N. Y., 1912), yields information as to the conditions surrounding book publishing, as does also Lea Brothers and Company, *One Hundred Years of Publishing, 1785-1885* (Phila., 1885), and J. H. Harper, *The House of Harper* (N. Y., 1912). C. C. Jewett, *Report on the Public Libraries of the United States* (Smithsonian Inst., *Rep. for 1849*), should be consulted on that subject. The new trend in journalism is best set forth in G. H. Payne, *History of Journalism in the United States* (N. Y., 1920), W. G. Bleyer, *Main Currents in the History of American Journalism* (Boston, 1927), and J. M. Lee, *History of American Journalism* (rev. edn., Boston, 1923), though much of value is still to be found in Frederic Hudson, *Journalism in the United States* (N. Y., 1873). The career of two important journals are traced in Allan Nevins, *The Evening Post* (N. Y., 1922), and F. M. O'Brien, *The Story of the Sun* (N. Y., 1918).

RELIGION

The source materials for a history of religion in this period are voluminous and of unknown extent. Students will wish to make preliminary use of W. H. Allison, comp., *Inventory of Unpublished Materials for American Religious History* (Wash., 1911); P. G. Mode, ed., *Source Book and Bibliographical Guide for American Church History* (Menasha, 1921); and S. M. Jackson, comp., "A Bibliography of American Church History, 1820-1893," *The American Church History Series* (13 vols., N. Y., 1893-1897), XII, 441-513. This series is a coöperative work and covers the history of the leading denominations and sects. The thirteenth volume, *A History of American Christianity* (N. Y., 1897) by L. W. Bacon, is the only attempt yet made to treat the whole subject synthetically and systematically. The title of H. K. Rowe, *The History of Religion in the United States* (N. Y., 1924), is misleading, though the work has its own value as a broad interpretation of outstanding phases of American religious development in terms of the social and economic background.

The religious press reached its period of greatest activity in the thirties and forties. Every denomination of any strength possessed a battery of such periodicals representing its different wings and activities. The proceedings and journals of most of the national church gatherings are also in print. In addition, a great many contemporary estimates and analyses of the general religious situation have come down to us. Among the more important are Robert Baird, *Progress and Prospects of Christianity in the United States* (London, 1851); Joseph Belcher, *Religious Denominations in the United States* (Phila., 1854); Henry Caswall, *America and the American Church* (London, 1839); P. O. Gorris, *The Churches and Sects of the United States* (N. Y., 1850); J. Lang, *Religion and Education in America* (London, 1848); Andrew Reed and James Mathewson, *Narrative of a Visit to the American Churches* (London, 1836); Philip

Schaff, *America* (N. Y., 1855); Edward Waylen, *Ecclesiastical Reminiscences of the United States* (N. Y., 1846); and Hermann Wimmer, *Die Kirche und Schule im Nord-Amerika* (Leipzig, 1853). The following official sources are indispensable for mission activities: American Home Missionary Society, *Reports* (1827-   ); American Board of Commissioners for Foreign Missions, *Annual Reports* (1810-   ); and *Home Missionary* (1828-   ).

The most satisfactory study of the Millerites is Clara E. Sears, *Days of Delusion* (Boston, 1924), based largely on the recollections of survivors. The literature on Mormonism is still largely colored by partisanship. The following works are among the best: E. H. Anderson, *Brief History of the Church of Jesus Christ of Latter Day Saints* (Salt Lake, 1902); F. J. Cannon, *Brigham Young and His Mormon Empire* (N. Y., 1913); W. E. La Rue, *The Foundations of Mormonism* (N. Y., 1919); and M. R. Werner, *Brigham Young* (N. Y., 1925). The last two volumes of J. G. Shea, *The Catholic Church in the United States* (4 vols., N. Y., 1886-1892), bear upon the rapid expansion of that church during the period. The impact of the slavery issue on religion is studied in J. N. Norwood, *The Schism in the Methodist Church, 1844* (Alfred Univ., *Studies*, I, 1923). On Unitarianism, J. W. Chadwick, *William Ellery Channing* (Boston, 1903), and G. W. Cooke, *Unitarianism in America* (Boston, 1902), should be consulted. Missionary activities may be traced in such works as J. O. Choules and Thomas Smith, *The Origin and History of Missions* (2 vols., Boston, 1837); Lewis Tappan, *History of the American Missionary Association* (N. Y., 1855); J. S. Dennis, *Centennial Survey of Foreign Missions* (N. Y., 1902); and W. E. Strong, *The Story of the American Board* (Boston, 1901).

HUMANITARIAN REFORM

As in the case of religious bodies, every reform organization of importance possessed one or more official or unofficial periodicals. From them may be gained a first-hand knowledge of their methods of propaganda and of their activities and accomplishments. Important for the antislavery movement are *The Liberator* (William Lloyd Garrison, ed., Boston, 1831-1865); *The Emancipator* (R. G. Williams, ed., N. Y. and Boston, 1834-1848); *The Philanthropist* (J. G. Birney and G. Bailey, eds., Cincinnati, 1836-1847); *The Genius of Universal Emancipation* (Benjamin Lundy, ed., various places, 1821-1838); *Herald of Freedom* (J. H. Kimball and others, eds., Concord, N. H., 1835-1846); and the *National Anti-Slavery Standard* (N. P. Rogers and others, eds., N. Y., 1840-1864). Temperance periodicals were even more numerous. During the latter half of the period there were never fewer than thirty weekly and monthly temperance journals in circulation; and the *Journal of the American Temperance Union*, founded in Philadelphia in 1837, was read all over the world. G. F. Clark, *History of the Temperance Reform in Massachusetts, 1813-1883* (Boston, 1888), 201-224, lists the temperance papers of that state. The chief organs of the peace movement were *The Harbinger of Peace* (later *The Calumet*, William Ladd, ed., 1828-1835) and the *American Advocate of Peace* (William Watson, first ed., 1834 to date, now *Advocate of Peace*).

ANTISLAVERY: The most complete bibliography of slavery and the slavery question continues to be W. E. B. Dubois, *A Select Bibliography of the Negro American* (Atlanta Univ., Publs., no. 10, 1905). The principal controversial pamphlets are listed in Albert Bushnell Hart, *Slavery and Abolition, 1831-1841* (*The American Nation, a History*, XVI, N. Y., 1906), 336-340. This volume presents a somewhat detailed account of the antislavery movement. Jesse Macy, *The Antislavery Crusade* (*The Chronicles of America Series*, XXVIII, New Haven, 1919), is a briefer narrative.

On special phases of the movement the following works should be consulted: E. L. Fox, *The American Colonization Society, 1817-1840* (Johns Hopkins Univ., *Studies*, XXXVII, no. 3, 1919); W. H. Siebert, *The Underground Railroad from Slavery to Freedom* (N. Y., 1898); C. G. Woodson, ed., *The Mind of the Negro as Reflected in Letters*

Written during the Crisis 1800-1860 (Wash., 1926); and biographies of the leading agitators.

WOMAN'S RIGHTS: The movement is shown in its historic setting in A. M. Schlesinger, *New Viewpoints in American History* (N. Y., 1922), chap. vi. The principal primary source is *The History of Woman Suffrage* (6 vols., Rochester, 1881-1922), written by Elizabeth Cady Stanton, Susan B. Anthony and others. The legal aspects receive attention in E. A. Hecker, *A Short History of Women's Rights* (N. Y., 1914).

PRISON REFORM: The most thorough account is O. F. Lewis, *The Development of American Prisons and Prison Customs, 1776-1845, with Special Reference to Early Institutions in the State of New York* (N. Y., 1924). Very valuable, though less detailed for the period, are F. H. Wines, *Punishment and Reformation* (rev. edn., N. Y., 1919), and H. E. Barnes, *The Repression of Crime* (N. Y., 1926). J. B. Lindsley, *Prison Discipline and Penal Legislation* (Nashville, 1874), traces the parallel movements in Europe and America. H. E. Barnes, *A History of the Penal, Reformatory and Correctional Institutions of the State of New Jersey* (Trenton, 1918), is a study of more than local importance. On the treatment of the insane during the period H. M. Hurd and others, *The Institutional Care of the Insane* (4 vols., Balt., 1916), is indispensable.

Important contemporary accounts of American penology are: Gustave de Beaumont and Alexis de Tocqueville, *Du système pénitentiare aux États-Unis* (Paris, 1833); Dorothea L. Dix, *Remarks on Prisons and Prison Discipline in the United States* (Phila., 1845); G. W. Smith, *Defence of the Pennsylvania System of Solitary Confinement* (Phila., 1833); F. C. Gray, *Prison Discipline in America* (London, 1847); and Sir Peter Laurie, *A Letter on the Disadvantages and Extravagance of the Separate System of Prison Discipline* (London, 1848).

TEMPERANCE: Much of value can be derived from such works as Daniel Dorchester, *The Liquor Problem in All Ages* (N. Y., 1888); J. G. Woolley and W. E. Johnson, *Temperance Progress of the Century* (Phila., 1903); E. H.

Cherrington, *The Evolution of Prohibition in the United States* (Westerville, 1920); and D. L. Colvin, *Prohibition in the United States* (N. Y., 1926). So far as the thirties and the forties are concerned, however, these studies are largely superseded by J. A. Krout, *The Origins of Prohibition* (N. Y., 1925), a thoughtful and detailed treatment which proceeds to the passage of the Maine liquor law of 1851.

COMMUNISTIC EXPERIMENTS: Detailed descriptions of the Utopian communities appear in J. H. Noyes, *History of American Socialisms* (Phila., 1870); Charles Nordhoff, *The Communistic Societies of the United States* (N. Y., 1875); and W. A. Hinds, *American Communities and Coöperative Colonies* (2d rev. edn., Chicago, 1908). Many of the societies have been written up separately, notably the following: Lindsay Swift, *Brook Farm* (N. Y., 1900); G. B. Lockwood, *The New Harmony Movement* (N. Y., 1905); Bertha M. H. Shambaugh, *Amana* (Iowa City, 1908); and Albert Shaw, *Icaria* (N. Y., 1884). A detailed bibliography of such individual histories is given in Hinds's volume in connection with his account of each community.

EDUCATION

The educational awakening receives appropriate emphasis in the standard manuals: E. P. Cubberley, *Public Education in the United States* (Boston, 1919); E. G. Dexter, *A History of Education in the United States* (N. Y., 1904); and R. G. Boone, *Education in the United States* (N. Y., 1889). The great storehouse of educational information and biography for the period is *The American Journal of Education* (Henry Barnard, ed., 31 vols., 1855-1870). A. D. Mayo has traced the awakening in every part of country in the following articles: "The Organization and Reconstruction of State Systems of Common-School Education in the North Atlantic States from 1830 to 1865," U. S. Commissioner of Education, *Rep. for 1897-1898*, I, 355-486; "The

Development of the Common School in the Western States from 1830 to 1850," *ibid. for 1898-1899,* I, 357-450; "The Organization and Development of the American Common School in the Atlantic and Central States of the South," *ibid. for 1899-1900,* I, 427-561; and "The Common School in the Southern States beyond the Mississippi River from 1830 to 1860," *ibid. for 1900-1901,* I, 357-401. Separate educational histories exist for many of the states, of which the following are typical: R. G. Boone, *History of Education in Indiana* (N. Y., 1892); E. A. Miller, *History of Educational Legislation in Ohio, 1803-1850* (Chicago, 1918); and J. P. Wickersham, *A History of Education in Pennsylvania* (Lancaster, 1886). E. W. Knight, *Public Education in the South* (Boston, 1922), is an excellent sectional study.

F. T. Carlton broke new ground in *Economic Influences upon Educational Progress in the United States, 1820-1850* (Univ. of Wis., *Bull.,* IV, no. 1, 1908). E. E. Brown, *The Making of Our Middle Schools* (N. Y., 1903), discusses the spread of academies and high schools, a subject further illustrated in G. F. Miller, *The Academy System of the State of New York* (Albany, 1922). On their respective subjects the following are standard works: C. A. Bennett, *History of Manual and Industrial Education up to 1870* (Peoria, 1926)—referring also to similar movements abroad; C. G. Woodson, *The Education of the Negro prior to 1861* (N. Y., 1915); S. C. Parker, *History of Modern Elementary Education* (Boston, 1912)—very good on the Pestalozzian movement in Europe and America; and A. C. Norton, ed., *The First State Normal School in America, Being the Journals of Cyrus Peirce and Mary Swift* (Cambridge, Mass., 1926)—written by the first principal and a member of the first class of the Lexington school. The two great leaders of the educational revival are studied in two articles by A. D. Mayo, "Horace Mann and the Great Revival of the American Common School, 1830-1850," and "Henry Barnard," U. S. Commissioner of Education, *Rep. for 1896-1897,* I, 715-767, 769-810, and in two books: B. A. Hinsdale, *Horace Mann and the Common School Revival in the United States*

(N. Y., 1898), and W. S. Monroe, *The Educational Labors of Henry Barnard* (Syracuse, 1893).

The best single discussion of the colleges of the period is to be found in C. F. Thwing, *A History of Higher Education in America* (N. Y., 1906). Separate histories, however, may be found of the more important institutions. J. M. Taylor, *Before Vassar Opened* (Boston, 1914), deals with the early history of the higher education of women in the United States.

SCIENCE

The most helpful guide to general scientific materials of the thirties and forties is Max Meisel, *A Bibliography of American Natural History; the Pioneer Century, 1769-1865* (Brooklyn, 1924). Scientific progress in a number of fields can be traced in *A Century of Science in America* (New Haven, 1918), written by E. S. Dana and other specialists. For special branches the following are authoritative and very useful for the period: E. F. Smith, *Chemistry in America* (N. Y., 1914); R. T. Young, *Biology in America* (Boston, 1922); G. P. Merrill, *The First One Hundred Years of American Geology* (New Haven, 1924); A. S. Packard, "A Century's Progress in American Zoology," *Am. Naturalist*, X (1876), 591-598; E. H. Clarke and others, *A Century of American Medicine, 1776-1876* (Phila., 1876); N. S. Davis, *Contributions to the History of Medical Education and Medical Institutions in the United States, 1776-1876* (Wash., 1877); and J. A. Taylor, *History of Dentistry* (Phila., 1922). Biographies of the leading scientists of the period are of great value, such as G. P. Fisher, *Life of Benjamin Silliman* (2 vols., N. Y., 1866); John Burroughs, *John James Audubon* (Boston, 1902); A. B. Gould, *Louis Agassiz* (Boston, 1901); and J. T. Morse, *Life and Letters of Oliver Wendell Holmes* (Boston, 1897). The founding of the leading scientific organization is set forth in two works by W. J. Rhees: *An Account of the Smithsonian Institution, Its Founder, etc.* (Phila., 1896), and *Smithsonian Institution: Documents Relative to Its Origin and History, 1835-1899* (2 vols., Wash., 1901).

THE FINE ARTS

The standard histories of American painting are all distinctly useful for the period: Sadakichi Hartman, *A History of American Art* (2 vols., Boston, 1901); Samuel Isham, *History of American Painting* (N. Y., 1905); and C. H. Caffin, *Story of American Painting* (N. Y., 1907). The advances in graphic art are recorded in F. Weitenkampf, *American Graphic Art* (N. Y., 1924). Lorado Taft very properly pays relatively little attention to the period in his *The History of American Sculpture* (rev. edn., N. Y., 1924). L. C. Elson, *The History of American Music* (N. Y., 1904), is an excellent general discussion which should be supplemented for this period by H. C. Lahee, *Annals of Music in America* (Boston, 1922); O. G. Sonneck, *Early Opera in America* (N. Y., 1915); and F. J. Metcalf, *American Writers and Compilers of Sacred Music* (N. Y., 1925).

Students of the stage will find F. C. Wemyss, *Chronology of the American Stage, 1752-1852* (N. Y., 1852), a useful compilation. A. H. Quinn, *A History of the American Drama from the Beginning to the Civil War* (N. Y., 1923), is a scholarly discussion of American playwriting. Mary C. Crawford, *The Romance of the American Stage* (rev. edn., Boston, 1925); T. A. Brown, *History of the New York Stage* (N. Y., 1903); Kate Ryan, *Old Boston Museum Days* (Boston, 1915); and M. J. Moses, *The American Dramatist* (rev. edn., Boston, 1926), are entertaining and informing. Arthur Hornblow, *A History of the Theatre in America* (2 vols., Phila., 1919), is a readable book though obviously drawn from comparatively few sources.

SOCIAL CUSTOMS AND SPORTS

The best work dealing with the relations of the sexes and family life is A. W. Calhoun, *Social History of the American Family* (3 vols., Cleveland, 1917-1919). Meade Minnigerode discusses the lighter phases of urban social life in the East in *The Fabulous Forties* (N. Y., 1924). Much light is thrown upon Southern social life by R. Q. Mallard, *Plantation Life before Emancipation* (Richmond, 1892); Edward Ingle, *Southern Sidelights* (N. Y., 1896); T. N. Page, *Social Life in Old Virginia before the War* (N. Y., 1897); and Eliza Ripley, *Social Life in Old New Orleans* (N. Y., 1912). W. E. Dodd, *The Cotton Kingdom* (*The Chronicles of America Series*, XXVII, New Haven, 1919), is an excellent summary.

The approved social usages of the period may be gleaned from the books of etiquette which appeared in such large numbers. The titles of some of the more popular manuals are cited in chapter vii of this volume. The attention given to correct dress is amply shown in the women's magazines of the time and also in such a book as C. W. Brewster, *National Standard of Costume* (Portsmouth, 1837). The clearest insight into manners and customs is, however, to be derived from the reminiscent writings of the people of the period. Besides the titles already noted under Personal Material, the following works are particularly helpful: W. H. Venable, *A Buckeye Boyhood* (Cincinnati, 1911); Lucy Larcom, *A New England Girlhood* (Boston, 1890); G. F. Hoar, *Autobiography of Seventy Years* (2 vols., N. Y., 1903); A. B. Longstreet, *Georgia Scenes* (Augusta, Ga., 1835); J. G. Baldwin, *The Flush Times of Alabama and Mississippi* (N. Y., 1853); S. L. Clemens (*pseud.* Mark Twain), *The Adventures of Tom Sawyer* (Toronto, 1876); and same author, *Adventures of Huckleberry Finn* (N. Y., 1885).

Outdoor pastimes are treated by contemporaries in the following works: Frank Forester, *Frank Forester's Field Sports of the United States and the British Provinces* (2 vols., N. Y., 1848); B. H. Revail, *Shooting and Fishing in the Rivers, Prairies and Backwoods of America* [1841-1849] (London, 1865); and C. A. Peverelly, *American Pastimes* (N. Y., 1866). Frederick William Janssen, *History of American Amateur Athletics and Aquatics* (N. Y., 1887), is enlightening for the period. *The Tribune Book of Sports* (N. Y., 1887), published by the *New York Tribune*, should also be consulted.

INDEX

367

INDEX

163

247; New Year's Day in, 161; and temperance, 263.

Newport, R. I., population of, 13; religion at, 184, 196.

Newspapers, official, 42, 142; used by reformers, 49; foreign-language, 119; support of, 106, 142; of Albany, 123; value as sources, 137, 141-142; price of, 142; methods of penny, 143; ease of establishing, 144. *See also* Periodicals, Press, and editors by name.

Niagara Falls, as honeymoon resort, 19.

Niles' Register, quoted, 54; position of, 247.

North, attitude of, towards social control, 36; agriculture in, 63-67; dress in, 141; dueling in, 161; attitude of, on slavery, 280; publicity in, 286; and Texas, 299-300; dissatisfaction in, 316-317; Free Soilers in, 318; and South, 336-337. *See also* Sectionalism, and states by name.

North American Review, quoted, 51; pays American authors, 249.

North Carolina, crops of, 68; railroad board of, 87; abolishes Negro suffrage, 285; gold in, 296.

Norwegians, immigration of, 121, 122.

Novels, historical, 247-248; popularity of, 255.

Nudity, on stage, 146; in art, 153; attitude toward, 233.

Nullification, by South Carolina, 168; Jackson and, 173-174.

OBERLIN COLLEGE, founded, 215; women at, 271.

Ohio, position of, 22, 36, 268, 318; constitutional convention of, 55; agriculture of, 63, 66; land grants to, 77; aliens in, 118, 125; New Englanders in, 123; and frontier, 128, 133; politics of, 164; Mormons in, 190; and slavery, 277; and Mexican War, 305.

Ohio Valley, elements of population in, 118, 123, 226; drinking in, 261; becomes section, 327.

Opera, cultivation of, 146, 237.

Oratory, form of, 19; in South, 28; at commencements, 204; taught, 206; literary, 254; on stump, 293.

Oregon, desired, 33, 134, 296; missions in, 125, 194, 329; land cheap, 131; trail to, 129; claims to, 194; dispute settled, 274, 302; joint occupancy of, 292; settlement of, 293, 295; conditions in, 300-301; in politics, 300-302; "reoccupation" of, 302.

Oregon Trail, 301, 308.

Organization, political, 168, 172; industrial, 334.

Owen, Robert, founds New Harmony, 189.

PAINTING, description of, 97, 231-232; income from, 106; and science, 240. *See also* painters by name.

Panic, of 1837, effect of, 37, 43, 106, 157-158, 272; of 1841, effect of, 37, 56.

Parkman, Francis, in West, 251, 294.

Parks, in cities, 14.

Parochial schools. *See* Education.

Parties. *See* Conventions, Organization, Political parties.

Partnership, importance of, 55; dangers of, 156; in law, 209.

Patent medicines, popularity of, 210, 268. *See also* Medicine.

Patriotism, power of, 177; in literature, 246; and Manifest Destiny, 307.

Patronage, and politics, 40, 310; of literature, 310.

Patti, Adelina, in America, 147.

Payne, J. H., writes songs, 237.

Peabody, George, brings foreign capital, 60.

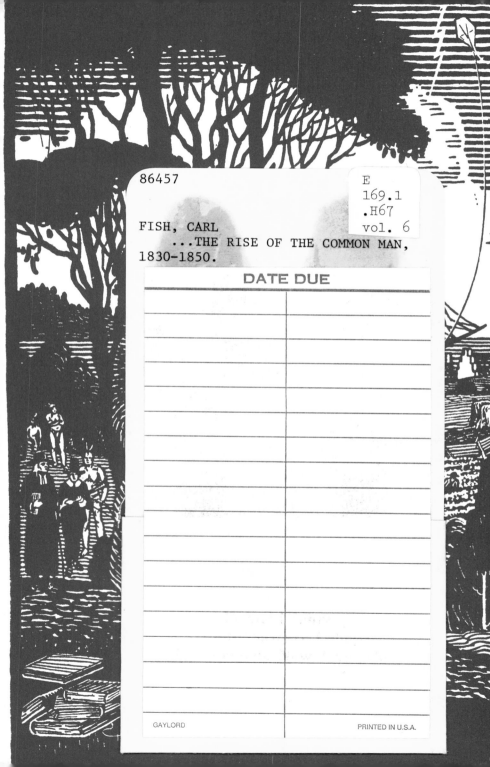

DATE DUE